Theodore Roethke

THE POET AND HIS CRITICS

Theodore Roethke

THE POET AND HIS CRITICS

RANDALL STIFFLER

AMERICAN
LIBRARY
ASSOCIATION
CHICAGO
AND LONDON
1986

THE POET AND HIS CRITICS

A series of volumes on the meaning of the
critical writings on selected modern British
and American poets.

Edited by CHARLES SANDERS, University of Illinois, Urbana

Robert Frost by Donald J. Greiner
William Carlos Williams by Paul L. Mariani
Dylan Thomas by R. B. Kershner, Jr.
Langston Hughes by Richard K. Barksdale
Wallace Stevens by Abbie F. Willard
T. S. Eliot by Robert H. Canary
Robert Lowell by Norma Procopiow

LIBRARY OF CONGRESS CATALOGING-IN-PUBLICATION DATA
Stiffler, Randall.
    Theodore Roethke : the poet and his critics.
    (The Poet and his critics)
    1. Roethke, Theodore, 1908–1963—Criticism and interpreta-
tions—History.   I. Title.   II. Series.
PS3535.039Z875   1986   811'.54   85-28676
ISBN 0-8389-0447-5

Printed in the United States of America.

For my father

Contents

Acknowledgments

I want to thank Charles Sanders of the University of Illinois, editor of the Poet and His Critics series, for his suggestion of this project and for his continued commitment to it. Herbert Bloom, senior editor of the American Library Association, also read drafts of this book; his responses were especially helpful to me in revising it. Others who have offered comments and encouragement and deserve my thanks are Duncan Carter of Boston University, Harry Crosby of Harvard University, Walter Kalaidjian of Mercer University, and John M. and Ann Hill of the University of Scranton. For their interest and patience, I wish also to thank Eric and Cynthia Stiffler, Jessica and Nathan, Thomas G. Mackey, my mother, Beth Stiffler (who supported this work at every turn and counter-turn of its progress), and my father, Harold Stiffler.

Introduction

Theodore Huebner Roethke was born in Saginaw, Michigan, in 1908 and died in 1963 on Bainbridge Island in the state of Washington. In the fifty-five years that he lived, Roethke published six collections of serious poetry, Open House (1941), The Lost Son and Other Poems (1948), Praise to the End! (1951), The Waking (1953), Words for the Wind (1958), and The Far Field (1964), and two works intended primarily for children, I Am! Says the Lamb (1961) and Party at the Zoo (1963). The Waking was a selection of poems from Roethke's three previous books, and Words for the Wind contained The Waking in its entirety, Roethke's Love Poems, and two important long poems, "The Dying Man" and "Meditations of an Old Woman." After Roethke died in 1963, his poems were newly gathered and published in what is now the most complete edition of his verse, The Collected Poems of Theodore Roethke (1966).

Though Roethke did not himself think his work was sufficiently recognized by the audience of his day, he received the kind of acclaim many poets would envy. In the course of his career, Roethke won numerous awards for his poetry, including two Guggenheim Fellowships; two Ford Fellowships, the second of which took him to Ireland and England; a Fulbright Lectureship in Italy; tenures at Breadloaf Writer's Conference and the Yaddo Writers Colony; the Pulitzer Prize for The Waking; the Bollingen Prize for Words for the Wind; and a National Book Award each for Words for the Wind and, posthumously, for The Far Field. In addition to being a celebrated poet, Roethke was an accomplished teacher of poetry and poetry writing. He taught at Lafayette College, Michigan State College, Pennsylvania State University, Bennington College, and the University of Washington where, in 1962, he was named Poet in Residence. Roethke was himself educated at the University of Michigan, where he later earned a master's degree, and did graduate work at Harvard.

Such a recitation of Theodore Roethke's fellowships, awards, and teaching positions presents an invalid image of this poet and his poetry, however. Though he taught for a living, Roethke was neither an academic nor an academic poet. By all accounts, though, when at his best, he was an unusually effective, demanding, and inspiring teacher. Since his death, Roethke's performance in the classroom has assumed almost legendary proportions, and the list of his students, especially those who worked with him at the University of Washington, includes the names of many important contemporary poets. Throughout his life, however, Roethke suffered from occasionally debilitating episodes of manic-depression. Outbreaks of this illness repeatedly interfered with Roethke's ability to teach in the classroom and, of more importance to some of his academic colleagues, to conform to those behaviors expected of a college professor. Roethke's transfers from university to university were not always, in other words, calculated moves up the academic ladder. As a result of his first breakdown in 1935, and his subsequent stay at Mercywood Sanitarium, for example, Roethke was not continued as a teacher at what was then Michigan State College.

The shower of recognition rained on Roethke toward the end of his career is also a little misleading. It might appear at first that Theodore Roethke's poetic career follows the course of other poets of the century: the poet, as an antenna of the race, is at first misunderstood, even reviled, until the rest of the race catches up and offers its acclaim. Theodore Roethke's first work won support from important reviewers of the day, however. He did not, it is true, receive an award for the volume of poetry (his second) that contains what many now see as his most original and important poetry, The Lost Son and Other Poems. It gained him an enthusiastic following, especially among certain innovative and experimental poets, however. With publication of his fourth major book, The Waking, and his fifth, Words for the Wind, Roethke lost some of that following. Outspoken experimentalists were not comfortable with the new direction in Roethke's verse these volumes indicated. For The Waking and for Words for the Wind, however, Roethke won three internationally significant awards. Awards were slower in coming to Theodore Roethke than he himself would have liked, perhaps, but when they did arrive toward the end of his career, an important portion of the audience he had earlier won had been alienated by his "betrayal" of experimental poetry. Roethke deserved awards, the betrayed might say, but unfortunately he received them at the wrong time in his career, and for the wrong volumes of his poetry.

Literary history tells us that, generally speaking, a poet's career can take one of three courses. In the first pattern, the poet begins precociously, develops meteorically, and dies young. The classic examples of this type of career are those of the Romantic poets Keats and Shelley. Keats died of tuberculosis at the age of twenty-five; Shelley, at twenty-nine, died by drowning. Other poets live longer and less dramatic lives, and their work develops more gradually. In the twentieth century, some of our greatest poets have sustained their powers to the ends of a long life: William

Butler Yeats, T. S. Eliot, Ezra Pound, Robert Frost, William Carlos Williams, Wallace Stevens, W. H. Auden. Though each of these
poets wrote significant verse as a young man, their greater work
came from their maturer years. The third kind of poetic career
yields the sad footnotes written about the poets of the first type
who live as long as poets of the second, even though the poetry in
them dies sooner. Samuel Taylor Coleridge led this kind of career,
and the poetic and mental powers of Ralph Waldo Emerson expired
years before his body.

In the twenty years since his death, Theodore Roethke's career
has been described in terms appropriate to all three of these popular notions of the poet's life. For example, though he was little
younger than the "ranking" modern poets of his day, Roethke was
often considered a merely "promising" and "developing" poet, even
after he was forty years old. Thus, when Roethke died at the age
of fifty-five, he died as a "younger" poet. This is Roethke on
his last afternoon, as described by Allan Seager in his 1968 biography of the poet, The Glass House:

> Mrs. Bloedel, her daughter, Mrs. Meadowcroft, who was visiting
> her parents from Switzerland, and the Meadowcrofts' governness
> were all at the swimming pool. Ted joined them and made some
> mint juleps which he put into the refrigerator. It was still
> hot at five in the afternoon and Ted said he was going to take
> a swim. The women were sitting at the edge of the pool talking,
> and, since they knew Ted swam well enough, paying little special
> attention to him. He dove in and swam to the shallow end. A
> moment or two later, they noticed him floating face down. The
> three women got him out of the water, his face blue, and Mrs.
> Meadowcroft tried mouth-to-mouth resuscitation while the others
> called Beatrice and a doctor. The doctor arrived, examined Ted,
> and pronounced him dead of a coronary occlusion. [p. 285]

Throughout the biography, Seager helps to perpetuate the romantic
image of the young poet, touched by madness (here, still athletic,
surrounded by juleps and women), cut off suddenly in the midst of
life. Laurence Lieberman implies a similar image of the poet in
his review of Roethke's last book. He notes that "moments of praise
and affirmation outweigh the gloomy passages, and even death becomes
a way of life" (p. 231), but Lieberman thinks that Roethke did not
live long enough to write his best poems: "one waits in vain for
the final flowering of his genius" (p. 230). Roy Harvey Pearce
takes a similar tack in his essay "The Power of Sympathy." Echoing the words of the Thunder in T. S. Eliot's The Waste Land,
Pearce argues that Roethke's "poems controlled, they sympathized.
They only began, at the end, fully to give" (p. 190). For Pearce,
Roethke's "beginning was in his end" (p. 197). Richard Eberhart
also suggests that Roethke's career corresponds to the Romantic
paradigm, in that he compares Roethke's work to that of James Agee,

John Brooks Wheelwright, and Theodore Spencer, three other poets who died young, but whose commitment to poetry was not so strong as Roethke's (pp. 612-20).

In fact, though, Roethke was fifty-five years old when he died, and he had seen five major volumes of poetry go into print, one of which was a "collected" poems of sorts, Words for the Wind. Of course, collecting poems is the crowning glory of the older poet's career, an option not afforded the Keatses and Shelleys, who die young. The quantity and scope of the major verse Roethke published while alive suggests that his death, though untimely, silenced his voice; it did not devastatingly foreshorten his career. One raises a central issue about his work in applying to Theodore Roethke the third popular concept of the poet's career. Some argue that Roethke completed his most important work with Praise to the End! in 1951. Well before he died on that August afternoon in 1963, it is suggested, the poetry died in Roethke, as it had for Emerson and Coleridge.

It is not, in fact, critical whether Roethke actually fits any one of these perceptions of poetic careers that literary history offers as examples. The poete maudit, the "good gray poet," are only images, but images that can affect evaluations of a poet's work. The first two images of the poet's career help to swell a poet's stature; the third diminishes it. Keenly aware of how such imagery works, critics can color the biographical facts (as we have seen Allan Seager do) to gain the polemical advantage. The shape of Roethke's career has thus become an important issue in the criticism because it is one way of influencing how Roethke eventually ranks among other twentieth-century American poets.

In the past thirty years, three different views of the shape of Roethke's career have emerged: the evolutionary, the disruptive, and the dialectical. Proponents of the evolutionary view argue that Roethke's poetry is of a piece, and that central concerns permeate all of his verse. These concerns emerge in the poems of his first book, develop as they persist in successive volumes, and are resolved triumphantly in the final work. Other critics think Roethke's poetry is not so well integrated, and support their position by pointing to the formal diversity of Roethke's poetry. They note that Roethke moves from the tightly controlled lyric style of Open House to the wildly associative style of the Lost Son narratives; he returns to rhymed and metered forms in The Waking and in Words for the Wind; and finally jumps back again to freer forms in the sweeping lines of the "North American Sequence." These shifts constitute disruption and indecisiveness in Roethke's development, these critics maintain, and such discontinuity argues persuasively against any claim that Roethke was a great American poet. For critics who understand Roethke's poems dialectically, however, the formal diversity of his verse is simply evidence of a dynamic of freedom and form, one of several important oppositions that animate his verse. According to these critics, contraries of theme, image, and style structure Roethke's poetry as a whole. From their point of view, antitheses are as valid as theses, though in fact most who stress the oppositions at work in Roethke's verse do prefer the poems of his most experimental periods. If not the most accurate of the three views of Roethke's career, the dialectical is now the most prevalent; it is versatile, too, for it has yielded both sympathetic and unsympathetic appraisals of Roethke's poetry. It might also be added that, unlike the evolutionary and the disruptive views, the dialectical perspective does not neatly correspond to any one of the three images of the poet's career offered by literary history.

In a sense, Theodore Roethke labored under a shadow all of his life due to the circumstances history handed him. His was not an unhappy childhood nor an unhappy life on the whole, but it is possible to argue that the great moment of American poetry in the twentieth century missed him; he was born a generation too late. He might lay greater claim to James Dickey's accolade of 1968, "The Greatest American Poet," were he to have been born in 1888, the year T. S. Eliot was born. In birth, as in other things, Ezra Pound preceded Eliot onto the stage: Pound was born in 1885. William Carlos Williams was born in 1883, Wallace Stevens in 1879, Robert Frost in 1874; it was Roethke's fate to be born twenty years after Eliot, in 1908. By the time Roethke reached the age of fifteen, Robert Frost had published North of Boston (1914), Mountain Interval (1916), and New Hampshire (1923), Wallace Stevens had written Harmonium (1923), William Carlos Williams had published Spring and All (1923), Ezra Pound had written a major poetic sequence, Hugh Selwyn Mauberley (1920), and T. S. Eliot had followed Prufrock and Other Observations (1917) with The Waste Land (1922). A year after the publication of Eliot's enormously influential poem, Theodore Roethke's father, Otto Roethke, died of cancer in 1923, in the "cruellest month" of that year. Roethke's own well-mannered first volume of poems did not appear until 1941, and twenty-two years later, Roethke himself was dead of heart failure, in August of 1963. Both Williams and Frost died in the year that Roethke died, and Eliot and Pound outlived Roethke. These poets, the founders of the high modern style, were old enough to be father to a younger Roethke, but while they lived, and even after they died, they were Roethke's major competition.

Roethke, it must be noted, benefited from the experiments of the great modern poets; some would say he benefited too much. It is a tribute to the change the moderns wrought on their audience that Roethke's own most challenging work was received in the way that it was. Some reviewers of The Lost Son and Other Poems (1948) and Praise to the End! (1951) were plainly baffled by Roethke's radically regressive poetics, but surprisingly few called him incompetent or obscure. Some actually blamed themselves for their incomprehension! Had they been unaccustomed to difficult poems like Eliot's The Waste Land, Roethke's critics probably would have received his experimental efforts more narrowly and less generously.

It would be misleading to compare Roethke's continuing critical reception to that of the modern poets, however. In comparison to the critical literature about T. S. Eliot, Ezra Pound, Wallace Stevens, or Robert Frost, Roethke's remains modest. (Another way of saying the same thing: the individual bibliographies of the modern poets are enormous.) In the past forty years, however, the poems of Theodore Roethke have inspired 11 books, three collections of critical essays, some 125 articles and chapters of books, 130 reviews and notices, five bibliographies and bibliographical essays, one concordance to the poems, one full-length biography, and numerous doctoral dissertations. Roethke's bibliography contains some 300 separate items, and it grows every year. The diversity of this secondary literature and its extent constitute one justification for this book. Twenty years after Roethke's death, it is appropriate to put the criticism of his poetry into perspective. That is not to suggest that Roethke's critics have finally agreed upon major issues in his work, however, but the arguments, the irreconcilable differences, it might be said, have sorted themselves out to some extent. This book is a guide to those issues, the major arguments about those issues, and the strengths and weaknesses of those arguments.

It is well, perhaps, to start with two contradictory or contrasting images of Theodore Roethke, or with one image and its shadow. In a sense, I have tried to make such a notion the structural principle of this book. The chronological career of Theodore Roethke organizes the chapters in the book, and like most discussions of Roethke's poetry, this one starts with the poems of Open House and ends with the poems of The Far Field. The first and the fifth chapters concern volumes of poetry, but chapters two, three, and four concern major segments of work, rather than titled volumes. Chapter two is devoted to the Greenhouse poems, the thirteen important poems which open Roethke's second volume. In the third chapter, I take up the Lost Son narratives, which first appeared in The Lost Son and Other Poems, were continued and reorganized in Praise to the End!, and were completed by The Waking. In the fourth chapter, I focus primarily on what Roethke called the "New Poems" of Words for the Wind. The fifth chapter is devoted to Roethke's last volume, The Far Field, with special attention to the "North American Sequence" and the "Sequence, Sometimes Metaphysical."

The chapters of this book follow the chronological order in which Roethke published the major segments and sequences of poetry, but within the individual chapters I have been directed by the emphases of Roethke's literary critics. As I have mentioned, one of my aims is to present, organize, and evaluate the major and representative statements of Roethke's critics. To achieve this, I have organized each of the chapters according to the major themes that Roethke's critics have deemed significant for understanding and evaluating his work. To some degree, these themes intersect with one another, but the ongoing critical debate over Roethke's poetry has revolved around five sometimes separable issues. Before Roethke's death and thereafter, critics have been concerned about (1) the shape of Roethke's career; (2) the range of Roethke's vision; (3) the mystical element of Roethke's poetry; (4) the extent to which Roethke was influenced by literary precedessors; and (5) the nature of Roethke's poetic methods. Where applicable within the context of the individual chapters of this book, I take up each of the issues cited above in the order mentioned. My intention in providing the thematic structure within the context of the larger chronological structure is to make that chronology meaningful, and to offer perhaps an alternative method of reading the book. One might get an overview of Roethke's "Literary Backgrounds and Sources" or his "Poetic Methods and Techniques" by reading the relevant section of all five chapters. One might construct a reception study by reading part one of each chapter because in part one I present reviewers' discussions of Roethke's volumes of poetry, and so forth.

It would be wrong to suggest that all of Roethke's major poetry equally illuminates all five of the major issues, however. The matter of literary influence is not a burning issue in discussions of Open House, for example. In Open House, most agree, Roethke imitates prior poetry. In the Lost Son narratives, Roethke's innovations are of more interest than their origins. In certain of the poems of Words for the Wind, however, some critics say Roethke's voice becomes an echo. In his later poetry especially the matter of influence strongly affects critical evaluations. Critics have indeed sought and addressed the sources and literary backgrounds for all of Roethke's poetry, but the issue of literary influence deserves (and gets) more emphasis in the fourth chapter than in the first, second, or third chapters. Thus, my secondary structure is not symmetrical. I devote considerable space to the methods of the Lost Son narratives in the third chapter, for example. In the fifth chapter, I devote considerable space to the view that "In a Dark Time" is a mystical poem. Such bulges of emphasis occur in each of the five chapters but I do not regret that. On the contrary, the bulges are especially pertinent to the study of Theodore Roethke's poetry, for they indicate centers of the critical debate.

Part of my intent in this book is to show clearly the variety of opinion and argument that Theodore Roethke's poetry has inspired in the past forty years. Roethke criticism is old enough to include many commentators and interpretations. Despite the quantity of published Roethke studies, however, it is an indication of the relative youth of Roethke criticism that so many of the essays are overviews of his poetry, rather than narrow and specialized studies. The criticism of other twentieth-century poets has developed beyond this phase: one could publish an essay entitled "The Poetry of Robert Frost" in 1950, perhaps, but not in 1985 or even in 1970.

As it is, however, the majority of essays on Roethke and almost all of the books have something to say about nearly every major segment of his work. Were Roethke criticism more specialized in subject matter, it would be easier to organize. One could collect the major readings of the major poems, the readings of Roethke as nature poet, as Romantic poet, as religious poet, and so forth. In order to retain a chronological coherence, however, it has been necessary for me to divide the many general readings into their parts, and to distribute their insights in the book where applicable. For this reason, the same essay may be mentioned in different places and in different contexts and as a result, some names and some works necessarily recur throughout the book. At other times, I cite authors and sources primarily to have mentioned them, so the reader can follow a particular argument to additional relevant sources. In addition to presenting, discussing, and evaluating the various arguments of Roethke's literary critics, I have in a number of places offered my own comments on Roethke's poems and essays. I have tried especially to comment in some detail on poems or sections of poems that have thus far gone unnoticed as well, of course, as discussing Roethke's best-known poems. Though certain of Roethke's poems are quoted here, this book is intended as an adjunct to Roethke verse. Some familiarity with major segments of his work is assumed.

Thoughout, I have also tried to indicate origins of influential arguments and insights. Two figures stand out in that regard, Kenneth Burke and Theodore Roethke. Though the borrowing is not always acknowledged, Burke's essay, "The Vegetal Radicalism of Theodore Roethke," has inspired many of Roethke's critics. Interestingly, his opinions and observations have been used both to attack and to defend Roethke's poetry, and I try to show that. Another major figure in Roethke criticism is Roethke himself. Unlike T. S. Eliot or Ezra Pound, Theodore Roethke was not a prolific writer of literary criticism, but where he describes his own work and comments on his poetic theory, Roethke's prose statements are interesting and useful. I frequently connect Roethke's poetry to his relevant prose writings, therefore, but I avoid the temptation, I hope, of lending Roethke's own critical opinions an unwarranted weight, and for good reason. With the exception of a few brief reviews, Roethke's prose is not literary criticism in any conventional sense. His essays concern the writing of poetry, and more particularly the writing of his own poetry. Roethke's prose is thus self-validating, in a sense more autobiographical than analytical. As such, his prose indicates what he thought he was doing and what he wanted to be doing in his poems, but whether he indicates in fact what he was doing is another issue entirely.

In commenting on the structure of "The Lost Son" in his "Open Letter," for example, Roethke sticks close to the text and gives accurate description. In describing the structure of <u>Words for the Wind</u>, however, Roethke's memory clearly lapses. In "Theodore

Roethke Writes," included in On the Poet and His Craft, edited
by Ralph J. Mills, Jr., Roethke describes the book's contents
this way:

> the first section of love poems in Words for the Wind contains
> pieces tender or highly romantic, others are "witty," coarse and
> sensual. . . . Then by way of contrast, there is a handful of
> light pieces and poems for children. . . .
> The third section of these later pieces consists of poems of
> terror, and running away--and the dissociation of personality
> that occurs in such attempts to escape reality. In these the
> protagonist is alive in space, almost against his will; his
> world is the cold and dark known to sub-human things. . . .
> There follows a series of poems dedicated to W. B. Yeats. . . .
> Finally comes a sequence of longish poems "Meditations of an
> Old Woman." [p. 58]

The sequence Roethke describes does not occur in Words for the
Wind. The "first section of love poems" he mentions must refer to
the "Shorter Poems, 1951-1953" because these clearly precede "by
way of contrast" the children's poems. (The section contains "The
Visitant," "A Light Breather," "Elegy for Jane," "Old Lady's
Winter Words," "Four for Sir John Davies," and "The Waking.")
None of these poems could be considered "coarse and sensual," however. Roethke must have had in mind his second set of love poems
in Words for the Wind, those called "Love Poems." "The Sensualists" in that section is perhaps the most "coarse" poem Roethke
wrote, and of course it is "sensual." The "third section" Roethke
mentions, which depicts "running away," must be, then, the section
called "Voices and Creatures." The poems "Snake" and "Slug" enter the world of "sub-human things." (The terms Roethke uses in
his essay, though, better describe the Lost Son narratives, especially "The Lost Son.") Following these, as Roethke notes, come
poems dedicated to W. B. Yeats, and the "Meditations." In his
prose writings, we must conclude from this example, Roethke can
be demonstrably fallible. Like his poems, Roethke's essays merit close analysis and evaluation. Rarely do they offer the last
word.

A few short notes: Despite its difficulties, the Collected
Poems of Theodore Roethke is the definitive version of Roethke's
poetry de facto. Thus, it is the source used throughout, and cited
parenthetically as "CP." Where indicated, Roethke's own prema-
ture collection of his poems, Words for the Wind (WW), is also
used because it contains preferable versions of certain poems.
In addition to Roethke's original poetry, two other important
primary sources cited parenthetically with abbreviation include:
On the Poet and His Craft (SP), a small selection of Roethke's

essays on poetry and teaching and his periodical reviews, edited
by Ralph J. Mills, Jr., and the Selected Letters of Theodore
Roethke (SL), also edited by Mills. Other sources of special
interest include Straw for the Fire, David Wagoner's selection
from Roethke's voluminous notebooks, and The Glass House, Allan
Seager's biography of Theodore Roethke. Last, though some sources
offer "Reth ke" as a second choice, the preferred pronunciation of
the name remains "Rĕt kē."

Bibliography

Burke, Kenneth
    1966. "The Vegetal Radicalism of Theodore Roethke," in Lan-
    guage as Symbolic Action, pp. 254-81. Berkeley: Univ. of
    California Pr. Appeared in Sewanee Review, pp. 68-108.
    Winter, 1950. Reprinted in Profile of Theodore Roethke,
    ed. William Heyen. Columbus: Merrill, 1971.
Eberhart, Richard
    1965. "On Theodore Roethke's Poetry," Southern Review Sum-
    mer, pp. 612-20.
Lieberman, Laurence
    1977. "Theodore Roethke," in Unassigned Frequencies: Ameri-
    can Poetry in Review, pp. 230-32. Urbana: Univ. of Illinois
    Pr.
Pearce, Roy Harvey
    1965. "The Power of Sympathy," in Theodore Roethke: Essays
    on the Poetry, ed. Arnold Stein, pp. 167-99. Seattle: Univ.
    of Washington Pr.
Roethke, Theodore
    1961. Words for the Wind: The Collected Verse of Theodore
    Roethke. Bloomington: Indiana Univ. Pr.
    1965. On the Poet and His Craft: Selected Prose of Theodore
    Roethke, ed. Ralph J. Mills, Jr. Seattle: Univ. of Washing-
    ton Pr.
    1966. The Collected Poems of Theodore Roethke. Garden City,
    N.Y.: Doubleday.
    1968. Selected Letters of Theodore Roethke, ed. Ralph J.
    Mills, Jr. Seattle: Univ. of Washington Pr.
    1972. Straw for the Fire: From the Notebooks of Theodore
    Roethke 1943-63, ed. David Wagoner. Seattle: Univ. of Wash-
    ington Pr.
Seager, Allan
    1968. The Glass House: The Life of Theodore Roethke. New
    York: McGraw-Hill.

CHAPTER 1

The Poems of Open House

The place one has to start in discussing Theodore Roethke's poetry is not, in all respects, the best place to start. "Begin with the rock;/ End with water," Roethke writes in "Bring the Day!" (CP, p. 77), but is the beginning of his poetry that rock? (The water with which to end will come later.) His beginning is not necessarily that rock, for an important part of understanding Theodore Roethke is realizing that he was a poet not wholly satisfied with the beginnings history gave him. He courageously and tirelessly sought deeper origins. He was, in essence, a poet of origins, and those beginnings did not clearly emerge in his first book of poems, Open House, published in 1941. Thus, a book about Roethke could well begin elsewhere. It could begin not with the historical beginning of Open House, but rather with the psychological or spiritual center Roethke approached in some of his later poetry. This hypothetical book might begin with the poems of 1948 and 1951, with the narrative poem "Where Knock Is Open Wide," for example; somewhere near the middle might appear a discussion of the poems of Open House. And yet, this conjectural book cannot be this book, and for a reason. When we ask first about beginnings, we ordinarily want to know about historical starts. We want the ready intelligibility that a sequence of historical events offers. To gain that intelligibility in the case of Theodore Roethke, we must sacrifice for the moment some perspective on his poetic project as a whole. Roethke was himself a "perpetual beginner," as we shall see, and he started and started again, in a series of seemingly endless regressions, in order to find the most solid place to start. For our purposes, though, and in order best to understand Roethke's urge to begin, our starting place must be at Open House, a "rock" of its own sort, at Roethke's chronological beginning.

Behind the excitement, the anticipation, the vision of where one would come to be, the urge to begin suggests also dissatisfaction with where one has, in fact, ended up. Theodore Roethke's verse addresses the full range of each of these contrary but related motives, though his is no simple journey from alienation to arrival.

1

In a sense, there are two Theodore Roethkes displayed in the poetry, each of whom offers a way of overcoming alienation and a way of arriving. Each is concerned with the self, and in that broad sense there is only one Theodore Roethke, but at different points in his career one or the other of the two poets and the two ways takes precedence. Prominent in the poems of Open House, for example, is Roethke's suspicion of the flesh, his faith in what he calls the "spare spirit." In some of his earliest poems, Roethke exhibits an almost Calvinistic sense of guilt and sin. Though at times in the poems of Open House he appears to want to liberate desire, he seems more forcefully to want to burn off the offending flesh, the "unhealthy elements" of the self, as James McMichael puts it in his essay, "The Poetry of Theodore Roethke" (p. 5). This Theodore Roethke, the "despiser of the body," is the poet often perceived in the poems of Open House and, once detected, followed throughout the career, as we shall see in the influential discussions of Ralph J. Mills, Jr., and Karl Malkoff. This is the Theodore Roethke who will later declare that "Being, not doing, is my first joy" (CP, p. 222). This Roethke seeks the "imperishable quiet at the heart of form" (CP, p. 188); he prefers the "still joy" (CP, p. 163), and wants to leave behind him, in his "long journey out of the self" (CP, p. 193), those "perpetual beginnings" that thin the "soul's substance" (CP, p. 171). This is the Theodore Roethke we find in "The Meditations of an Old Woman," in the "North American Sequence," and in the "Sequence, Sometimes Metaphysical." This Roethke values spirit over flesh and, like the roses in his father's greenhouse, he reaches out of himself toward the light, leaving behind him the body. Many who have defended Theodore Roethke's poetic reputation in the past twenty years have focused primarily on this Roethke, and on those poems where "nobility/at odds with circumstance" (CP, p. 239) comes to a place of balance, as the rose in the sea-wind at the end of the "North American Sequence" marks and shares a boundary with the fresh water and the salt.

At the same time, however, there is another Theodore Roethke evident in the Collected Poems and, to an extent, evident in the poems of Open House. Less articulate, he tells us, less prone to categories and valuations, this Roethke thrives on action, excess, and sensuality. This Roethke is the "roaring boy," commandant of the "sleek captains of intuition" (CP, p. 169), for whom reason is "that dreary shed, that hutch for grubby schoolboys!" (CP, p. 92). While we might call the first of the Roethkes a reflective and philosophical man, this second Roethke comes closer to the mystic (in the strict sense of the term), who concentrates on experiencing, rather than articulating, the "eternal things" (CP, p. 241). Of the two Roethkes, the second comes to the fore in the Greenhouse poems and the Lost Son narratives, but it takes some effort to detect this Roethke in the poems of Open House. Given as they are to celebrating excesses, overeating, bad manners, and obesity, the two sections of nonsense and children's poems emerge also from the second Roethke. Though almost universally ignored in recent criticism, those less serious poems have an important place in the Collected Poems; they help to indicate that Roethke's was not an unbroken journey from the intuitive to the philosophical. Within individual books and even within individual poems, Theodore Roethke's two emphases coexist and often collide, but that part of him which was the philosophical poet did come to the fore in his last poems.

In his poetry, Roethke establishes a tension between flesh and spirit, between desire and the extinction of desire. He also phrases this central tension as one between darkness and light. A long literary and religious tradition has filled the imagery of light and darkness with associations, and in much of his work Roethke uses the associations in accord with the tradition. That is, light (and its attendant, the soul or the spirit) is presented as good, and darkness (and its attendant, the flesh or desire) is presented as evil. Most critics observe this opposition. They see the "journey out of the self" as a move from the fleshly to the spiritual, from the darkness to the light. At one level, of course, Roethke's poetic career supports such a reading, but throughout the long journey there are strong indications that Roethke himself is not nearly so comfortable with the tradition as many would have us believe.

Traditionally in the Western world, light is aligned with the mind and with reason, and darkness is associated with the body and with desire. Roethke is unwilling to celebrate reason, however, nor is he willing to devalue the body's desire entirely. For Roethke, the traditional opposition between darkness and light cannot be a complete one. As we shall see, he finds crucial inspiration in darkness and desire. Darkness and light and flesh and spirit are contraries for Roethke, not opposites. Unwilling to set darkness and light and body and spirit into complete opposition, Roethke is nonetheless willing to exploit the ready conflict that literary and religious tradition can provide any Western poet who speaks in the polarizing terms.

In some of his poems, Roethke manages to balance both terms in the dialectic, but in others the bias toward the light and the spirit, inherent in religious and literary tradition, powerfully asserts itself. That influence is compounded by Roethke's use, in his later work, of two poets themselves directed by the traditional imagery, T. S. Eliot and William Butler Yeats. A number of critics have charged that Roethke's later poetry is unduly influenced by those potent poetic voices, but Roethke's more signal problem in exploiting the conflicts inherent in the traditional imagery was that he was intuitively opposed to the notion that any conflict was entailed by those images. He was thus in conflict with himself, because so many of his poems indicate that he could see goodness in the dark, could see dangers in the light. He would not do so consistently, however. That he could at all separates

him from other poets of his generation, and it remains one of his
major contributions to a generation of contemporary poets, part
of whose project is to explore in more detail the resources of
this unorthodox poetic imagery.

In the last year of his life, Roethke appears to have detected
the two contrary motives in his work. In his statement delivered
at Northwestern University in February of 1963, and later published
as the essay "On 'Identity,' " Roethke reflected on the poems of
Open House, and corrected a mistake that he then saw in them: "the
spirit or soul--should we say the self, once perceived, becomes the
soul?--this I was keeping 'spare' in my desire for the essential.
But the spirit need not be spare: it can grow gracefully and beautifully like a tendril, like a flower. I did not know this at
the time" (SP, p. 21). Later, in a paragraph editor Ralph J. Mills,
Jr., says was marked by Roethke for deletion, Roethke continues,
"but the young often do have an acute sense of defilement, a hatred
of the body . . . [Roethke here quotes the last seven lines of
a poem from Open House, "Epidermal Macabre," and comments], . . .
Hyperbole, of course, but behind it is still the same desire for
a reality of the spirit. Again I was wrong. For the body should
be cherished: a temple of God, some Christians say" (SP, pp. 22-23).

It is difficult to determine exactly why Roethke wanted to omit
his reflections on "Epidermal Macabre." Perhaps he thought the
paragraph itself descended to piety in the conclusion, or that he
had aligned himself too closely with Christian notions of the body.
Perhaps he found himself recanting a former poem unnecessarily. In
any case, it is clear that marking the paragraph for omission does
not mean Roethke thought it contained an inaccuracy, for in the
passage he simply makes more pointed the attitude he had earlier
implied. Earlier in the essay, in lines he did not mean to omit,
Roethke says, "nor need this final self, or spirit, be a foulness,
a disgusting thing from which we should be delivered" (SP, p. 22).

Reviews and Overviews

The first readers of Open House did not have to confront the
problem of where to start with Roethke's poetry. They were offered
the start, the only beginning, the one book, Open House. The book
contained forty-five short and formal lyric poems, arranged in five
numbered sections. (When Roethke selected poems from Open House
to include in The Waking and Words for the Wind, he chose only
seventeen of the original forty-five poems.) When Open House was
published in March of 1941, it was by no means a major event in
American poetry, nor has it been seen as such since then. Open
House was neither ignored nor applauded enthusiastically, but reviewers were nearly unanimous in finding merit in the forty-five
poems. W. H. Auden, Babette Deutsch, John Holmes, Rolfe Hum-

phries, Yvor Winters, and others received the well-mannered poems
of Roethke's first book graciously, if not enthusiastically. Primarily, the reviewers directed their attention to Roethke's technique, singling out poems like "The Adamant" for special comments:

> Thought does not crush to stone.
> The great sledge drops in vain.
> Truth never is undone;
> Its shafts remain.
>
> The teeth of knitted gears
> Turn slowly through the night,
> But the true substance bears
> The hammer's weight.
>
> Compression cannot break
> A center so congealed;
> The tool can chip no flake:
> The core lies sealed.
>   [CP, p. 9]

Praise for Open House was leavened with qualifications, however,
and with suggestions for improvement. Interestingly--and percep-
tively--Roethke's first readers viewed Open House as what it was,
a first book of poems, an apprentice work, and viewed its poet
as a skilled newcomer who had yet to come fully into his own. The
reviewers were not above offering specific suggestions, directing
their comments primarily to matters of technique. For example,
Stephen Baldanza noted too much restraint and caution in Roethke's
first poems; W. H. Auden thought Roethke might broaden his interests
and reading; and, after noting how Roethke's natural descriptions
evoke emotion through "exactness of epithet" and simplicity of diction, Louis Forster, Jr., called for "experimentation with metrical
irregularity," for "greater boldness" (p. 224).
     When Open House was the only volume of Roethke's poems available
to readers, little attention was directed to the poetic vision that
the poet might be developing. The immediate reaction to Roethke's
first book focused upon his technical virtuosity, rather than upon
the nature of his thematic explorations. That distinction is an
important one to make, for critical discussion of Open House in
the decades after its publication has reversed that emphasis.
Most critics cite Open House today to show that Roethke's mature
verse had its roots in his first book, or to show emphatically that
it did not. The somewhat modest first poems in Roethke's Open
House have, therefore, become controversial ones. Where the first
reviewers stood together in their general appreciation of Roethke's
beginnings, the critical opinion of Roethke's first book in the
years since has divided considerably.
     Current critical opinion of Open House might be divided into

two camps: one group reacts very negatively to Roethke's first
poems both on stylistic and thematic grounds. Individual poems
in Open House still inspire enthusiastic commentary ("The Adamant,"
"Open House," and "The Premonition" are frequently cited), but a
number of critics think Open House as a whole does not add evidence
indispensable for understanding Roethke's mature vision or his
most innovative poetic technique. Some who otherwise like Roethke's verse have little patience with the poems of Open House. For
example, in his essay of 1965, "That Anguish of Concreteness,"
W. D. Snodgrass wrote that the poems of Open House are "old-
fashioned and prerevolutionary"; some verge on "sentimentality and
ladies' verse" (p. 79). The same year, Louis Martz argued in "A
Greenhouse Eden" that "the celebration of the naked bone, the spare
spirit, and the sealed core is not the central mode of Roethke; it
is indeed the very opposite of his true motion, which is to unseal,
to let flow forth, to nourish into growth" (p. 20). In 1968, in
"Theodore Roethke and the Landscape of American Poetry," C. W.
Truesdale reiterated that evaluation by saying that Open House
"unmistakably suggests the wrong kind of future" for Roethke
(p. 345). More recently, in Theodore Roethke's Dynamic Vision,
Richard Blessing observes that Roethke's first book "buzzes
with various promises, most of them misleading" (p. 40). Many
critics think that Open House is the wrong place to start in discussing Roethke's poetry, and their impatience with the early poems
makes itself evident: though nearly every book or full-length essay
on Roethke begins with some attention to Open House, in their discussions these critics move as briskly as possible through Open
House in order to get to Roethke's more innovative work.

   Not all recent critics are as impatient with Roethke's Open
House as are these individuals, however. John Wain's reading of
Open House in "The Monocle of My Sea-Faced Uncle" is surely excep-
tional in that he thinks the "direction in which his [Roethke's]
gift was moving must have been evident to the attentive reader
from the beginning" (p. 69). But the first major attempt to
disclose connections between Roethke's Open House and his later
poetry was offered by Ralph J. Mills, Jr. In Theodore Roethke,
his brief overview of the majority of Roethke's poetry, Mills
argues that the poems of Open House constitute the first step
in what was to become Roethke's lifelong poetic project, the
"journey out of the self." According to Mills, Roethke's poetry
as a whole is a "restless quest for that communion in which self
and creation are joined" (p. 8), and in the poems of Open House
Mills sees Roethke examining two subjects central to his poetic
project: "the correspondence between the poet's inner life and
the life of nature, and the strengths or weaknesses of the individual psyche" (p. 10). The second of these two subjects is
more prominent in the early stages of Roethke's quest, Mills
says, and in Open House Roethke explores, tests, and establishes
the self, a term Mills defines as "a principle of identity and

of being which is generally spiritual in character but also reaches into the realm of the physical" (p. 8). Mills believes that the "journey out of the self" is fundamental to Roethke's poetry, but Mills wants to argue, paradoxically, that the self remains essentially intact in the course of this journey. The "journey out of the self," in fact, is predicated upon strengthening, not weakening, the self. When "self and creation are joined," Mills believes, the self is not dismantled but fulfilled. Mills does not suggest that this ultimate end is achieved in Open House, of course, but he does see Roethke preparing for that goal in these first poems by fortifying the self, by defining it.

Where Mills believes that Roethke values equally the spirit and the flesh in the poems of Open House, Karl Malkoff notes in his book, Theodore Roethke: An Introduction to the Poetry, that the central opposition of Open House is "between flesh and spirit . . . between analysis and intuition" (p. 38). Malkoff draws that conclusion based on his reading of Open House as well as on his study of the uncollected poems written contemporaneously with--but not published in--Open House. (Many of these poems appear in Mills's edition of the Selected Letters of Theodore Roethke.) According to Malkoff, the central tension most evident in the unpublished work is nonetheless available to the reader of Open House. In his widely acknowledged reading of the book, Malkoff argues, like Mills before him, that Open House is concerned primarily with the definition of the self. The five numbered sections of Open House mark the stages in the gradual acquisition of that self-knowledge. In the poems of part 1, Malkoff says, the poet moves "from analytic probing to vision as a means of knowing the self" (p. 32). In part 2, the self is "seen in terms of the correspondence between inner and outer reality" (p. 33). In the third part, the self is illuminated "by nonbeing, by negation." Part 4 moderates the seriousness of the third part, and here the self is viewed from the "distance of comic perspective." In the fifth and last part, the self is presented in its "social context" (p. 33). By this, Malkoff later explains, he means the love poem, for "the only form of social behavior that was, for Roethke, the stuff of poetry was the most personal and private of all, love" (p. 34). Malkoff concludes by observing that "the structure of Open House is far more complicated than that of any other book by Roethke" (p. 33). Malkoff's assertion about the structure of Open House has since been persuasively refuted, as we shall see, but his reading is useful in raising a major issue in Roethke's poetry, the tension between spirit and flesh.

In "Circling toward the Pain: Open House," the first chapter in Theodore Roethke, a volume in the Twayne series, George Wolff acknowledges Malkoff's argument by observing that one might organize Roethke's first poems structurally. Wolff sees the subjects of the five numbered sections of Open House as "the sick spirit, nature, the flesh and the spirit, sex and writing, and . . . the problems of American society," in that order (p. 23). Wolff thus agrees with Malkoff's structural reading to a large extent, but he departs significantly from Malkoff in that he prefers to read Open House in thematic rather than structural terms. In order to do this, Wolff ignores Roethke's organization of the poems in Open House. He collects the poems into five groups of his own making. As the title of his chapter indicates, Wolff will discuss the central themes of these five new groups of poems from the "most emotionally distant to the one that most closely approaches the painful center" (p. 23).

Wolff's first theme involves "natural description laden with implications of another order of experience" (p. 24). Poems containing this theme include "The Premonition," "The Light Comes Brighter," and "Night Journey," the poem Wolff finds the best in the book. Though at an emotional distance from the "painful center," poems addressing the first theme are among the "best poems in Open House," he argues, because they depict "symbolic landscapes" much as do the Greenhouse poems several years later (p. 24). With the second theme, the "spiritual power of vision," Roethke "approaches more closely the underlying emotional core of Open House" (p. 25). Recapitulating Malkoff's opposition between spirit and flesh, Wolff suggests that vision (in the sense of eyesight) is the "mode of perception most amenable to the imagination, most likely to become visionary" (p. 26). By valuing eyesight above the other senses that "deal more corporeally with their objects," Roethke moves toward the spirit and away from the flesh, Wolff says. This theme appears in "Prayer" and in "The Signals." The third theme "grew out of Roethke's personal experiences with manic-depressive psychosis." Poems like "Feud" and "Death Piece" show that "invention or creativity can cure an inherited curse" (p. 26), but Wolff himself seems somewhat confused by the purpose of this third theme. In a note, he remarks that he "can find no evidence that Roethke thought his mental illness was hereditary" (p. 135), and Wolff seems relieved to take a "step closer to the emotional core" with his fourth theme, the "defensiveness of the spare spirit" (p. 27). "Long Live the Weeds," "Epidermal Macabre," and "Open House" incorporate this theme of discorporation. Wolff sees connections between "Open House" and Roethke's last work, in that he was "denying the value of the body and its appetites . . . being more otherworldly than he would ever be again until the last poems in his final book" (p. 29). In poems containing the fifth theme, Roethke "does not speak of tactics for containing or detoxifying the emotions at the core; he presents the emotions directly." Wolff cites "The Gentle" and "On the Road to Woodlawn" as "explicit statements of the horrors of madness and death" (p. 29), and he implies that the "painful center" Roethke finally arrives at in such poems he will

speak from again in the poems of The Lost Son. Wolff's reading
is an attempt to detect in the poems of Open House a premonition
of the more emotionally charged Greenhouse poems published in
1948, but his is no advance over Karl Malkoff's flawed, though
more plausibly based, study. As Wolff's interpretation illustrates,
useful discussion of the themes of Open House requires recourse
to poems other than those that appear within the two boards of the
book itself.

Neal Bowers focuses more directly on the matter of the relationship between spirit and flesh in Roethke's early poems in his book
Theodore Roethke: The Journey from I to Otherwise, one of the
most recent discussions of the issue. Bowers appears at first to
agree with Mills's perception of Roethke's perilous balance of spirit and flesh. Bowers writes that "the early poems, particularly
those of Open House, represent a preliminary excursion along the
road of the mystic quest" (p. 71). Like Malkoff, however, Bowers thinks the movement of the poems in Open House is "away from
flesh and analytical thought"; Bowers stresses both the antirational
and the anticorporeal qualities of the poems (p. 70). Mills finds
Roethke's mystical quest to be ultimately successful, but Bowers
believes Roethke's entire project involves an "impossible contra-
diction" (p. 209). Roethke's "struggle for identity inevitably
necessitated the loss of his identity," Bowers concludes; "his desire was to attain ultimate union, but he could not bear to pay
the ultimate cost, the loss of his own individual identity" (pp.
208-9). Bowers traces the roots of that paradox to Roethke's earliest poems, to Open House. There, according to Bowers, Roethke
displays a fatal ambivalency toward "ultimate union." Bowers notes
that Roethke is both fascinated by dying and haunted by dying, and
he cites as examples the poems "Prayer before Study" and "Epidermal Macabre," the latter reprinted here:

> Indelicate is he who loathes
> The aspect of his fleshy clothes,--
> The flying fabric stitched on bone,
> The vesture of the skeleton,
> The garment neither fur nor hair,
> The cloak of evil and despair,
> The veil long violated by
> Caresses of the hand and eye.
> Yet such is my unseemliness:
> I hate my epidermal dress,
> The savage blood's obscenity,
> The rags of my anatomy,
> And willingly would I dispense
> With false accouterments of sense,
> To sleep immodestly, a most
> Incarnadine and carnal ghost.
>   [CP, p. 19]

On purely thematic grounds, Bowers appears to be correct in his interpretation, but after a closer look at the tone of "Epidermal Macabre," it is clear that the speaker of this poem is in complete control of his emotions. In "Epidermal Macabre," as well as in "Prayer before Study," deliverance from the body is a subject for humor more than terror, as evidenced in "Epidermal Macabre" by Roethke's witty use of rhymed couplets, his polysyllabic rhyme ("obscenity"/"anatomy"), and his clever and learned pun in the concluding line.

Like Karl Malkoff before him, Richard Blessing examined Roethke's undergraduate papers, his notes, and his uncollected poems, but based on much the same evidence Blessing draws conclusions very different from Malkoff's. In his reading of Open House in his book, Theodore Roethke's Dynamic Vision, Blessing argues that Roethke chooses very early to side with the "dynamic values of change, growth, and development as opposed to the static virtues of order and stability" (p. 14). In that respect, Blessing's is a negative reading of Open House: he finds most important what he sees Roethke working to avoid or restrain. Blessing disagrees with Malkoff that Roethke takes a first step toward the spirit in Open House; he disagrees with Wolff that Roethke's first poems circle toward and then disclose the "pain." For Blessing, Roethke's major achievement in Open House is his discovery, however tentative, of a "force that floods, swells, and finally bursts--the concept of a terrible energy straining to be free" (p. 45). In Open House, that "energy" (source of what Blessing will come to call Roethke's "dynamic vision") is "most keenly felt through its absence" (p. 39). Energy is potential only in Open House, and disclosed primarily when the barriers erected to contain it topple down, as in "Idyll," "Sale," and "The Reminder" (p. 51). The poem "Highway: Michigan" can become a figure for the volume as a whole, Blessing suggests. In it, finally, energy goes wild and "the body, the machine, cannot withstand the terrible energy within" (p. 47). Blessing likens the situation of that poem to Roethke's situation as a poet. In Open House, the "formal arrangement of words which is the poet's 'machine' is never quite up to the pace" (p. 47).

In addition to questioning the prevalent view that Roethke works to suppress the flesh, the body, source of wnat he calls "energy," Richard Blessing also offers a convincing refutation of Karl Malkoff's analysis of the five numbered sections of Open House. In response to Malkoff, Blessing observes, for example, that "the first section is no more 'personal pronoun' than the others, if by that one means that the poetry of the section is written in the first person" (p. 41). Because the poems contained in Open House, as well as the lines and stanzas within those poems, are curiously "interchangeable" ones, as we shall see, Blessing thinks the structure of Open House is "not so much complex and subtle as it is artificial and tenuous" (p. 42).

Roethke himself offers corroborating evidence on the structural point. In a letter to Ben Belitt dated August 8, 1938, Roethke says of Open House, "[Stanley] Kunitz arranged it" (SL, p. 68), and in responding to a comment by Katherine Anne Porter about the structure of Open House, Roethke writes, "the point you made about the arrangement [of Open House] is absolutely right, of course; as a matter of fact, I had already moved these pieces, which might have been written by almost anyone, to the center of the book" (SL, p. 89).

Malkoff's complex rationale for the structure of Open House will not stand up to careful scrutiny, therefore, but that in itself does not utterly invalidate his argument. Malkoff's major contribution to discussion of Open House is his identification of Roethke's interest in the "spare spirit"; that notion has repeatedly been seen as a central concern in Roethke's first book and in his poetry as a whole. Malkoff has isolated only part of the dialectic, however. To Malkoff's emphasis on the spirit we need to add Richard Blessing's countering argument. Blessing balances Malkoff's view by identifying and then emphasizing the undercurrent of dynamic energy that obtrudes in Open House sporadically. If we look at the poems Roethke wrote shortly after 1941 and did not include in his first book, it is possible to see more clearly that the parallel thematic concerns do emerge in Open House. In important respects, the poems of Open House continue into and culminate in parts 2 and 3 of his second book, The Lost Son and Other Poems, published in 1948.

As Karl Malkoff has pointed out, the poems of parts 2 and 3 of The Lost Son appeared in periodicals between 1941-44, and the Greenhouse poems of part 1 appeared between 1946-48 (p. 45). In other words, the poems of parts 2 and 3 preceded the composition of the poems of part 1. No doubt realizing that the Greenhouse poems were among the strongest and most accessible in the book, Roethke functionally suppressed the connections between Open House and The Lost Son by relegating poems more reminiscent of Open House to the less prominent second and third parts. Of course, there was nothing underhanded in so doing, but Roethke's own structural decision emphasizes the differences rather than the similarities between Open House and the Greenhouse. Roethke's arrangement of poems in his second volume is thus an assertion of a literary identity, not a historical one. (To show that in the later 1930s and 1940s Roethke graduated from "the support of formal verse" to try to "re-create the process of perception in the act of writing" [p. 417], Don Bogen has charted Roethke's stylistic transition through three poems, "Genesis" [dating from the mid-1930s], "On the Road to Woodlawn" [from the late 1930s], and "Cuttings" [from the mid-1940s], in his essay, "From Open House to the Greenhouse: Theodore Roethke's Poetic Breakthrough.") In order to account for that literary identity, we need to look at how poems in parts 2 and 3 of The Lost Son connect Open House and the

Greenhouse thematically. When filtered through the second and
third parts of The Lost Son, it should be clearer that Roethke's
early commitment to the "spare spirit" in the poems of Open House
is not as complete as Karl Malkoff argues. Nor, by reading parts
2 and 3 of The Lost Son as if they follow the poems of Open
House, need one postulate the existence of a mysterious poetic
breakthrough to account for the radically different, highly accomplished Greenhouse poems of part 1 of The Lost Son. By reading
parts 2 and 3 of The Lost Son as if they are parts 6 and 7 of Open
House, by coming into Roethke's Open House through the back door,
as it were, it is possible to clarify the thematic concerns of
Open House and show the connectedness rather than the disruption
between Roethke's first book and his famous Greenhouse poems. As
an additional advantage of this procedure, the reader can get a
taste of Roethke's more accomplished work within the discussion
of his apprentice poems.

Roethke's "Poetic Breakthrough"

The two major themes of parts 2 and 3 of The Lost Son are Roethke's dissatisfaction with his fellow humans and with society, and
his eventual discovery of the more fufilling society offered by
what he will call the minimal creatures. In the seven poems of
part 2 of The Lost Son, Roethke writes about other persons and
about himself in the social context of those other persons more
directly than he does anywhere else in his poetry. (Some critics
make much of this fact, as we shall see in chapters 4 and 5.)
Roethke's relationship to the persons depicted in the poems of
part 2 involves unresolved conflicts, however, even in those poems
where he seems most engaged by other people, as in "My Papa's
Waltz," for example. In this frequently anthologized poem, Roethke depicts himself as a little boy clinging to his father, Otto,
but he also communicates in the poem the fear his father inspires.
He hints at his brutality:

> The whiskey on your breath
> Could make a small boy dizzy;
> But I hung on like death:
> Such waltzing was not easy.
>
> We romped until the pans
> Slid from the kitchen shelf;
> My mother's countenance
> Could not unfrown itself.
>
> The hand that held my wrist
> Was battered on one knuckle;

> At every step you missed
> My right ear scraped a buckle.
>
> You beat time on my head
> With a palm caked hard by dirt,
> Then waltzed me off to bed
> Still clinging to your shirt.
>   [CP p. 45]

Roethke introduces an additional bit of conflict into the family scene by mentioning his mother's dissatisfaction with her husband's behavior.

In the other poems of the second section, the variety of his difficulty in relating to other people becomes prominent. In "Pickle Belt," Roethke describes an adolescent, presumably himself, who is sexually excited by the woman who works beside him in the factory, but the occasion offers him only frustration and discomfort. In the concluding quatrain of the poem, the "perplexed" youth stands "in his shrunken britches,/Eyes rimmed with pickle dust,/ Prickling with all the itches/Of sixteen-year-old lust" (CP. p. 46). In "Dolor," a grown-up Roethke reflects in the first person upon his experience as a teacher. The images Roethke creates and the despair he communicates carry none of the excitement that Roethke himself could generate in the classroom:

> I have known the inexorable sadness of pencils,
> Neat in their boxes, dolor of pad and paper-weight,
> All the misery of manilla folders and mucilage,
> Desolation in immaculate public places,
> Lonely reception room, lavatory, switchboard,
> The unalterable pathos of basin and pitcher,
> Ritual of multigraph, paper-clip, comma,
> Endless duplication of lives and objects.
> And I have seen dust from the walls of institutions,
> Finer than flour, alive, more dangerous than silica,
> Sift, almost invisible, through long afternoons of tedium,
> Dropping a fine film on nails and delicate eyebrows,
> Glazing the pale hair, the duplicate grey standard faces.
>   [CP, p. 46]

The major point of the fourth poem in the section, "Double Feature," seems to be to make the reader feel sorry for the speaker. By presenting him lonely and isolated, hoping for something else, however, the poem continues the impression of Roethke's distance from and difficulty with other people. "Double Feature" is not one of the best poems in the section, and Roethke omitted it from his selection in Words for the Wind. Roethke does not court sympathy in "The Return." Like a cornered animal, he turns on his pursuers, though it should also be noted that some of Roethke's animosity is

directed in this poem at himself. In that respect, with its mention of "that self-infected lair," Roethke's "The Return" has some
of the character of his student James Wright's "Inscription for the
Tank." Where Wright finds finally the value of his life in his
poem, however, Roethke resolves in his piece merely to be defiant:

> I circled on leather paws
> In the darkening corridor,
> Crouched closer to the floor,
> Then bristled like a dog.
>
> As I turned for a backward look,
> The muscles in one thigh
> Sagged like a frightened lip.
>
> A cold key let me in
> That self-infected lair;
> And I lay down with my life,
> With the rags and rotting clothes,
> With a stump of scraggy fang
> Bared for a hunter's boot.
>   [CP, p. 47]

In the subsequent poem, "Last Words," the "fine fuming stink of
particular kettles" and the "Frigidaires snoring the sleep of plen-
ty" inspire a dissatisfaction reminiscent of that in "Dolor" (CP,
p. 48). Roethke's desire to escape the "Muttony tears falling on
figured linoleum," the "psyche writhing and squirming in heavy wool-
en," and the "worm of duty" results in his direct request to be
liberated. The vague "something else I was hoping for" of "Double
Feature" becomes in "Last Words" an appeal to an equally vague
"mistress of lost wisdom": "Come out of a cloud, angel with several
faces,/Bring me my hat, my umbrella and rubbers,/Enshroud me with
Light! O Whirling! O Terrible Love!" (CP, p. 48).
     The angel does not come out of the cloud in the last poem in the
second section, however, nor does the section end with the plea
of "Last Words." It concludes, rather, on a distinctly misanthropic note, and in a poem Roethke chose also to exclude from Words
for the Wind. While asking that "the blessings of life, O Lord,
descend on the living," on the children "staring from newsprint"
(CP, p. 48), Roethke asks also in "Judge Not" that on "drunkards
howling" and on "women, their eyelids like little rags" Death should
come down (CP, p. 48). Thus, Roethke's distance from human beings
could not be more total. He concludes the second section of The
Lost Son by positioning himself nearer God and Death than the human
beings he has depicted.
     Roethke's alienation from other persons is the central problem
of part 2 of The Lost Son, and at places in the section, that ali-

enation is transformed into misanthropy. Some of those sentiments
might be traced to the poems of part 4 of Open House, poems that
Karl Malkoff has observed are "comic" and satiric. Such poems
include "Poetaster" (CP, p. 24), "My Dim-Wit Cousin" (CP, p. 25),
and especially "Academic": "The stethoscope tells what everyone
fears:/You're likely to go on living for years,/With a nurse-maid
waddle and a shop-girl simper,/And the style of your prose growing
limper and limper" (CP, p. 23). With its almost nursery rhyme
use of wit and terror, there is a similarly comic spirit to "The
Bat," a poem from part 2 of Open House. "The Bat" does conclude
with what some might see as a misanthropic metaphor, however: "For
something is amiss or out of place/When mice with wings can wear
a human face" (CP, p. 16). In order to identify as closely as he
does with the bat, of course, Roethke must distance himself from
the human perspective. That identification and that distance will
become trademarks of his Greenhouse and Lost Son poems.

Roethke's more fundamentally negative sentiments toward other
people appear elsewhere in Open House, a book, it might be said,
about closing rather than opening the self to others. In "To My
Sister," for example, Roethke counsels his sister to remain aloof
from others:

> O my sister remember the stars the tears the trains
> The woods in spring the leaves the scented lanes
> Recall the gradual dark the snow's unmeasured fall
> The naked fields the cloud's immaculate folds
> Recount each childhood pleasure: the skies of azure
> The pageantry of wings the eye's bright treasure.
>
> Keep faith with present joys refuse to choose
> Defer the vice of flesh the irrevocable choice
> Cherish the eyes the proud incredible poise
> Walk boldly my sister but do not deign to give
> Remain secure from pain preserve thy hate thy heart.
> [CP, p. 5]

In and of itself, and as opposed to "spirit," "flesh" is not the
problem here. Other people are the problem, and how they hurt one
another through inevitably failing attempts at loving. Roethke's
desire to sustain the "proud incredible poise" by not giving shall
return as an important problem in his later Love Poems. "To My
Sister" is additionally notable in that Roethke breaks from the
rigidities of stanza and rhyme so typical of Open House, approxi-
mating a stream of consciousness by suppressing most punctuation.
Doing so, of course, amid more considered and formal poems allows
the reader to discount "To My Sister" as anomalous, to see that
the poem is intended as a fit of distemper. In this respect, the
poem not only talks about remaining shielded from others; it pro-

tects itself stylistically and thus discourages too intent an analysis.

Other poems in Open House, "Reply to Censure" and its attendant "Silence" (which might be read as a kind of "Fear of Censure"), outline Roethke's hostility toward the hostile and insensitive audience, and "Silence" ends with the same reluctance to risk opening oneself to others ("What shakes my skull to disrepair/Shall never touch another ear" [CP, p. 22]) as does "To My Sister" and its even better-known antecedent, the title poem "Open House":

> My secrets cry aloud.
> I have no need for tongue.
> My heart keeps open house,
> My doors are widely swung.
> An epic of the eyes
> My love, with no disguise.
>
> My truths are all foreknown,
> This anguish self-revealed.
> I'm naked to the bone,
> With nakedness my shield.
> Myself is what I wear:
> I keep the spirit spare.
>
> The anger will endure,
> The deed will speak the truth
> In language strict and pure.
> I stop the lying mouth:
> Rage warps my clearest cry
> To witless agony.
>   [CP, p. 3]

In fact, "Open House" discloses fewer intelligible "secrets" than is usually supposed, since an undercurrent of "rage," Roethke promises us, will transform even his "clearest cry" (i.e., "Open House") into "witless agony." Thus, Roethke actually advances a negative attitude toward language in the poem: he has "no need for tongue" and he advances the antipoetic sentiment that actions speak louder than words: "the deed will speak the truth/In language strict and pure" (CP, p. 3). By framing it with comments critical of language and communication, Roethke announces in "Open House" his reluctance to become entangled with the major means of relating to other human beings. Instead of being an introduction to his book that invites the reader to follow, Roethke's inaugural poem shuts the door on language.

Had Roethke pursued in a conventional way the misanthropic strain evident in parts of his early poetry, his verse might have developed in the direction of explicit social or cultural criticism. That

Roethke did not develop in that way is the subject of much discussion, as we shall see, but it is important to note that his gradual retreat from society betrays no artistic inadequacy on his part. The early misanthropic strain led him to consider the value and significance of what he termed the minimal creatures. That move was a creative act, a discovery, an artistic choice with important ramifications for the remainder of Roethke's verse. James McMichael highlights the momentousness of Roethke's shift in attention in his essay, "The Poetry of Theodore Roethke," by suggesting that Roethke was faced with an important spiritual alternative early in his career. Using a theological discourse that somewhat misrepresents Roethke's aims, McMichael writes that Roethke had available two avenues toward God as outlined by the philosopher Blaise Pascal: the way of the infinitely large and the way of the infinitely small. (In the hands of the most gifted poets, of course, the particular becomes universal and the universal illuminates each particular.) In the earliest stages of his career, Roethke tentatively explored both of Pascal's avenues but, as McMichael observes correctly, Roethke chose the way of the microcosm. Roethke exhausted the macrocosmic tendencies of Open House in the misanthropic poems of part 2 of The Lost Son, and he prepared for his finest delvings into the microcosm with the quasi-Greenhouse poems of part 3 of The Lost Son.

Just as the misanthropic tendency is evident in Roethke's concern for aloofness from others in certain poems in Open House, so his identification with the minimal world is prefigured in a generalized way in his first book. The term in Open House that will flower into the principle of identification with the minimal world is "blood," a term Roethke does seem to denigrate in Open House. In Open House, Roethke appears to value the clarity he can receive through his eyes rather than the murkier kind of affinity he can sense through the unruly, more intuitive "blood." Roethke's mistrust of the "blood" comes across clearly in "Prayer":

If I must of my Senses lose,
I pray Thee, Lord, that I may choose
Which of the Five I shall retain
Before oblivion clouds the brain.
My Tongue is generations dead,
My Nose defiles a comely head;
For hearkening to carnal evils
My Ears have been the very devil's.
And some have held the Eye to be
The instrument of lechery,
More furtive than the Hand in low
And vicious venery--Not so!
Its rape is gentle, never more
Violent than a metaphor.
In truth, the Eye's the abettor of

> The holiest platonic love:
> Lip, Breast and Thigh cannot possess
> So singular a blessedness.
> Therefore, O Lord, let me preserve
> The Sense that does so fitly serve,
> Take Tongue and Ear--all else I have--
> Let Light attend me to the grave!
> [CP. p. 8]

A similar valuation of the eyes appears in "Orders for the Day" (CP, p. 7).

In opposition to the primacy of the "eyes," Roethke puts the dysteleological "rage" he associates with "blood" and "confusion." "Blood" has two separable but connected meanings in Roethke's early verse. On the one hand, it indicates rather explicitly his family relationships and inheritances. On the other, it alludes to an intuitive means of sensing the world around one. Apparently, Roethke works out a more uncompromising attitude toward the first meaning of the term than he does toward the second. In Open House, Roethke included several poems highly critical of "blood" in the sense of inheritance, suggesting that an important theme for his work would be conflict with the past, with tradition, with family, in the mode later refined by Robert Lowell. As other poems in Open House indicate, however ("The Premonition," "The Reminder"), Roethke's relationship with his family was decidedly not antagonistic. Though at times uneasy, Roethke's relation to his family, and to his father in particular, was essentially affectionate, even adoring. "Feud" (CP, p. 4), "Prognosis" (CP, p. 5), "Orders for the Day" (CP, p. 7) and other poems that allude, as in "Sale," to some "taint in a blood that was running too thin" (CP, p. 32) are, in fact, dead ends and wrong directions. Roethke's later poetry, of course, shows that his future as a poet lay in turning repeatedly to his past.

Roethke is less emphatic in condemning "blood" as an epistemological principle. Roethke's misgivings about his blood relations survive to a degree in the misanthropic poems of part 2 of The Lost Son, but in part 3 he celebrates the attributes of growth and vitality, qualities we might associate with his term "blood." The early opposition between the "eyes" and the "blood" that Roethke elaborates in Open House is one whose importance to Roethke's larger poetic vision must not be misinterpreted, therefore. In the early work, Roethke seems to side with the higher and more rational faculties associated with eyesight, but in fact his exploration of the darker, more intuitive areas aligned with the "blood" affords him sympathy with the minimal creatures.

An indication of the direction Roethke eventually was to take occurs in "The Signals," a poem in Open House, where he counters his earlier affections for eyesight with this self-study of a deeper kind of perception:

Often I meet, on walking from a door,
A flash of objects never seen before.

As known particulars come wheeling by,
They dart across a corner of the eye.

They flicker faster than a blue-tailed swift,
Or when dark follows dark in lightning rift.

They slip between the fingers of my sight.
I cannot put my glance upon them tight.

Sometimes the blood is privileged to guess
The things the eye or hand cannot possess.
                                        [CP, p. 8]

The privileged blood of the final stanza, blood which turns its
"private substance into green" in "The Light Comes Brighter"
(CP, p. 11), is the intuition, the feeling, the tie of kinship
that will grow to fruition in the Greenhouse poems.

In the third part of The Lost Son, Roethke was to acknowledge
more forthrightly the ambivalences, the opportunities, and the dangers that a poem such as "The Signals" implied. "River Incident,"
the second poem of part 3, and a poem Roethke chose to omit from
Words for the Wind, illustrates those ambivalences. In a sense,
"River Incident" is filled with menace, but Roethke would repeatedly and more confidently take the risk to earn the psychological
insights such circumstances could provide:

A shell arched under my toes,
Stirred up a whirl of silt
That riffled around my knees.
Whatever I owed to time
Slowed in my human form;
Sea water stood in my veins,
The elements I kept warm
Crumbled and flowed away,
And I knew I had been there before,
In that cold, granitic slime,
In the dark, in the rolling water.
                                        [CP, p. 49]

In "The Minimal," another poem from part 3 of The Lost Son,
Roethke moves even farther from human beings and nearer the perspective he would perfect in his Greenhouse poems. The poem is
less specific and less focused than the Greenhouse poems, however.
Roethke addresses tiny creatures, "the minimal," in somewhat generalized terms, and he ranges more freely through their habitat

than elsewhere he will allow. The Greenhouse Roethke would not tolerate such giant, such human, steps among the minimals. At the same time, the hallmarks of the Greenhouse poems appear here. In "The Minimal," we find a remarkably condensed and precise diction that yields a sense of dramatic action; and subjects we might turn from in disgust, were we ever so myopically to see them, we find rendered with respect and, frequently, with sympathy.

> I study the lives on a leaf: the little
> Sleepers, numb nudgers in cold dimensions,
> Beetles in caves, newts, stone-deaf fishes,
> Lice tethered to long limp subterranean weeds,
> Squirmers in bogs,
> And bacterial creepers
> Wriggling through wounds
> Like elvers in ponds,
> Their wan mouths kissing the warm sutures,
> Cleaning and caressing,
> Creeping and healing.
>
> [CP, p. 50]

Such a poem reflects and provides experience of a dimension human beings do not customarily measure. Roethke achieves that through the originality of his perspective and through technique. Here, the terminal masculine rhymes, predictably spaced, that were so typical of the poems of Open House, give way to less obtrusive rhyming effects. In "The Minimal," Roethke dramatizes an almost sickeningly intimate contact with his subjects, in that the little doers of the poem, the sleepers, nudgers, squirmers, and creepers-- and Theodore Roethke through them--finally are immersed, by virtue of rhyme, in "warm sutures." Roethke moves a great distance from other human beings by bending to the minimal creatures, but he himself does not lose his humanity in so doing, it must be said. Roethke will bring to bear on these entities beneath the nose the human eye full of its ambivalency.

We have seen how the twelve poems of parts 2 and 3 of The Lost Son help us to read Open House because they point up the essential motives often obscured and confused in that first book. It is clear from the poems of part 2 of The Lost Son that conflicts expressed in Open House will not be resolved by love of human beings, and it is clear from the poems of part 3 that Roethke's project for addressing those conflicts will tend toward a more radical immersion in the stuff of creation, rather than toward an escape into a more rarefied spiritual sublime. In other words, the poems of parts 2 and 3 of The Lost Son directly counter what are often taken as the very values forged in Open House.

That does not mean, of course, that love of humanity and interest in the spirit are entirely absent from Open House or from Roethke's later works. Those two themes do not come out of Open House, how-

ever, to take center stage in The Lost Son, and this fact changes
the way we might read Open House. Once the misanthropic tendencies of part 2 become prominent, for example, the roots of that
strain emerge more strongly in Roethke's first book. Once Roethke's turn from man to the elements and the minimal creatures in
part 3 is observed, his rejection of "blood" and "rage" in Open
House appears less convinced. By bidding temporary farewell to
humanity, and by pursuing rather than fleeing the motive behind
the vague terms "blood" and "rage," Roethke constructs his relation to the minimal creatures.

Literary Backgrounds and Sources

One would think that the matter of discussing the literary origins
of a significant poet's early work would be a rather neutral and
academic venture. That is not the situation in the case of Theodore Roethke, because he has been accused in his later work of being inordinately affected, even overpowered, by the styles and voices
of other poets. Much discussion of the literary origins and predecessors of Roethke's early work has a hidden agenda, therefore.
Some critics want to show that from the start Roethke leaned too
heavily on earlier work; others seek to show that Roethke asserted
his individuality even when he was learning his craft and openly
acknowledging the distinctive voices of his teachers. However, certain objective observations can be made about the roots of Roethke's
first works, but for these we probably should not turn to Roethke
himself. "I am influenced too much, perhaps, by natural objects,"
Theodore Roethke wrote in an essay entitled "Some Self-Analysis"
as an undergraduate at the University of Michigan (SP, p. 4), but
the influence that shows most powerfully in his first book of poems,
Open House, comes from books rather than from nature. In his review of Open House, W. H. Auden observed and forgave that fact,
and he offered Roethke some advice. He wrote that Roethke "has
read quite enough English poetry for a bit, and should now read
not only the poetry of other cultures, but books that are neither
poetry nor about poetry" (p. 31). Auden implied also that Roethke
might range more freely into alternative and longer poetic forms,
perhaps in noniambic meter. In "The Objective Ego," an essay published some two decades later, Stephen Spender would suggest more
specifically that Roethke's early work echoes Emily Dickinson,
Walt Whitman, Robert Frost, W. H. Auden, Edmund Blunden and, in
the poem "To My Sister," Spender himself (pp. 7-8), but most readers
of Open House would agree with Rolfe Humphries's earlier assess-
ment. In his review, Humphries identified somewhat backhandedly
the literary source of Open House by cautioning Roethke that the
"personal-metaphysical rock will not yield ore indefinitely" (p.
62). Stylistically and thematically, it is generally agreed that

the most prominent literary predecessors of Open House are the seventeenth-century metaphysical poets and poets contemporary with Roethke who were themselves influenced by the metaphysicals.

Reference to the metaphysical tradition corroborates a great deal of Karl Malkoff's interpretation of Open House, and so he treats the matter confidently in his book, Theodore Roethke: An Introduction to the Poetry. Malkoff argues that Roethke turned to the metaphysical and "neo-metaphysical" poets because they shared with him a "similar perception of reality" (p. 19). "Like [John] Donne," Malkoff observes, Roethke "was torn by the split between flesh and spirit; like [George] Herbert, he was tormented by the near impossibility of faith; like [Henry] Vaughan, he sought the eternal in the temporal" (p. 19). Thematic connections also explain Roethke's interest in certain twentieth-century neo-metaphysical poets, a number of whom Roethke knew intimately. According to Malkoff, Roethke's obsession with the spirit/flesh conflict attracted him to his contemporaries W. H. Auden, Elinor Wylie, Leonie Adams, and Louise Bogan, who were also concerned with that thematic opposition. Aware, however, that discussion of Roethke's literary influences can play into the hands of his opponents, Malkoff is careful to credit Roethke with originality, even at this early stage of his career. As with the seventeenth-century metaphysicals, the twentieth-century poets echoed in Open House "loomed in the background," Malkoff adds, "as reasonably well assimilated influences" (p. 9).

In his book, Theodore Roethke's Dynamic Vision, Richard Blessing agrees that the metaphysical poets affected Roethke, but predictably Blessing counters Karl Malkoff's emphasis on the metaphysical origins of the spirit and flesh dichotomy. Blessing thinks Roethke's verse is animated by an appreciation of motion, by a quest for a "dynamic vision," not by an eventual conquest of spirit over flesh. Thus, Blessing believes Roethke appreciated the seventeenth-century metaphysical poet Henry Vaughan because of Vaughan's "belief that God manifests Himself as pure motion and energy" (p. 16). Both Malkoff and Blessing acknowledge Roethke's indebtedness to metaphysical poets and issues, but clearly they disagree on what use Roethke made of those things.

Judging from the exception that Jenijoy La Belle takes to Malkoff's argument in her book, The Echoing Wood of Theodore Roethke, the fact might be overlooked that Karl Malkoff is actually quite generous to Roethke in his discussion of the literary influences in Open House. La Belle's book is the major work on the nature and extent of Roethke's literary influences. It is an indication of the importance of this issue, in the case of most poets a narrow and specialized subject, that one of the small handful of book-length studies of Roethke is devoted to the matter of literary influence. La Belle's central point is that Roethke's use of his literary heritage was creative, not slavish or ventriloquial. La Belle begins to establish her point by discussing the origins of the poems of

Open House. Against Malkoff, La Belle insists at the outset of her book that "Roethke almost never modeled his poems after the general style of any literary period or tradition; instead, he imitated the distinctive pattern of individual authors" (p. 13). For that reason, she thinks Malkoff's discussion of literary influences is much too general when, for example, he remarks that the poem, "The Adamant," belongs to the "metaphysical tradition." La Belle sets for herself a much more ambitious project: she says "we must find the particular author and even the particular work that the modern poet is responding to" (p. 15). Her book is replete with such discoveries and specific findings. In that respect, Jenijoy La Belle has provided Roethke's readers an invaluable service in capably seeking out individual poets, poems, and lines and phrases that Roethke borrows and echoes in her overall aim to show that "Roethke makes use of a tradition not just in some general sense, but through a unique borrowing of particular portions from other poems" (p. 17).

Described in that way, it would seem that Roethke's use of other works of literature is much like the allusive method of T. S. Eliot and Ezra Pound. Roethke quotes or paraphrases others in only a few cases, however, and in his prose writings he repeatedly rejects the allusive technique, which he says results in what he calls the "referential poem" (SP, p. 62). La Belle is thus at pains not to identify Roethke's use of literary predecessors with that of Eliot or Pound. She stresses the uniqueness of Roethke's borrowings, but that is a uniqueness not always easy to see. The distinction La Belle offers between Roethke's method and the better-known allusive technique becomes blurred at times. At any rate, if Roethke's borrowing from literary tradition is different from Eliot's or Pound's, it would seem that each gained much the same thing. La Belle says as much. Her description of one facet of Roethke's poetic method, in fact, might as easily apply to the allusive method of T. S. Eliot: "one way in which a poet can increase the density and range of meaning in a poem is to borrow a well-known image from another poet, since that single image will bring into his poem some of the meanings and attendant associations it had in the original work" (p. 18). To illustrate this point, La Belle details how Roethke ties his poem, "The Premonition," to works of the metaphysical poet John Donne. In so doing, La Belle says, in order to "enlarge the meaning of his poem, Roethke relied not only upon his own awareness of a literary tradition, but also upon the reader's awareness of this tradition" (p. 19). The difference in method, it appears, and it seems a difference in degree not in kind, is that Eliot and Pound quote, paraphrase, and parody liberally; Roethke more distantly and less frequently only echoes.

In addition to examining in detail Roethke's specific use of sources, La Belle also looks at the attitude he displays toward literary tradition itself. Roethke does not use the stuff of literature solely as a means of widening the references of his poems.

Roethke's relationship to his literary ancestors goes beyond the matter of technique. He takes his literary relationships personally, and as we shall see in the fourth chapter, that sometimes assumes an almost spiritual significance. An intriguing description of how Roethke personalized his relations to his literary predecessors in his early verse does appear in "How to Write like Somebody Else," however. There, Roethke gives indications of how he came to be himself by imitating the model of Elinor Wylie and by having a "spiritual romance" with Léonie Adams (SP, p. 64). The inspiration for Jenijoy La Belle's concept of Roethke's relationships with other poets may derive from this expression of Roethke's admiration for Léonie Adams. Roethke is referring to the poem, "Country Summer":

> I hate to abandon that poem: I feel it's something Miss Adams and I have created: a literary lovechild. Put it this way: I loved her so much, her poetry, that I just had to become, for a brief moment, a part of her world. For it is her world, and I had filled myself with it, and I had to create something that would honor her in her own terms. That, I think, expresses as best I can what really goes on with the hero- or heroine-worshiping young. I didn't cabbage those effects in cold blood; that poem is a true release in its way. I was too clumsy and stupid to articulate my own emotions: she helped me to say something about the external world, helped me convince myself that maybe, if I kept at it, eventually I might write a poem of my own, with the accent on my own speech. [SP, p. 66]

In his first book, though, Roethke conceives of the literary tradition as a burden inherited from the past, La Belle argues. She reads some of the poems of Open House as being explicitly about problems an author has in dealing with the literary past. She cites the intensely confrontational poem, "Feud," as evidence that Roethke is essentially oppressed by the weight of literary tradition:

> Corruption reaps the young; you dread
> The menace of ancestral eyes;
> Recoiling from the serpent head
> Of fate, you blubber in surprise.
>
> Exhausted fathers thinned the blood,
> You curse the legacy of pain;
> Darling of an infected brood,
> You feel disaster climb the vein.
>
> There's canker at the root, your seed
> Denies the blessing of the sun,
> The light essential to your need.
> Your hopes are murdered and undone.

> The dead leap at the throat, destroy
> The meaning of the day; dark forms
> Have scaled your walls, and spies betray
> Old secrets to amorphous swarms.
>
> You meditate upon the nerves,
> Inflame with hate. This ancient feud
> Is seldom won. The spirit starves
> Until the dead have been subdued.
>   [CP, p. 4]

Unlike "Open House," the poem it follows in the book, "Feud" is written in the second person. It reads like an accusation. That accusation is directed at the "ancestral eyes," indeed, but an equal animosity is leveled at the "you" of the poem. The "you" is depicted as standing at the degenerated end of a genealogical line. That accounts for the impotence of this person, and for the frustration he feels at being called upon, with what he sees as diminished abilities, to match the ancestral models held up to him. It should be noted, however, that "Feud" does not make explicit reference to literary ancestors or to the problems of literary inheritance, to problems Harold Bloom would call the "anxiety of influence." The terms of "Feud" are more generalized than that. There is thus less specific internal evidence in "Feud" that supports La Belle's reading than she would have us suppose.

Other poems in Open House treat the matter of literary inheritance more specifically, La Belle counters. She thinks that the poem "Sale," which appears in the fifth and last part of Open House, offers Roethke a way to deal with the burdens of literary tradition, of influence:

> For sale: by order of the remaining heirs
> Who ran up and down the big center stairs
> The what-not, the settee, the Chippendale chairs
> --And an attic of horrors, a closet of fears.
>
> The furniture polished and polished so grand,
> A stable and paddock, some fox-hunting land,
> The summer house shaped like a village band stand
> --And grandfather's sinister hovering hand.
>
> The antimacassar for the sofa in red,
> The Bechstein piano, the four-poster bed,
> The library used as a card room instead
> --And some watery eyes in a Copley head.
>
> The dining room carpet dyed brighter than blood,
> The table where everyone ate as he should,

The sideboard beside which a tall footman stood
--And a fume of decay that clings fast to the wood.

The hand-painted wall-paper, finer than skin,
The room that the children had never been in,
All the rings and the relics encrusted with sin
--And the taint in a blood that was running too thin.
                                        [CP, p. 32]

In "Sale," she says, Roethke conceives of literary tradition as a
houseful of furniture. Poetry "is cluttered with the furnishings
of our literary ancestors," she writes. "To prepare for his 'open
house,' Roethke had to throw out the inessential fixtures--the
antimacassars, Chippendale chairs, and hand-painted wallpaper"
(p. 8). Similarly, La Belle thinks that "On the Road to Woodlawn," the last poem in the third part of Open House, is less a
reflection of Roethke's grief at the death of his father than it
is a "funeral" for sentimental literary diction (p. 91):

I miss the polished brass, the powerful black horses,
The drivers creaking the seats of the baroque hearses,
The high-piled floral offerings with sentimental verses,
The carriages reeking with varnish and stale perfume.

I miss the pallbearers momentously taking their places,
The undertaker's obsequious grimaces,
The craned necks, the mourners' anonymous faces,
--And the eyes, still vivid, looking up from a sunken
     room.
                                        [CP, p. 22]

Jenijoy La Belle thinks that Roethke in his first book applied
techniques and ideas learned from earlier poets, and exhibited those
borrowings in discernible ways, but more importantly he was conscious of the fact that he was doing those things. His borrowings
indicate the choices he was making for his own verse, La Belle says.
Based on her reading of "Open House" and "Sale," La Belle concludes
that Roethke "wanted to associate himself with a tradition that was
likewise 'strict and pure'--that he select--in effect, create--his
own tradition, discarding what was worthless, to provide himself
with the proper milieu for the creation of his poetry" (p. 8),
and in this respect she does agree with Karl Malkoff's emphasis.
Though she admits that some of Roethke's echoing of other poets and
poems was probably unconscious, and attributable to the enormity
of his "elephantine memory," she is intent on showing that in his
borrowings from his literary predecessors Roethke was both conscious
and creative (p. 16).
    Poems like "Feud," "Sale," and "On the Road to Woodlawn" need

not be read solely as Roethke's reflections upon literary tradition, however. La Belle finds it useful for her argument to see
Roethke's literary ancestors represented in many of his early poems, and to see their protagonists as a struggling young Theodore
Roethke, but the connections, though available, are not essential
to the poems. Each of these poems might be understood in terms
nearer the ones they present. The ill-tempered spirit of some
of these poems, their animosity toward human beings and toward
being human, translates into the misanthropic view Roethke offers
in part 2 of his second book, and the central theme of "Feud,"
"Sale," and "On the Road to Woodlawn" might better be seen as an
early and sometimes overgeneralized effort to broach, through a
kind of displacement, the issue of the father and the son, the issue Roethke would explore to enormous depth in the Lost Son narratives.

Poetic Method and Technique

As the reviews of Open House indicate, Roethke's first poems
were perceived as modest achievements in existing poetic forms
rather than as innovations of new form. If anything, later readers have been less enthusiastic about Roethke's early technical
accomplishments. Though, as we shall see, some critics treat
the subject in and for itself, most treat the poetic of Open
House because of the contrast that style affords for the later
Greenhouse and narrative poems, or because of the comparison it
offers for the Love Poems of Words for the Wind. The most useful
and effective discussions of the poetic of Open House have been
attempts to characterize the nature of Roethke's poetic language
and efforts to reconstruct the steps in his poetic method. The
least instructive discussions of Roethke's early technique have
been detailed traditional prosodic analyses. Those discussions
point up the inherent flaws in prosodic analysis itself, however, rather than limitations on the part of those who have used
it.
In his essay of 1954, "The Poetry of Theodore Roethke," one
of the first full-length essays devoted to the subject, Hilton
Kramer put Roethke's poetic into useful perspective by observing
that language in the poems of Open House has a "conventional
relationship to subject, calling attention to itself as little as
possible" (p. 133). Kramer evidently shared some of the first reviewers' sensitivity to traditional poetic form, but readers raised
on looser, more open poetic forms will probably disagree with Kramer's contention. They will find that the formal qualities of the
Open House poems, their regular meters and predictable rhymes, call
considerable attention to themselves, so much so, perhaps, that

their forms render meaning nearly impenetrable. In that respect, ironically, Roethke's first poems, that reviewers found so accessible because so familiar in form and so well behaved, may become for subsequent readers those in his canon that are among the most difficult to appreciate. And yet Kramer is right in his observation that the poems of Open House are "objective," in a sense, existing "in the observable world, the world which our reason unfolds to us in waking experience" (p. 133). William Meredith draws a similar conclusion in his essay of 1965, "A Steady Storm of Correspondences." Meredith says that "it seems to have been the aesthetic premise of the first book that poetry is obliged to set experience in order" (p. 38).

In what remains one of the best essays on Theodore Roethke, "The Vegetal Radicalism of Theodore Roethke," first published in 1950, Kenneth Burke first noted the extent to which Roethke relies on intuitions rather than ideas, especially in his Greenhouse poems and the Lost Son narratives. In his essay "Theodore Roethke and the Failures of Language," published twenty years later, Jerome Mazzaro has expanded on Burke's original observation to illustrate two modes of discourse Roethke uses, the Brahmin, associated with Burke's ideas, and the primal, associated with Burke's intuitions. Mazzaro thinks Roethke's drive in the direction of a Brahmin language in the poems of Open House is more complex and less assured than does Hilton Kramer. Mazzaro does not view the poems or the poetic of Open House as the first step in a methodical "journey out of the self." He sees in the poems Roethke's uncomfortable realization of a "widening separation of inner and outer worlds blocking his development through a failure of language to act properly as a mediator of deeds and rage" (p. 63). In other words, language fails in Open House, and Mazzaro thinks Roethke perceived the failure. In order to compensate for the failure, Roethke used "wit" to tie together the separated worlds of "primal and educated languages" (p. 69). Some of the difficulty lay in Roethke, too, Mazzaro argues. Roethke lacked confidence in himself because of what and where he came from. Thus, through a poetic method of imitating respectable, traditional forms, Mazzaro says, Roethke worked to "shun out of embarrassment" his upbringing in the German-American world of Saginaw, Michigan (p. 72). Roethke's own experience provided the impulses for the poetry, what Kenneth Burke had called intuitions, but Mazzaro thinks Roethke felt it necessary to tame those impulses: "out of his primal German-American 'gut' responses, Roethke chooses what can be blurred and warped into an educated, imitative Brahmin diction" in the poems of Open House (p. 67). Though his psychological account of the origins of the language of Open House may not be compelling, Mazzaro's distinction between Brahmin and primal diction is very useful; it can be applied elsewhere in Roethke's poetry.

Some critics have simply responded to the Brahmin diction of Open House either negatively or appreciatively; others have tried to explain more analytically how the verse of Open House works. In his book The American Moment: American Poetry in Mid-Century, Geoffrey Thurley dismisses the poems of Open House as "rhythmic academicism" (p. 92). On the other hand, in his study of modern English and American prosody, Sound and Form in Modern Poetry, Harvey Gross finds in the poem "Night Journey" a "purity of language and firmness of rhythm Auden rarely achieves" (p. 283). Since W. H. Auden is an acknowledged master of technique, Gross's remark is high praise, indeed. Clearly, Thurley's and Gross's aesthetic reactions to the poetic of Open House are irreconcilable, but Bernard Heringman, for one, understands how critical responses can be so different. In his essay "Roethke's Poetry: The Forms of Meaning," he notes that "I cannot get around the subjectivity of my material. The rhythm of a passage as I hear it will usually be a little different from what you hear; the patterns of feeling evoked will probably differ much more" (p. 567). (Roethke knew this, of course, and commented on it in his essay, "How to Write like Somebody Else" [SP, p. 62].) In an attempt to see if there is any objective pattern to the verse that affects the intuitive response, Heringman presents a very detailed technical analysis of Roethke's more formal poems, concentrating especially on the trimeter and pentameter works in Open House and Words for the Wind. Heringman is strongest in describing the successive shortening of lines that Roethke characteristically uses as a closing device, but he has larger aims. He observes that "The Adamant" and the later "Words for the Wind" are similarly metered and rhymed, and yet the former poem has a "powerful sealing-in motion" while the latter has a "very open, freely flowing motion" (p. 569). He calls these the two "motions" and "manners" in Roethke's verse, the "bone spareness and tendril grace" (p. 569). Form alone cannot account for the different responses to the poems, however, and in the end Heringman cannot draw firm conclusions based only on his technical analysis alone. He must conclude that "we cannot find in Roethke's work as a whole that he used strict trimeters whenever he was dealing with hemmed-in feelings, or slant-rhyme whenever he described nature, or frequent adjectives in all his long-line poems" (p. 569). That conclusion should not come as a surprise, though, for content always modifies form (or should do so), and thus it modifies also a reader's response.

As Heringman's essay indicates, the traditional prosodic analysis is not the best way to investigate Roethke's early poetic methods. Readers do not respond only to formal qualities of verse; they respond also, and usually more vigorously, to the content. The poet, however, especially the apprentice poet, may be directed more significantly by the form of the poem, especially if that poet is working from established models. Richard Blessing comes to that conclusion in his analysis of Roethke's early poetic technique in his book, Theodore Roethke's Dynamic Vision. Blessing bases his argument on a study of the poems in Open House as well

as on the uncollected poems, many of which are available in the
Selected Letters of Theodore Roethke, and on a study of Roethke's
notebooks. Drawing on these sources, he shows that form alone
exercised considerable influence over Roethke's working methods
in his apprentice years.

In his essay "How to Write like Somebody Else," Roethke observed
that "imitation, conscious imitation, is one of the great methods,
perhaps the method, of learning to write" (SP, p. 69). Blessing
argues that the early Roethke carried that imitativeness to a certain extreme: "Roethke the apprentice was not above pulling out a
stanzaic 'mold' and filling in the blanks. The early notebooks
contain several such 'molds,' some of them with lines scratched in
here and there as if the pouring had begun and stopped" (p. 54).
Blessing provides convincing illustrations for his conclusion, and,
by speculating upon the nature of Roethke's early poetic method,
Blessing explains why some readers think the poems of Open House
sound formulaic and mechanical:

> He seems to have worked on as many as four or five poems at
> one time, juggling them from page to page, abandoning one to
> work on another which, in turn, would be abandoned either for
> the first poem or for yet another. Sometimes he seems to fit
> lines or short stanzas from one poem into another, usually with
> surprisingly little modification. He gets away with it, clearly,
> because of the remarkable sameness in tone, vocabulary, meter,
> and rhyme of those early pieces. They are poems assembled from
> parts which are often all but interchangeable, and the notebooks
> are crammed with isolated lines or couplets--almost always in iam-
> bic tetrameter or trimeter, almost always with perfect rhymes or
> ending with words which will be easy to rhyme on--lines which
> seem to be waiting for a poem that they can be squeezed into or
> tacked onto. [pp. 28-29]

Roethke's obsessively imitative method was not the only impulse at
work in the early verse, however. Blessing cites applications of
the notion, espoused in Roethke's essay, "Some Remarks on Rhythm,"
that "some words . . . are so drenched with human association, they
sometimes can make even bad poems evocative" (SP, p. 80). Roethke's means of freeing the mind, of tapping the resources of the
unconscious, becomes more important as a principle and more sophisticated as a method in his Greenhouse poems and in the Lost Son
narratives, but Blessing finds evidence of this more spontaneous
direction in Roethke's early work. He observes in Roethke's notebooks that "in his effort to break loose, to stimulate his imagination, Roethke often begins by doodling with unusual, or what
he hopes are unusual, combinations of adjectives and nouns" (p.
29).

The imitative method is indeed pronounced in Open House as, in fact, it is often evident in the first work of any developing poet. A skilled teacher of verse-writing himself, Roethke knew imitation of received poetic forms helps to discipline and direct the imagination. Only after learning the fundamentals, after gaining a certain amount of technical control, can the poet best profit from releasing the deeper resources of the unconscious. It would appear, then, that the imitative method and the method of free association could not coexist, but Blessing argues to the contrary that imitativeness can gain the poet the same benefits as more associative writing. Imitativeness helped Roethke free his imagination, Blessing says. He suggests that "Roethke's need to rhyme, the need to maintain a rhythm and to keep regular stanzas, are ways of distracting the conscious mind long enough to allow something from the subconscious mind to slip past" (pp. 31-32), a view Roethke may have shared or might have agreed with. In fact, Roethke did believe that freer methods of composing conceal dangers, for later in his career, in "Some Remarks on Rhythm," he said that "the writer in freer forms must have an even greater fidelity to his subject matter than the poet who has the support of form. He must keep his eye on the object, and his rhythm must move as a mind moves, must be imaginatively right, or he is lost" (SP, p. 83).

For the most part, discussions of the poetic of Open House have not achieved their stated or implied aim: they have not satisfactorily revealed, in the language of technique alone, how or why Roethke moves from the tightly controlled "received" forms of Open House to the more innovative "organic" forms of The Lost Son and Other Poems. Critics can agree, though, after the fact, that the direction in which Roethke's technique was moving is best illustrated in Open House by the poem "The Premonition," a work which, as Louis Martz writes in "A Greenhouse Eden," "suggests a way out of this metaphysical sealing" more characteristic of the poems of Open House (p. 20). Since "The Premonition" is probably the best and most distinctive poem in Open House, it is interesting that Roethke omitted it from his selection of poems from Open House for The Waking and for Words for the Wind, but he was right to do so. "The Premonition" is radically different from the other poems in Open House in terms of tone as well as form. As we have seen, Roethke's attitude toward the past in Open House is at times antagonistic; "The Premonition" displays quite a different sentiment:

> Walking this field I remember
> Days of another summer.
> Oh that was long ago! I kept
> Close to the heels of my father,

Matching his stride with half-steps
Until we came to a river.
He dipped his hand in the shallow:
Water ran over and under
Hair on a narrow wrist bone;
His image kept following after,--
Flashed with the sun in the ripple.
But when he stood up, that face
Was lost in a maze of water.
                                        [CP, p. 6]

The poem moves from the present through memory to a specific
instance resurrected from the past, in a way that will become
characteristic of the Greenhouse poems. In addition, the poem
appears on the page in a block of print; unlike most other poems
in Open House, "The Premonition" is not split into symmetrical
stanzas, nor can it be. It contains thirteen lines. Again different from other poems in Open House, the rhyme in "The Premonition"
is unobtrusive. It is feminine or slanted ("remember"/"summer",
"kept"/"steps"), asymmetrically located to a degree, and behind
the frequent anapests and the inversions, the meter is a very irregular iambic. The poem is a premonition for the child of the
death of the father that the adult now remembers. In terms of
his poetry as a whole, the poem is a technical premonition of
the loosened but more penetrating style that Roethke will realize
in the poems of his second book, The Lost Son and Other Poems.

The critical debate over the significance of Roethke's Open
House is not over, but agreement on several issues has emerged.
It is clear that an argument that Roethke was a major American
poet of the twentieth century cannot rest solely on the basis of
poems in Open House, though several poems in the book endure and
are always included in any sample of Roethke's verse in major an-
thologies. It is clear also that in Open House Roethke raises an
issue fundamental to his poetic vision, the dialectical interplay
of spirit and flesh, though critics disagree over what to make of
Roethke's bias toward the spirit in his earliest work. The prevalent view is that Roethke inaugurates his "journey out of the self"
in Open House by valuing spirit over flesh. Study of the poems
Roethke wrote after 1941 indicates, however, that Roethke exagger-
ates the extent of his desire for a "spare spirit" in the poems of
Open House, and that exaggeration should not be reflected in critical interpretations. In terms of poetic style, it is generally
agreed that the origins of forms Roethke imitates in his first work
lie in metaphysical poetry, that he does use imitation as a poetic
method, and that, technically, the poems of Open House introduce
Roethke as a competent craftsman. Thus, as a means of establishing himself as a poet in his day for the audience of his day, Open

House was for Theodore Roethke an excellent place to start. The book launched Roethke's career, it earned him recognition that was professionally useful, and it established him as a young poet in his generation worth watching. As critical discussions of the book show as clearly, though, later readers have asked different things of Roethke's Open House than did his first reviewers. They have made considerable stylistic and thematic demands of the book, and in so doing have, perhaps, asked more of Open House than it can possibly support. Instead of seeing that as an indication of the failure of Roethke's first efforts, however, we might better take it as an indication of the great expectations aroused by the poems that follow Open House.

Bibliography

Auden, W. H.
1941. "Verse and the Times," Saturday Review Apr. 5, pp. 30-31.
Baldanza, Stephen
1941. Commonweal June 13, p. 188.
Blessing, Richard A.
1974. Theodore Roethke's Dynamic Vision. Bloomington: Indiana Univ. Pr.
Bogen, Don
1980. "From Open House to the Greenhouse: Theodore Roethke's Poetic Breakthrough," Journal of English Literary History 47, pp. 399-418.
Bowers, Neal
1982. Theodore Roethke: The Journey from I to Otherwise. Columbia: Univ. of Missouri Pr.
Burke, Kenneth
1966. "The Vegetal Radicalism of Theodore Roethke," in Language as Symbolic Action, pp. 254-81. Berkeley: Univ. of California Pr. Appeared in Sewanee Review, pp. 68-108. Winter, 1950. Reprinted in Profile of Theodore Roethke, ed. William Heyen. Columbus: Merrill, 1971.
Deutsch, Babette
1941. "Three Generations in Poetry," Decision Aug., pp. 60-61.
Forster, Louis, Jr.
1941. "A Lyric Realist," Poetry July, pp. 222-25.
Gross, Harvey
1968. Sound and Form in Modern Poetry: A Study of Prosody from Thomas Hardy to Robert Lowell. Ann Arbor: Univ. of Michigan Pr.
Heringman, Bernard
1974. "Roethke's Poetry: The Forms of Meaning," Texas Studies in Literature and Language 16, pp. 567-83.

Holmes, John
1941. "Poems and Things," Boston Evening Transcript Mar. 24,
p. 9.
Humphries, Rolfe
1941. "Inside Story," New Republic July 14, p. 62.
Kramer, Hilton
1954. "The Poetry of Theodore Roethke," Western Review Winter,
pp. 131-46.
La Belle, Jenijoy
1976. The Echoing Wood of Theodore Roethke. Princeton:
Princeton Univ. Pr. In her book, La Belle acknowledges
material from these articles:
1971. "Theodore Roethke and Tradition: 'The Pure Serene of Memory in One Man,' " Northwest Review: Theodore Roethke Special
Issue Summer, pp. 1-18.
1973. "Roethke's 'I Knew a Woman,' " Explicator Oct., item 15.
1975. "Martyr to a Motion Not His Own: Theodore Roethke's
Love Poems," Ball State University Forum Spring, pp. 71-75.
1975. "Theodore Roethke's Dancing Masters in 'Four for Sir
John Davies,' " Concerning Poetry Fall, pp. 29-35.
1976. "Out of the Cradle Endlessly Robbing: Whitman, Eliot,
and Theodore Roethke," Walt Whitman Review pp. 75-84.
1976. "Theodore Roethke's 'The Lost Son' : From Archetypes to
Literary History," Modern Language Quarterly Spring, pp. 179-
95.
1980. "William Blake, Theodore Roethke, and Mother Goose:
The Unholy Trinity," Blake Studies Summer, pp. 74-86.
Malkoff, Karl
1966. Theodore Roethke: An Introduction to the Poetry. New
York: Columbia Univ. Pr.
Martz, Louis
1965. "A Greenhouse Eden," in Theodore Roethke: Essays on
the Poetry, ed. Arnold Stein, pp. 14-35. Seattle: Univ. of
Washington Pr.
Mazzaro, Jerome
1980. Postmodern American Poetry. Urbana: Univ. of Illinois
Pr. pp. 59-84. Appeared as "Theodore Roethke and the Failures
of Language," Modern Poetry Studies July 1970, pp. 73-96.
McMichael, James
1969. "The Poetry of Theodore Roethke," Southern Review Win-
ter, pp. 4-25. Reprinted in Profile of Theodore Roethke, ed.
William Heyen. Columbus: Merrill, 1971.
Meredith, William
1965. "A Steady Storm of Correspondences: Theodore Roethke's
Long Journey Out of the Self," in Theodore Roethke: Essays on
the Poetry, ed. Arnold Stein, pp. 36-53. Seattle: Univ. of
Washington Pr.

Mills, Ralph J., Jr.
1963. Theodore Roethke. Minnesota Pamphlets on American Writers, no. 30. Minneapolis: Univ. of Minnesota Pr.
Roethke, Theodore
1965. On the Poet and His Craft: Selected Prose of Theodore Roethke, ed. Ralph J. Mills, Jr. Seattle: Univ. of Washington Pr.
1966. The Collected Poems of Theodore Roethke. Garden City, N.Y.: Doubleday.
1968. Selected Letters of Theodore Roethke, ed. Ralph J. Mills, Jr. Seattle: Univ. of Washington Pr.
Seager, Allan
1968. The Glass House: The Life of Theodore Roethke. New York: McGraw-Hill.
Snodgrass, W. D.
1965. " 'That Anguish of Concreteness': Theodore Roethke's Career," in Theodore Roethke: Essays on the Poetry, ed. Arnold Stein, pp. 78-93. Seattle: Univ. of Washington Pr.
Spender, Stephen
1965. "The Objective Ego," in Theodore Roethke: Essays on the Poetry, ed. Arnold Stein, pp. 3-13. Seattle: Univ. of Washington Pr.
Thurley, Geoffrey
1978. The American Moment: American Poetry in Mid-Century. New York: St. Martin's Pr.
Truesdale, C. W.
1968. "Theodore Roethke and the Landscape of American Poetry," Minnesota Review, pp. 345-58.
Wain, John
1965. "The Monocle of My Sea-Faced Uncle," in Theodore Roethke: Essays on the Poetry, ed. Arnold Stein, pp. 54-77. Seattle: Univ. of Washington Pr.
Winters, Yvor
1941. "The Poems of Theodore Roethke," Kenyon Review Autumn, pp. 514-16.
Wolff, George
1981. Theodore Roethke. Boston: Twayne.

Additional Reading

Belitt, Ben
1941. "Six Poets," Virginia Quarterly Review Summer, pp. 462-63.
Bogan, Louise
1935. "Stitched in Bone," in Trial Balances, ed. Ann Winslow, pp. 138-39. New York: MacMillan.

Bonner, Amy
1941. "The Poems of Theodore Roethke," New York Times Book Review Oct. 5, pp. 9, 12.
Ciardi, John
1959. "My Papa's Waltz," in How Does a Poem Mean? Boston: Houghton Mifflin.
Colussi, D. L.
1969. "Roethke's 'The Gentle,' " Explicator 27, item 73.
Cruz, I. R.
1977. "Roethke's 'The Return,' " Notes on Contemporary Literature 7, 1, pp. 8-9.
Curley, Dorothy Nyren
1960. "Roethke, Theodore (1908-1963)," in A Library of Literary Criticism. New York: Frederick Ungar Co.
Hayden, Mary H.
1971. "Open House: Poetry of the Constricted Self," in Northwest Review: Theodore Roethke Special Issue Summer, pp. 116-38.
Holmes, John
1934. "Theodore Roethke," American Poetry Journal 17, p. 2.
Lane, Gary, ed.
1972. A Concordance to the Poems of Theodore Roethke. Metuchen, N.J.: Scarecrow Pr.
Martz, William J.
1966. The Achievement of Theodore Roethke: A Comprehensive Selection of His Poems with a Critical Introduction. Glenview, Ill.: Scott, Foresman.
McFarland, Ronald E.
1981. "Roethke's 'Epidermal Macabre,' " Concerning Poetry 4, 2, pp. 16-22.
McLeod, James R.
1971. Roethke: A Manuscript Checklist. Kent, Ohio: Kent State Univ. Pr.
1973. Theodore Roethke: A Bibliography. Kent, Ohio: Kent State Univ. Pr.
Moul, Keith R.
1977. Theodore Roethke's Career: An Annotated Bibliography. Boston: Hall.
Nicholson, C. H. and W. H. Wasilewski
1978. "Roethke's 'Interlude,' " Explicator 36, 3, pp. 26-27.
Perrine, Laurence
1977. "The Theme of Theodore Roethke's 'Interlude,' " Notes on Modern American Literature 1, item 23.
Porter, Kenneth
1971. "Roethke at Harvard 1930-1931 and the Decade After," Northwest Review: Theodore Roethke Special Issue Summer, pp. 139-48.
Roethke, Theodore
1941. Open House. New York: Knopf.

Sweeny, John L.
  1941. "New Poetry," Yale Review Summer, pp. 817-18.
Walker, Ursula Genug
  1968. Notes on Theodore Roethke.   Charlottesville: Univ.
  of North Carolina Pr.
Walton, Edna Lou
  1941. "Bridges of Iron Lace," New York Herald Tribune Book
  Review Aug. 10, p. 4.
Westfall, Jeff
  1979. "Roethke's 'Dolor,' " Explicator Spring, pp. 25-27.

CHAPTER 2

The Greenhouse Poems

Theodore Roethke's second book, The Lost Son and Other Poems, was published in 1948. It contains the Greenhouse poems, the thirteen short pieces that make up part 1, and the Lost Son narratives, four of which make up part 4. Parts 2 and 3, of course, include important individual poems that help clarify Roethke's move from an imitative and traditional style in Open House to the original and experimental style of parts 1 and 4 of The Lost Son. In 1948, Roethke did not name the poems of part 1 the "Greenhouse poems," nor did he do so later when he reprinted all of the original Greenhouse poems, with one addition, in The Waking (1953) and Words for the Wind (1958). In those collections he simply identified the Greenhouse section as "from The Lost Son and Other Poems, 1948." In critical discussions, however, the Greenhouse poems have earned their own name, and though they are only a part of Roethke's second book, they have often been accorded the recognition usually reserved for a major long poem or for an important volume.

The Greenhouse poems are based on Roethke's childhood experience in the extensive greenhouses his father and uncle, Otto and Charles Roethke, owned in Saginaw, Michigan, and they are significant reenactments of that experience. Louis Martz observes in his 1965 essay "A Greenhouse Eden," for example, that the Greenhouse poems are "one of the permanent achievements of modern poetry" (p. 27); they are poems Roethke "never surpassed" (p. 35). Roethke's accomplishment is all the more startling for the reader who turns the page on "Night Journey," the last poem in Open House in both Words for the Wind and the Collected Poems, and comes upon "Cuttings," the first of the Greenhouse poems. As we have seen in chapter one, Roethke's decision to make the Greenhouse poems part 1 of The Lost Son instead of part 3 (where they should go chronologically) intensifies this contrast between his first and second books. Roethke helped to create the impression that something dramatic, even mysterious, happened to transform him from the workmanlike writer of Open House to the masterful poet of The Lost Son and Other Poems.

Allan Seager contributes to what mystery surrounds the origins of The Lost Son and Other Poems in his biography of Roethke, The Glass House. Roethke wrote the poems of the book between 1943 and 1947 while a teacher at Bennington College, and Seager's image of Roethke, in the heat of composing at Shingle Cottage at Bennington, is inevitably cited as evidence of the extraordinary origins of The Lost Son and Other Poems. While he was writing the poems, according to Seager, Roethke was "drinking a lot as a deliberate stimulus . . . popping out of his clothes, wandering around the cottage naked for a while, then dressing slowly, four or five times a day" (p. 144). Seager does not say Roethke wrote The Lost Son and Other Poems because of this behavior, but he does mention the parallel between Roethke's achievement of a childlike perspective in his second volume and what he calls this "birthday-suit motif" (p. 144). Perhaps Roethke was trying to experience the vulnerability of the child or to enact symbolically the regression to the child's point of view, but his behavior, though indeed interesting, does not readily translate into discernible poetic principles. Roethke's own discussion of his poetic principles in the "Open Letter," his essay on method, repays attention more fully than does speculation about Seager's curious anecdote.

While some notion of Roethke's "poetic breakthrough" needlessly mystifies the origins of The Lost Son and Other Poems, therefore, it does affirm the importance of the book for Roethke's poetry. For the first time in his career, Roethke displays in the Greenhouse poems the breadth of his poetic abilities by treating a novel subject from a unique perspective in an accomplished and original voice. The Greenhouse poems are thus vital in Theodore Roethke's own poetic development and are telling signals of Roethke's later poetic directions. At the same time, the poems are achievements in and of themselves, and are important in American poetry. They contain the beginnings of what has become a widespread poetic vision.

The first innovation for Roethke is his focus, in the Greenhouse poems, on a sustained project, his effort to accumulate out of little poems the sense of a long poem. In contrast, Roethke's first volume contains highly resolved individual poems with comparatively little connection to one another. Roethke allows the Greenhouse landscape to extend beyond the confines of the individual poem, however, and in so doing he prepares for the longer, more ambitious poems he writes later in his career. Critical readings of the Greenhouse poems as a single, largely integrated effort are the subject of the first part of this chapter, as well, especially, as the impact on that whole of Roethke's addition of a fourteenth poem to the sequence, "Frau Bauman, Frau Schmidt, and Frau Schwartze."

Others have constructed long poems, of course, but Roethke's treatment of his subject is something new in American poetry. His Greenhouse poems open new territory for poetry and expand its boundaries, for no one before him had entered the life of the minimal world with such authenticity, nor had anyone perceived that world through the perspective of the child. Though the language used in

the Greenhouse poems is that of an adult reliving, through an especially acute memory, the child's experience, the perceptions
disclosed are those of a child.   Roethke's ability to phrase that
child's experience in the language of the articulate man accounts
for the accessibility of the Greenhouse poems, and it also differ-
entiates their voice from that of the so-called infancy narratives
of Praise to the End!, where Roethke experiments with the language
of the child.   It is additionally notable in the Greenhouse poems
that Roethke does not sentimentalize either plant or child, nor does
he limit the implications of the Greenhouse world by drawing conclusions about its significance.   Those implications, whether philosophical, psychological, or mystical, are left unstated in the Greenhouse poems, so in "Roethke's Minimal Mysticism," the second part
of this chapter, we look at the different interpretations of Roethke's complex perspective on his Greenhouse world.
    Part three of this chapter contains a discussion of the literary
origins of Roethke's Greenhouse perspective and an attempt at plac-
ing him into the larger context of American poetry, and the fourth
and final section focuses on the poetic of the Greenhouse poems.
Theodore Roethke did not invent "open" poetry or the organic poetic
form, of course, and certain formal devices and strategies organize
the individual Greenhouse poems.   Those can be identified, but they
function in a way particular to these poems. They seem to emerge,
somehow naturally, from the contents of the poems, and thus forms
are not imported from without, as they were in the poems of Open
House.   In addition to a unique poetic vision that he offers, then,
Roethke shows for the first time in his Greenhouse poems that he
and not the form is the master of his poem.

Overviews and Organizations

    Individually, the Greenhouse poems are representations of Theo-
dore Roethke's childhood experiences of a Greenhouse world.   The
poems have so much in common, though, that it is reasonable to
argue that they work together to create a coherent whole. Two opposed perspectives of that whole have emerged in the past twenty
years.   Some think Roethke's Greenhouse poems are carefully se-
quenced, and chronicle the growth of the protagonist from infant to
adolescent.   This view was most clearly advanced by Karl Malkoff in
1966, in his book Theodore Roethke: An Introduction to the Poetry.
The argument has since been reformulated by George Wolff in his
study, Theodore Roethke.   Others think the dynamic of the Greenhouse poems is not sequential but is cyclical.   The poems alter-
nate between emphasis on the two aspects of Roethke's Greenhouse
world, its heaven and its hell.   Jarold Ramsey has most fully argued that view in his essay "Roethke in the Greenhouse," published
in 1972.

Like the flowers surrounding him, according to Karl Malkoff, the boy represented in the Greenhouse poems grows and comes of age in the course of the sequence. Malkoff argues that there is a "general sense of growth uniting the poems" (p. 50). In "Cuttings," the first poem in the sequence, Roethke stoops to the minimal things. His viewpoint is indistinguishable from theirs, Malkoff suggests, because no identity has distinguished itself yet. The poem simply describes:

> Sticks-in-a-drowse droop over sugary loam,   ‒
> Their intricate stem-fur dries;
> But still the delicate slips keep coaxing up water;
> The small cells bulge;
>
> One nub of growth
> Nudges a sand-crumb loose,
> Pokes through a musty sheath
> Its pale tendrilous horn.
>
> [CP, p. 37]

The second poem, "Cuttings (later)," marks a change in perspective. The tentative "nub" of the first poem becomes an individual ego straining upwards, and in the second paragraph of the poem Roethke introduces the first-person pronoun to indicate that:

> I can hear, underground, that sucking and sobbing,
> In my veins, in my bones I feel it,--
> The small waters seeping upward,
> The tight grains parting at last.
> When sprouts break out,
> Slippery as fish,
> I quail, lean to beginnings, sheath-wet.
>
> [CP, p. 37]

By the time of the sixth poem, "Orchids," the child is an adolescent, Malkoff says, and in the seventh poem, "Moss-Gathering," he makes connections between behavior and consequence and wrestles with his own sexuality. After reveling in the experience of gathering moss, "the kind for lining cemetery baskets," Roethke reflects

> . . . afterwards I always felt mean, jogging back
>   over the logging road,
> As if I had broken the natural order of things in
>   that swampland;
> Disturbed some rhythm, old and of vast importance,
> By pulling off flesh from the living planet;
> As if I had committed, against the whole scheme of
>   life, a desecration.
>
> [CP, p. 40]

As he matures, Malkoff says, Roethke recognizes also that other
persons, too, if they have a similarly close relation to the plants
and creatures, can coexist in and be party to the spirit he senses
in his Greenhouse world. In the eighth poem, "Big Wind," where
the greenhouse is threatened by a violent storm, Roethke works side
by side with adults, like one of them, to help save the greenhouse
(he uses the plural pronoun, "we"), and in the ninth poem, "Old
Florist," he celebrates

> That hump of a man bunching chrysanthemums
> Or pinching-back asters, or planting azaleas,
> Tamping and stamping dirt into pots,--
> How he could flick and pick
> Rotten leaves or yellowy petals,
> Or scoop out a weed close to flourishing roots, . . .
> Or stand all night watering roses, his feet blue
>   in rubber boots.
>   [CP, p. 42]

In the last poems of the sequence, Malkoff says, the boy has come
of age. In "Child on Top of a Greenhouse," he looks down on the
greenhouse for the first time and he looks beyond it:

> The wind billowing out the seat of my britches,
> My feet crackling splinters of glass and dried
>   putty,
> The half-grown chrysanthemums staring up like
>   accusers,
> Up through the streaked glass, flashing with sunlight,
> A few white clouds all rushing eastward,
> A line of elms plunging and tossing like horses,
> And everyone, everyone pointing up and shouting!
>   [CP, p. 43]

In Karl Malkoff's reading, then, the Greenhouse poems might be
divided into four parts that correspond to stages in the protagonist's growth. The first five are about birth; the next three
are about "self-conscious sexuality"; the next three concern the
"tenders of the greenhouse"; and the last three present the "triumph and terror of emerging from the greenhouse world of childhood"
(pp. 50-55). Malkoff's numbers total fourteen and not thirteen
poems, it will be noticed. He includes in his scheme the disputed
poem "Frau Bauman, Frau Schmidt, and Frau Schwartze" and finds a
place for it in his third grouping.

Karl Malkoff's discussion convincingly shows the dynamic varia-
tions of Roethke's perspective in the Greenhouse poems. He shows
that the perspective shifts, but it does not shift so systematically
as he suggests. The voice of "Child on Top of a Greenhouse" is

clearly more sure of itself than is the subdued voice of "Cuttings," and thus in very general terms it is true that the Greenhouse sequence charts a development of the protagonist's personality. Upon closer examination, however, the sequence does not move neatly from infancy to independence. "Cuttings (later)" does indeed rouse the subjective "I" from the objectivity and anonymity of the previous "Cuttings," but "Root Cellar," the third poem, returns to the objective point of view, as do "Forcing House," "Orchids," "Old Florist," "Transplanting," "Flower Dump," and the last poem in the sequence, "Carnations." The protagonist's own address of the Greenhouse may come to the fore in the later poems in the sequence, but a sense of the maturation of his point of view is only one thing that structures the poems.

In Theodore Roethke, published in 1981, George Wolff complicates Karl Malkoff's organization of the Greenhouse poems. Wolff is interested primarily in discovering the peculiar qualities of the voice in the Greenhouse, and to that end he notes the dramatic nature of the poems (he opposes it to the "discursive talk about emotions" he finds characteristic of Open House [p. 33]), and he concludes that the "drama lies in his [the boy's] regressions into the terrifying parts of his past . . . and in his sudden progressions into a greater maturity" (p. 33). It would appear at first, then, that Wolff observes a dialectical play of opposites at work in the Greenhouse poems, a structure quite different from Malkoff's. In fact, however, Wolff returns to Malkoff's scheme, for he thinks Roethke alerts us to the wider meaning of his poems "by their arrangement in a sequence from birth to death" (p. 34).

His organization helps to illuminate the dramatic context of poems early and late in the sequence, for Wolff is right, broadly speaking, in observing that we begin with tiny shoots, in the spring probably, in "Cuttings" and "Cuttings (later)," and we end with the shriveled plants of "Flower Dump" and the beginning of autumn in "Carnations." The main focus in "Flower Dump," however, is the "one tulip on top,/ One swaggering head/ Over the dying, the newly dead" (CP, p. 43), and in "Carnations" Roethke creates an image of perfect balance rather than death. Of more damage to Wolff's reading, though, is the fact that the other poems in the section seem only tenuously intertwined with the theme Wolff observes. Their order, in fact, might be changed to strengthen Wolff's argument. For example, "Orchids" should probably go earlier in the sequence, since it is filled with images of "infants" and "cradles" (CP, p. 39), and "Root Cellar" might well go nearer the end, since it describes harvested roots and bulbs. Like Malkoff's earlier interpretation, then, George Wolff's is helpful in distinguishing a tendency in the Greenhouse poems, but again like Malkoff's, his does not account comprehensively for all the connections between the poems.

In "Texture and Form in Theodore Roethke's Greenhouse Poems," his essay published in 1971, John D. Boyd counters Karl Malkoff's view of the Greenhouse sequence by suggesting that the poems are not much of a sequence at all. Boyd notes that the individual Greenhouse poems are very sophisticated in structure, but he doubts that a similar sophistication obtains with the structure of the sequence as a whole (p. 424). He thinks that the order of the poems in the section is "inspired improvisation" (p. 424), a point with which Charles Molesworth agrees in his essay on Roethke in The Fierce Embrace. According to Molesworth, the poems are "a loose system of conduits" that communicate the exchange between the "clearly personal" and the world outside the self (p. 26). More interested in discovering the reasons behind the "organic unity" of individual poems (p. 418), Boyd believes the poems "owe much of their 'writhing life' to [the] crackling atmosphere of contending opposites" (p. 412). The contraries Boyd mentions include the static versus the dynamic, active versus passive, stillness versus movement, struggle versus surrender, and life versus death (pp. 412-13), and these mark also the peaks and valleys Jarold Ramsey observes. Ramsey is the main exponent of the second major structural overview of the Greenhouse poems.

By focusing on the discontinuities rather than the continuities between adjacent poems, Jarold Ramsey argues in his essay "Roethke in the Greenhouse" that the essential direction of the Greenhouse poems is cyclical instead of sequential. The poet's psyche, Ramsey says, "moves in clearly defined cycles of ascent and decline, bloom and wilt and bloom again" (p. 39). Ramsey's cycles occur not only between adjacent poems but within individual poems themselves, and can be observed, for example, in the dilation of "Child on Top of a Greenhouse," which is then answered by the return to earth of "Flower Dump," a return answered yet again at the conclusion of the same poem by the emerging tulip. Ramsey's point of view is supported to a degree by Roethke's own pronouncements about the poetics of "The Lost Son." In his "Open Letter," Roethke remarks that "any history of the psyche . . . is bound to be a succession of experiences, similar yet dissimilar. There is a perpetual slipping-back, then a going-forward; but there is some 'progress' " (SP, p. 39). In addition, Ramsey can connect the cycles he observes in the Greenhouse to Roethke's manic-depressive illness, though he is careful not to reduce the poems to the "cyclicity of his [Roethke's] own mental life" (p. 47).

For Ramsey, Roethke's "progress" is most evident in "Carnations," the last poem in the section. The cyclical motion of the remainder of the Greenhouse poems is put into dramatic relief, Ramsey suggests, because in "Carnations" that alternation is temporarily stayed when Roethke presents, not a vision of death as George Wolff says, but a "mood of composed, expectant contemplation of permanent natural forms" (p. 47):

> Pale blossoms, each balanced on a single jointed
> stem,
> The leaves curled back in elaborate Corinthian scrolls;

And the air cool, as if drifting down from wet
   hemlocks,
Or rising out of ferns not far from water,
A crisp hyacinthine coolness,
Like that clear autumnal weather of eternity,
The windless perpetual morning above a September cloud.

[CP, p. 43]

Most critics, it must be said, view "Carnations" as a compelling conclusion to the Greenhouse poems. In "Carnations," Louis Martz writes, "the sequence ends with the triumph of art" (p. 27), and Sandra Spanier has constructed a reading of the sequence that emphasizes that perception. In her essay, "The Unity of the Greenhouse Sequence: Roethke's Portrait of the Artist," she organizes the poems into six stages in the " 'life cycle' of a work of art" (p. 54). Essentially the same criticisms Louis Martz levels at the fourteenth Greenhouse poem, "Frau Bauman, Frau Schmidt, and Frau Schwartze," might be raised against "Carnations," however. In language and in imagery, "Carnations" differs significantly from the other original Greenhouse poems. The poem looks like a sentence, as George Wolff has pointed out, but it contains "no main verb" (p. 42), and the verb carries the burden in the other Greenhouse poems. (Wolff agrees with Ramsey's evaluation of the poem, though; he approves the "timeless peace" of the poem [p. 42].) In addition, the language of "Carnations" is fundamentally foreign to the language of the greenhouse. It is language more characteristic of the Theodore Roethke who values stasis and balance rather than activity. The language in the other Greenhouse poems is never "crisp," however; it is fleshy and "slug-soft," intentionally dense, even cloying. Nor, in the other poems, does Roethke stray so far from the greenhouse for his language. In "Carnations," he alludes to "elaborate Corinthian scrolls" (CP, p. 43), and he reaches out of the greenhouse itself to end in the sky. If we have learned anything from the other Greenhouse poems, we know that nothing stays still there, nor would Roethke want it to. "Carnations," however, concludes with motion frozen. It provides the pause in which to place the poems of parts 2 and 3 before, in part 4, Roethke takes up his radical poetics of regress and progress again. As a conclusion, then, and perhaps so that it might finally be the conclusion, "Carnations" seems to have been imposed on the rest of the poems. In order to indicate that there is "progress" in the sequence, it appears, Roethke disengages "Carnations" from the necessary cyclicity, the "perpetual slipping-back," that Ramsey thinks is fundamental to the Greenhouse poems.

Roethke's "Carnations" poses a certain problem for interpretation, but its central image provides a metaphor for evaluating the two structural alternatives we have seen. The Greenhouse poems support both sequential and cyclical readings, more or less, and it might seem important to decide for one of the two alternatives. We may

instead try to see, however, how Roethke makes two irreconcilable
structures coincide. Though not a long poem in the conventional
sense, taken together the Greenhouse poems convey a poetic vision.
Parts of that vision conform to a linear, a sequential notion of
history. The poems do follow a general trend from infancy to maturity, from spring to fall, from birth to death, as Karl Malkoff and
George Wolff have pointed out. In the Greenhouse world of Theodore
Roethke, however, history is not only linear, it is also cyclical,
as Jarold Ramsey has shown. In the Greenhouse world, of course,
death follows birth, but rebirth also follows death. Out of winter
comes the spring, a fact only imaginable in the linear scheme of
history. The imagination of Roethke's protagonist is subject to
both ways of experiencing history, and to do justice to that imagination, one needs to keep both structuring principles in mind when
reading the Greenhouse poems.

Most critics do not object to the pause that is "Carnations,"
but a number do regret what Louis Martz calls the "intrusion" into
the Greenhouse of the poem "Frau Bauman, Frau Schmidt, and Frau
Schwartze" (p. 27). This poem constitutes one of the two significant textual problems in Roethke's poetry. (The other involves the
proper sequence of the Lost Son narratives.) "Frau Bauman, Frau
Schmidt, and Frau Schwartze" did not appear in the original Greenhouse poems of The Lost Son and Other Poems. Roethke published it
in 1952 and inserted it between "Old Florist" and "Transplanting"
in the Greenhouse poems printed in The Waking (1953) and in Words
for the Wind (1958) (Martz, pp. 27-28). (Incidentally, when Martz
refers to "Roethke's collected verse" in his essay [p. 27], he means
Words for the Wind.) Since the first edition of the Collected
Poems (1966) reprints The Lost Son in "its first integrity" (Martz,
p. 29), the poem does not appear in that volume at all. In later
printings of the Collected Poems, however, the three Fraus reemerge:

> Gone the three ancient ladies
> Who creaked on the greenhouse ladders,
> Reaching up white strings
> To wind, to wind
> The sweet-pea tendrils, the smilax,
> Nasturtiums, the climbing
> Roses, to straighten
> Carnations, red
> Chrysanthemums; the stiff
> Stems, jointed like corn,
> They tied and tucked,--
> These nurses of nobody else.
> Quicker than birds, they dipped
> Up and sifted the dirt;
> They sprinkled and shook;
> They stood astride pipes,
> Their skirts billowing out wide into tents,

Their hands twinkling with wet;
Like witches they flew along rows
Keeping creation at ease;
With a tendril for needle
They sewed up the air with a stem;
They teased out the seed that the cold kept asleep,--
All the coils, loops, and whorls.
They trellised the sun; they plotted for more than
   themselves.

I remember how they picked me up, a spindly kid,
Pinching and poking my thin ribs
Till I lay in their laps, laughing,
Weak as a whiffet;
Now, when I'm alone and cold in my bed,
They still hover over me,
These ancient leathery crones,
With their bandannas stiffened with sweat,
And their thorn-bitten wrists,
And their snuff-laden breath blowing lightly over
   me in my first sleep.

[WW, pp. 47-48]

No one disputes that "Frau Bauman, Frau Schmidt, and Frau Schwartze" is a good poem. William Meredith considers it the "greatest one" in the Greenhouse sequence (p. 40), and Karl Malkoff embraces the poem because it elaborates the theme he notices in "Old Florist" and "Transplanting." For Malkoff, "Frau Bauman, Frau Schmidt, and Frau Schwartze" also concerns the adult "manipulators of this vegetable world," and he thinks the poem was "placed appropriately" (p. 54). Louis Martz offers a more compelling argument against inclusion of the poem in the Greenhouse sequence, however. Martz observes that "Frau Bauman, Frau Schmidt, and Frau Schwartze" is different from the Greenhouse poems in its use of allusion ("the three workers are like Fates"), in its style (which creates "distance . . . between the child and the adult") and in its "careful literary echo of Yeats's poem, 'The Magi' " (p. 28). (In her book The Echoing Wood of Theodore Roethke, Jenijoy La Belle notes an echo of Yeats's "Lines Written in Dejection" [p. 142].) Martz does not fault the poem for any of these differences from the others in the sequence, but in that it departs from "the natural idiom and the localized greenhouse imagery of the original sequence" and "breaks the natural, intimate presence of those earlier poems," Martz thinks that it does not belong in the Greenhouse sequence (p. 28).

Martz's argument is a compelling one and his observations are widely cited. Not everyone concurs with his conclusion, however. For example, George Wolff agrees that "Frau Bauman, Frau Schmidt, and Frau Schwartze" is significantly different from the other Greenhouse poems, and he even reiterates Martz's evidence. Wolff says the poem departs from its neighbors; it depicts the "poet's present adult life" and is "drawn from memory." Inexplicably, however, Wolff is comfortable in reading the piece as the "tenth Greenhouse Poem" (p. 40). Robert Phillips is guilty of a similar inconsistency in his book The Confessional Poets. Phillips acknowledges that "first editions of the book [The Lost Son and Other Poems] did not contain the poem: Roethke appended it later" (p. 116), but Roethke later inserted the poem between "Old Florist" and "Transplanting." He did not place it at the end of the sequence, where it now appears in the Collected Poems. It is hard to see why, therefore, Phillips has been persuaded that "it seems singularly appropriate that the section should conclude with 'Frau Bauman, Frau Schmidt, and Frau Schwartze' " (p. 116).

"Frau Bauman, Frau Schmidt, and Frau Schwartze" is a fine poem and it should appear somewhere in Roethke's canon. That somewhere should not be between "Old Florist" and "Transplanting" for the reasons Louis Martz advances in his discussion. At any rate, "Frau Bauman . . . " should not appear where it does in the current Collected Poems. The compromise position of printing "Frau Bauman . . ." at the end of part 1, without note or comment, is a poor solution to the textual problem. New readers of Roethke's Greenhouse poems will surely be misled into thinking that "Frau Bauman . . . " is more than "at the end" of the section. They will think that it is the conclusion of the Greenhouse sequence, and that conclusion is one Roethke very certainly did not intend.

Roethke's Minimal Mysticism

Virtually all critics agree that Theodore Roethke's Greenhouse poems are more than finely drawn botanical descriptions. The poems mean more than they say and appear to imply a world-view, a philosophy, even a spiritual position. It is easier to talk about such implications when discussing Roethke's later poems, his "Sequence, Sometimes Metaphysical" and his "North American Sequence," however. In those poems, Roethke addresses spiritual matters explicitly. In the Greenhouse poems Roethke does not use philosophical or religious discourse or imagery. In the Greenhouse poems, he presents only perceptions, images, and dramatic situations, but one can get the impression that these Greenhouse experiences imply considerably more, not only for an imaginative reader but for Theodore Roethke as well. As might be expected, Roethke's own complex perspective on the Greenhouse has been widely discussed. One thing that will strike the reader of such interpretations is the ease with which Roethke's perspective can be phrased in the language of mystical experience. That is appropriate, we will see, for the language of mysticism can describe Roethke's immersion in his Greenhouse world, but mystical discourse is not native to Roethke's Greenhouse and it can misrepresent his perspective. Mystical discourse contains implications quite foreign to Roethke's perspective and critics who apply it suggest too frequently that the Greenhouse Roethke is more "other-worldly" than he really is.

Stanley Kunitz, Roethke's lifelong friend, was one of the first to discuss Roethke's Greenhouse perspective in detail and in its own terms. His insightful review of The Lost Son and Other Poems, "News of the Root," which appeared in Poetry in January of 1949, remains important because he identifies comprehensively the ambivalence of Roethke's perspective on his Greenhouse world, and unlike most of the first reviewers of The Lost Son and Other Poems, he argues for a major connection between the Greenhouse poems and the narrative poems that make up part 4 of the book. According to Kunitz, the Greenhouse world, for Theodore Roethke, is more than a remembered place or thing. Some critics read Roethke's love of the Greenhouse world as a mystically significant empathy, but Kunitz thinks Roethke's identification with the Greenhouse world is essentially secular, though especially intense. He cites as one example of Roethke's profound feeling his depiction in "Big Wind" of a greenhouse's weathering and then triumphing over a violent storm:

> But she rode it out,
> That old rose-house,
> She hove into the teeth of it,
> The core and pith of that ugly storm,
> Ploughing with her stiff prow,
> Bucking into the wind-waves
> That broke over the whole of her,
> Flailing her sides with spray,
> Flinging long strings of wet across the roof-top,
> Finally veering, wearing themselves out, merely
> Whistling thinly under the wind-vents;
> She sailed until the calm morning,
> Carrying her full cargo of roses.
>
> [CP, p. 41]

The greenhouse has "gender and personality" Kunitz says, and Roethke speaks of it "con amore" (p. 84).

The greenhouse breeds and nurtures beautiful and valuable things, and Roethke is enamored of those, of course. In "Carnations," for example, the last of the Greenhouse poems, Roethke presents admiringly an image of what a greenhouse can achieve. Kunitz thinks it a mistake to trace or limit Roethke's love of the Greenhouse world to his simple aesthetic appreciation of flowers, however. The poems themselves present a more complex and comprehensive experience of the Greenhouse world, Kunitz says. He argues that Roethke's major interest in the poems is the entire journey of the plants in the

greenhouse, their striving to become something more, what Kunitz
terms the plant's "green force, its invincible Becoming" (p. 84).
That journey is a difficult one, and Roethke depicts in the Greenhouse poems an array of "malevolent forces" that tries to arrest
the plants' development. In the Greenhouse world, Kunitz says,
"underness is everywhere" (p. 84).

    The benevolent aspect of the Greenhouse world is the easy one to
see, of course, and even Roethke, apparently, was not immediately
aware of the broader range of his own poems. In 1953, however,
in his statement, "An American Poet Introduces Himself and His
Poems," Roethke came to agree with Kunitz's observation and acknowledged that the greenhouses "were to me, I realize now, both
heaven and hell" (SP, p. 8). In none of the Greenhouse poems is
the infernal aspect more evident than in "Weed Puller":

> Under the concrete benches,
> Hacking at black hairy roots,--
> Those lewd monkey-tails hanging from drainholes,--
> Digging into the soft rubble underneath,
> Webs and weeds,
> Grubs and snails and sharp sticks,
> Or yanking tough fern-shapes,
> Coiled green and thick, like dripping smilax,
> Tugging all day at perverse life:
> The indignity of it!--
> With everything blooming above me,
> Lilies, pale-pink cyclamen, roses,
> Whole fields lovely and inviolate,--
> Me down in that fetor of weeds,
> Crawling on all fours,
> Alive, in a slippery grave.
>
> > [CP, p. 39]

Thus, Roethke's immersion in his Greenhouse world is no escapist's
remove to a childhood fantasy. The Greenhouse world is not innocent
of death and decay. They exist in the greenhouse, too, and perhaps
more terribly because the perspective Roethke presents in the Greenhouse poems is that of a boy, not that of a towering man.

    In addition to doing justice to Roethke's complex vision of the
Greenhouse world, Kunitz observes a connection between the Greenhouse poems and the Lost Son narratives of part 4. Much of the
book, Kunitz notes, "proliferates from a single root-cluster of images" (p. 83), and he is certainly right that imagery introduced in
the Greenhouse poems functions importantly in the Lost Son narratives. "The Return," for example, the fourth part of "The Lost
Son," and the fifth part of "The Shape of the Fire" both read much
like Greenhouse poems. The concluding image in the latter poem
is reminiscent of the "crisp hyacinthine coolness" of "Carnations."
Most critics now discuss the two sections of the book separately,

however, especially since Roethke worked the first installment of his narratives into the longer sequence he later titled Praise to the End! On this point most readers agree with the simplification of Kunitz's argument at the outset of Kenneth Burke's essay, "The Vegetal Radicalism of Theodore Roethke." There, Burke suggests that the best approach to the Lost Son narratives is through the more accessible Greenhouse poems.

Literary critic and theorist Kenneth Burke was also a close friend of Roethke's. The two met at Bennington College, and Brendan Galvin has argued in "Kenneth Burke and Theodore Roethke's 'Lost Son' Poems" that Burke's theoretical positions had considerable impact on the poems of Roethke's second volume. Burke's essay on Roethke, "The Vegetal Radicalism of Theodore Roethke," first published in 1950, has certainly had great impact on literary criticism of the poet. Burke's essay is probably the single most widely cited interpretation of Roethke's work, and deservedly so, but in at least one case an insight usually credited to Burke is anticipated or paralleled by Stanley Kunitz. There need be no suspicion that Burke appropriated Kunitz's idea of Roethke's ambivalent perspective toward the Greenhouse world, however. Even though Kunitz's "News of the Root" was published well before "The Vegetal Radicalism of Theodore Roethke," it is clear from Roethke's letter to Burke on February 8, 1949, that Burke was already at work on his essay before that date, and of course Burke read Roethke's Greenhouse and narrative poems as they were being composed (SL, p. 148).

Kenneth Burke explains Roethke's perspective in the Greenhouse poems by citing the vision of existence presented by the nineteenth-century French symbolist poet, Charles Beaudelaire, in his famous sonnet "Correspondances." At times, Beaudelaire says, a person may be privileged to see the world as alive with meanings and implications. These connections, the coherence one feels and sees, Beaudelaire terms "correspondances." They imply the existence of a different sphere, the surreal world, which can penetrate into our own. Burke notes the influence of Beaudelaire's view, and says it especially informs the "somewhat mystic ars poetica of so many contemporary poets" (p. 264). In that group Burke positions Roethke, but he does not suggest that Roethke's perspective in the Greenhouse poems is essentially mystical or maturely surreal. Burke thinks that "in describing the flowers objectively . . . he [Roethke] comes upon corresponding human situations, as it were by redundancy" (p. 264). Taking his cue from a misprinting of the word "perverse" in an early version of "Weed-Puller," Burke argues that the Greenhouse poems are "pre-verse." "In the flowers," Burke writes, Roethke "was trained to a symbolic vocabulary of subtle human relations and odd strivings, before he could have encountered the equivalent patterns of experience in exclusively human terms" (p. 265). Burke traces the disarming quality of innocence and understatement in the poems to Roethke's having "noted these forms before he felt the need for them, except vaguely and 'vatically' " (p. 265). A later

Roethke might have constructed or assigned emblematic values to the flowers in his greenhouse, but instead he simply resurrected experience of those things and their environment. For Burke, the special strength of the Greenhouse poems lies in that suggestiveness. It derives from Roethke's unwillingness or his inability to state conclusively the significance of the correspondences one might draw between vegetable and human being.

The criticisms of Kenneth Burke and Stanley Kunitz have established the foundations for much subsequent discussion of Roethke's Greenhouse perspective, though others have derived different implications from their assumptions. Like Burke and like Kunitz, Ralph J. Mills, Jr., observes also the "disturbing quality" of the Greenhouse poems in his little book, Theodore Roethke, published in 1963. Mills locates that disturbance in the reader's response to the poems, however, rather than in Roethke's ambivalent perspective on the Greenhouse world. One is disturbed by the Greenhouse poems, Mills says, because they "surpass the barriers of privacy to delineate hidden patterns in creation" (p. 14). In so saying, Mills acknowledges the surreal dimension Kenneth Burke points out; Mills's own statement, in fact, might be taken as a short definition of a major surrealist intention. Mills goes on to counter two major criticisms of Roethke's work as a whole by arguing that the Greenhouse poems thus suggest a wider poetic vision than usually thought possible for Roethke, and they offer also, implicitly, a sweeping social criticism. Mills thinks it valuable "for the scientific, technological mind of contemporary man to countenance such images of his origins, of archaic sources of life he shares with lesser forms than himself" (p. 14).

James Dickey thinks Roethke's Greenhouse perspective is of anthropological rather than social interest. In his review of the "Sequence, Sometimes Metaphysical" for Poetry in 1964, Dickey characterizes Roethke as one of the "great Empathizers." Roethke's poetry is best, Dickey argues, when there is a "mindless, elemental quality in the sound of his voice, something primitive and animistic, something with the wariness and inhuman grace of the wild beast, and with it another thing that could not be and never had been animal-like" (p. 150). Dickey comes close to suggesting that Roethke could achieve a sort of mystical identification with nature but he stresses that "spirit to him [Roethke] was meaningless without body" (p. 151). For Dickey, Roethke was a man "animal enough to enter half into unthinking nature and unanimal enough to be uneasy there" (p. 150).

In his essay of 1965, "The Objective Ego," Stephen Spender separates completely the two aspects of Roethke's perspective that James Dickey noted. Spender distinguishes between the " 'I' which becomes . . . dissolved in the object, and the 'I' which stays outside the object" in the Greenhouse poems (p. 10). In using language almost always reserved for describing mystical experience, of course, Spender implies that the perspective of the first of these "I's"

is somehow mystical. John D. Boyd goes further than that in his
essay "Texture and Form in Theodore Roethke's Greenhouse Poems,"
published in 1971. Boyd obliterates Spender's distinction between
the two "I's". He attributes "the sense of aliveness" so notable
in the Greenhouse poems to the first "I," to "an interpenetration
or coalescence of subject and object" (p. 411). That "coalescence,"
of course, is a main feature in any definition of mystical experience. By the time of Boyd's reading, then, Roethke's Greenhouse
perspective has become a largely mystical one.

In his essay of 1968, "Theodore Roethke's Minimals," William
Heyen tries to provide an analytic basis for his discussion of
Roethke's Greenhouse perspective. Kenneth Burke's discussion of
"correspondence" and Ralph J. Mills's comment on the "hidden pattern" in the Greenhouse provide a point of departure for Heyen. In
the Greenhouse poems, Heyen says, Roethke "begins to develop a
personal symbolism of minimals" (p. 361). Before The Lost Son
and Other Poems, Roethke used the imagery of the minimal creatures
traditionally. Heyen says the plants in Open House, for example,
"depending on the season, are suggestive of death or regeneration"
(p. 361). In the greenhouse, however, traditional symbolic references shatter. In his discussion of "The Lost Son," Ralph J. Mills,
Jr., commented that "one could . . . draw up two lists, of his positive and negative imagery" (p. 42). In order to analyze Roethke's
"personal symbolism," Heyen has done this. Drawing on the Lost
Son narratives and on "Meditations of an Old Woman," Heyen connects minimal to meaning. When a child "appears in a Roethke poem," Heyen says, "spiritual crisis is imminent" (p. 364). A dog
represents "repressed animality" (p. 369), a horse is the "antithesis of man's spiritual nature" (p. 369), a bird is the "image of
spiritual being" (p. 371), and a rose is the "image of the perfect
harmony of the spirit with its cosmos" (p. 375). Such cross-refer-
encing may be instructive, especially to the beginning reader baffled by the narrative poems, but Heyen's equations sharply limit
the complexities of Roethke's perspective on the minimal world.
Heyen does acknowledge that Roethke's perspective is more suggestive than he himself allows, however. In the Greenhouse, Heyen
says, the minimals become "at once beautiful and fearful" (p. 363),
a complexity of perspective Heyen's own system of symbolic allegiances does not adequately express.

In his reading, William Heyen narrows too much the meaning the
Greenhouse poems can support, but his analytically based discussion is more instructive than merely impressionistic interpretations
inspired by the suggestiveness of the poems. In the section on
Roethke in his book, The Confessional Poets, Robert Phillips alternates between the reductive and the tenuously analogical in his
interpretation of the Greenhouse poems. Of the "one nub of growth"
in "Cuttings," for example, he writes that "it can and must be
likened to the human spirit which miraculously survives even when
severed from the parent plant" (p. 111), and the poem "Root Cellar"

"is a symbol for the poet's psyche, that dark and deep-down place in which 'Nothing could sleep'" (p. 111). Such readings, of course, shrink and oversimplify these poems. The following analogy certainly stretches the poem "Big Wind": "first, the greenhouse as a ship is a metaphor for Roethke's life. . . . Seeing the greenhouse as an ark, his father as Noah and Roethke as Noah's son, the flowers instead of beasts as cargo, we can entertain the notion that the young Roethke was afraid to learn to sail the sea of passions in order to reach the mountain of salvation" (p. 114).

In his 1974 book, Theodore Roethke's Dynamic Vision, Richard Blessing looks more closely at the special quality in the Greenhouse poems that can motivate interpretations such as Robert Phillips's. Blessing is alert to Roethke's "sense of the terrible and beautiful dynamism of life" (pp. 5-6), but he adds that Roethke invites us to "meditate on the energies displayed" within the poems; he asks us also "to supply abstractions . . . to do more work, to join in the act of creation" (p. 69). To Blessing's credit, he applies his own hand lightly in formulating abstractions. He notices, for example, that the "terrible energy of tropism, the mysterious forces by which plants grow down to their food and reach upward toward the light . . . is an analogy which fits Roethke's creative struggle, but it fits other struggles as well" (pp. 69-70). Though Blessing acknowledges the "dynamic vision" at work in the Greenhouse poems, his primary interest is in the poems' impact on the reader. The transaction "between reader and poem is much more dynamic," he says (p. 69). While he overstates the case in concluding that the meanings of a plant in Roethke's poetry and in the world are identical, and that Roethke "has left the range of interpretation almost as wide as did the original greenhouse in which he grew up" (p. 68), Blessing's analysis does focus attention on how a reader responds to the Greenhouse poems.

Rosemary Sullivan's discussion in Theodore Roethke: The Garden Master returns to more traditional ways of explaining Roethke's unique Greenhouse perspective. According to Sullivan, that perspective is attributable to Roethke's notion of a "profound correspondence between mind and nature" due, she says echoing James Dickey, to "the primitive animistic cast of his mind" (p. 74). Sullivan argues that Roethke does not subscribe to classic statements of the doctrine of correspondence; he does not believe "that every physical entity corresponds to a spiritual essence" (p. 74). Roethke does believe that nature is "sacramental," however. "In moments of intensity," she says, "natural objects could sound deep responses within the individual convincing of a coinherence of interior being and exterior world" (p. 74). (Sullivan's statement amounts to a paraphrase of Beaudelaire's poem, "Correspondances.") Philosophical precedents for such a view exist additionally in the works of Swedish mystic Emanuel Swedenborg and German mystic Jakob Boehme, but Sullivan thinks Roethke's vision came from experience: it "is less a philosophical conception than an animistic belief" (p. 75).

To get the proper perspective on Sullivan's statement of Roethke's religious and philosophical position in the Greenhouse poems, we need to look at its source in Nathan A. Scott, Jr.'s lengthy essay, "The Example of Theodore Roethke," in The Wild Prayer of Longing. Scott's discussion is unique in Roethke criticism in that he approaches the poet's vision through the avenue of existential theology rather than through traditional literary criticism. According to Scott, Roethke believes through "lively intuition that both the human and the nonhuman modes of existence are animated and empowered by some primal reality, which may be denominated simply as Being itself" (p. 85). Others may have articulated the results of a similar "lively intuition" in the form of pantheism or animism, but Scott sees neither of those world-views as Roethke's fundamental orientation to his world. Roethke does not indicate that each and every creature contains a spark of spirit that is eventually released from the imprisoning body. Roethke's "minute particulars," Scott writes, "are never swallowed up in some vast encircling unity in which all diversity and distinction are ultimately annulled" (p. 103). Roethke's apprehension of nature is more akin to what Martin Buber called the I-Thou relation.

Roethke's is no pantheist's or animist's vision, Scott says, nor is it any traditional version of the doctrine of correspondences. Roethke "has no interest at all in devouring his snails and frogs and slugs and fungi in some system of moralizing analogy" (p. 92). He "lets things be" (p. 92). Nor, most significantly, was Roethke's perception essentially mystical, Scott points out, for Roethke "had no desire to transcend the finites and definites that make up the common occasions of life" (p. 102). Not a pantheist, a moralizer, or a mystic, then, Roethke was in fact what Scott calls a "sacramentalist," the term Rosemary Sullivan later borrows. By "sacramentalist" Scott means that type of imagination in which the reasoning powers have been "so hushed as to permit an attitude of simple enchantment before the irrevocability whereby the things and creatures of this world are what they are, in their utter specificity" (p. 77). Because he may experience that enchantment, it is "man's principal obligation to offer, in turn, a humble pietas as his primary response to the mysteriousness with which all created things reflect the splendid fecundity and holiness of Being" (p. 87). Roethke does this in his work, Scott argues, and he concludes that "there is rarely to be found in our period a book of poetry so predominantly psalmic and doxological as Roethke's" (p. 80).

Nathan A. Scott, Jr., provides valuable clarification of philosophical and religious terminology in his enthusiastic appraisal of Roethke's perspective and performance. Despite Scott's discussion and Sullivan's reiteration, however, the trend in Roethke criticism is to see his Greenhouse perspective in secular terms,

as exemplified recently by George Wolff's discussion in <u>Theodore</u>
<u>Roethke</u>. We have already seen in the first part of this chapter
that George Wolff reformulates Karl Malkoff's argument about the
structure of the Greenhouse poems; later in his discussion Wolff
shifts attention from conceptual and thematic content to his main
interest, what he calls the "implied human presence" in the Greenhouse poems (p. 35). Wolff derives his observation from Kenneth
Burke's introductory comment in "The Vegetal Radicalism of Theodore Roethke" that the "thirteen flower poems" are "clearly the
imagistic figuring of a human situation" (p. 254). In Wolff's
view, that "figuring" translates into a version of the pathetic
fallacy: "the quality of life the plants experience reflects the
quality of the emotional and spiritual life of the poet" (p. 35).
"Cuttings (later)," for example, is a kind of projection or transformation of Roethke's own experience rather than an identification
with some "heroic struggle" of the plants (p. 37). In depicting
the stems as "cut" and "struggling" and the limbs as "lopped,"
Roethke figures his own pain, and in noticing the "resurrection,"
the "new life," and the "seeping" and "parting" (CP, p. 37), he indicates his aspirations. Contrary to Wolff's interpretation, however, the plants in the greenhouse do not stand simply as symbols
or indicators of the protagonist's feelings. They have a life
apart from his, and he apart from theirs. In "Cuttings (later)"
the protagonist disassociates himself from the plants in the conclusion. Their struggle is successful, over, and done by the end
of the poem but his has only begun. After finishing "Cuttings
(later)," we need to return to the beginning of the poem. Another
"urge" and "wrestle" is in the offing, now, and in our second reading the struggle will not be experienced by the plants. George
Wolff is correct to note the importance of the connection between
the plants and the "implied human perspective" in the Greenhouse
poems, but to explain that connection Wolff dissolves the distinction between the two worlds that Roethke also makes so evident.
Wolff does not lay the issue to rest, then. His reading eventually
resurrects the matter of the special empathy, the unique perspective,
that Roethke displays in the Greenhouse poems.

   Theodore Roethke's complex perspective on the Greenhouse world
remains a lively topic in the criticism, it should be obvious, but
some agreement on the issue has emerged. Most critics acknowledge
that Roethke portrays his Greenhouse world as a mixture of heaven
and hell. The Greenhouse world is not Eden or a remembered world
of innocence lost. Critics agree also that Roethke endows the
Greenhouse world with a significance we do not ordinarily associate
with minimal things or plants. He makes that significance especially dramatic because he approaches the minimal creatures on their
own terms, as a creature of the same size as they. Through memory
the adult speaker of the poems diminishes himself to the more vul-
nerable stature of the child. Instead of towering over the flowers
and plants, as his father does, as he would do, the boy remembered

sees the vegetation eye to eye. From that point of view, the greenhouse creatures loom large with intensified meaning. Features of
the Greenhouse world correspond to more momentous things, but the
intimate relationship of subject and object in the Greenhouse poems does not easily translate into any traditional or religious
view. Nonetheless, most critics sense a spiritual dimension to
Roethke's perspective in the poems, as we have seen, and they have
tried in a variety of ways to account for that. In that respect,
one might do worse than return to (or begin with) the clear and
simple reasoning of Stanley Kunitz in his retrospective on Roethke,
"Poet of Transformations," published in 1965. Kunitz says Roethke stoops to the minimals because they are minimals, because "these
are creatures still moist with the waters of the beginning" (p.
100). Roethke was interested in such beginnings, of course, because
as he said, "to go forward as a spiritual man it is necessary first
to go back" (SP, p. 39).

Literary Backgrounds and Sources

No one hears loud echoes of other poets in the Greenhouse poems.
In them, it is agreed, Roethke speaks in an original and authentic
voice; he creates poetic forms of his own devising; he treats a
subject that before him no one had approached; and he presents, of
course, a complex and innovative perspective. For these reasons,
the integrity of Theodore Roethke's poetic voice is not a major
issue in criticism of the Greenhouse poems. When critics say
Roethke's verse shows too much influence, owes too much to other
poets, those critics are not referring to the Greenhouse poems.
The primary source of the poems is experience, and experience of
nature especially, accessed by the memory. Much critical effort,
we have seen, has been devoted to interpreting Roethke's approach
to that experience, often in philosophical or religious terms,
though two substantial works do focus on how literary backgrounds
inform the Greenhouse poems.
Jenijoy La Belle's The Echoing Wood of Theodore Roethke and
Jay Parini's Theodore Roethke: An American Romantic represent
two quite different approaches to the subject. As we have seen
in her discussion of the literary backgrounds of Open House, La
Belle is not satisfied to refer Roethke's poems to some general
intellectual movement or literary tradition. Her entire method is
predicated on detecting the specific poet and even the specific
poem upon which Roethke drew in constructing his own literary tradition. On the other hand, Jay Parini wants to show that Roethke
is a twentieth-century representative of American Romanticism, and
he follows a quite different method. Parini does not isolate Roethke's specific borrowings from Romantic poets and Romantic poems;
he discovers in Roethke's poetry the Romantic concepts and atti-

tudes they illustrate.   La Belle's method is inductive and precise;
Parini's is deductive and more general.   Of the two treatments, La
Belle's is probably more useful for the reader in search of the
literary backgrounds of Roethke's individual poems.   The rigor
of her method, however, the strength of her book as a whole, is,
in her discussion of the Greenhouse poems, a significant obstacle
for La Belle.   Jay Parini's purpose can be satisfied by detecting
Romantic aspects in Roethke's poems, but La Belle's method demands
the specific reference.   Her discussion becomes a tribute to the
originality of the Greenhouse poems because she herself must admit that specific literary precedents for the poems are especially
difficult to find.

According to La Belle, the important literary figure behind the
Greenhouse poems is the Romantic poet William Wordsworth, both in
his life and work.   "Roethke's relationship with Wordsworth is much
more than a matter of verbal or even thematic echoes," La Belle
writes (p. 42).   Roethke's use of Wordsworth transcends the specific of the detectable literary echo because Roethke "felt a sympathetic companionship with Wordsworth's life as well as with his
art" (p. 43).   Roethke empathized with Wordsworth's life, La Belle
says, because "in their childhoods both poets had profoundly intense and memorable experiences in nature," and he empathized with
Wordsworth's writings because those were "transmutations of these
experiences into poetry" (p. 43).   As evidence for the latter point,
La Belle draws a connection between Roethke's poem "Moss-Gathering" and Wordsworth's "Nutting."   She rejects out of hand Karl
Malkoff's interpretation of "Moss-Gathering" in Theodore Roethke:
An Introduction to the Poetry.   Malkoff's psychoanalytic interpretation that the poem is essentially about masturbation is a
"limiting critical perspective," La Belle says (p. 28).   By reading "Moss-Gathering" in the context of Wordsworth's "Nutting," La
Belle finds that both Roethke and Wordsworth feel guilty over their
actions in the "bower" of nature, both poets "invest nature with
qualities of human feeling," and "the incident is for both poets a
central experience in the development of their poetic faculties"
(p. 29).   Wordsworth learns "a new awareness of his relationship
to and sympathy with nature" and Roethke learns that "nature is
pervaded by a spiritual presence . . . [and] it is informed with
order" (p. 29).

La Belle can make the case that Wordsworth was an important source
for Roethke.   The phrase "Praise to the end!," for example, title
for one of Roethke's volumes, comes from Wordsworth.   But are the
Greenhouse poems a conscious borrowing from or echoing of William
Wordsworth?   The answer must be a qualified "no."   In discussing
the Greenhouse poems, La Belle must enlarge her pool of evidence to
include lives of the poets as well as their works.   Her argument
about the literary backgrounds of the Greenhouse poems is therefore
not so strong as is her detailed discussion of Roethke's more obvious uses of the "great dead."   La Belle admits that "parallels be-

tween Roethke and Wordsworth do not in every case point to actual sources" (p. 42), and at her most rigorous, La Belle herself would question the strength of conclusions based on such soft echoes.

In The Echoing Wood of Theodore Roethke, Jenijoy La Belle collects a host of instances of Roethke's literary borrowings and then arranges those citations in order to reconstruct what might be construed as the anthology of poems that Roethke's own poems direct us to read. In his book, Theodore Roethke: An American Romantic, Jay Parini begins with a set of characteristically Romantic ideas and then proceeds to discover those ideas in Roethke's poetry in an effort to show that Roethke is an American Romantic poet. Parini refers Roethke's poems to a generalized tradition and not, as La Belle would prefer to do, to individual poets and poems that the poet has chosen to constitute his tradition. The range of material Parini may cite, therefore, is considerably broader than La Belle would allow. Parini succeeds in showing a number of important connections between the Romantic world-view and similar notions in Roethke's poetry and poetic methods, but the main criterion Parini appears to exercise is that the source cited be recognizably Romantic. For that reason, some of the connections he finds are weak or misleading. In addition to his excursions into literary and intellectual history, Parini explicates many of Roethke's poems at length. He comments on nearly all of them, in their chronological order, whether the poem exhibits Romantic attributes or not. As an unfortunate result, Parini's central thesis, that Roethke is essentially a Romantic American poet, periodically gets overshadowed, even lost, in the course of his running commentary.

According to Parini, among the characteristically Romantic biases that Roethke exhibits in his verse are a reliance on the lyric, the quintessentially Romantic form (p. 33); a preference for feeling over reason, for emotion over intellect (p. 33); a use of what Parini calls "normal speech patterns" instead of poetical diction (p. 34); a "recognition that man is cut off from nature" (p. 4) which combines with the notion that the "source of real knowledge is within him [man] already" (p. 11); and an assumption that poetry should not merely imitate reality but should "embody" it (p. 51). To greater or lesser extent, each of these views can be found in Roethke's work but it takes little reflection to see they are not perfectly applicable. Roethke departed from the "lyric" mode in his experimental Lost Son narratives, of course, and in them he went beyond "normal speech patterns" indeed. Nor in the Greenhouse poems, in particular, does Roethke demonstrate much evidence of being estranged from nature. To the contrary, some of the anxiety in those poems derives from his visceral recognition that he, too, is part of nature.

Parini is probably farthest from the mark when he discusses Roethke's sense of the poet's role. While it may be true that "Roethke's poetics hark back to German Romantic theory and Cole-

ridge, although his personal sources were Wordsworth and Emerson"
(p. 30), the conclusion Parini draws from the connection is simply
not appropriate: "fundamental to this system is the concept of
poet as prophet," Parini writes. "The poet becomes a priest of
the imagination, a secular clergyman. But the cost of this special
role is alienation from the mainstream of society; the seer appears
to outsiders as a madman, the poete maudit of nineteenth-century
French letters" (pp. 30-31). At this point, Parini is not talking
about Theodore Roethke anymore. As we have seen, Roethke refuses
to draw moral implications in his Greenhouse poems. He rejects the
hortatory stance of Blake, Shelley, Whitman, or in Roethke's own
day, Allen Ginsberg, poets ordinarily thought of as "prophetic."
One can argue that Roethke assumes a public stance in his later poems, in the "North American Sequence," for example, but in the
Greenhouse poems and in the Lost Son narratives, Roethke neither
achieves nor aspires to the prophetic. Simply because other poets,
specifically Romantic poets, have taken on the role, it is certainly
too much to say that Roethke assumes the mantle of "secular clergyman." And Roethke would probably cringe at the suggestion that he
was a "seer" seen as a "madman" or a "poete maudit." The pain and
embarrassment of his manic-depressive episodes aside, Roethke wanted
to be remembered as a poet of affirmation. His poems bear out that
desire. At the least, the work of Theodore Roethke reads quite
differently from that of Charles Beaudelaire, Arthur Rimbaud, or
Edgar Allan Poe.

If one must draw a label out of literary history to describe
Roethke's poetic vision as a whole, the term "Romantic" probably
fits better than most others. Jenijoy La Belle implies that in
connecting the Greenhouse poems to William Wordsworth, and in
pointing out how Roethke's own allegiances and practices align
with a number of important Romantic concepts, Jay Parini wants to
show it explicitly. However, neither Parini nor La Belle makes it
necessary to know such connections for an understanding of Roethke's
Greenhouse poems in particular. The more that Jay Parini seeks to
show how Roethke conforms to this or that Romantic precept, the
more Roethke's poetry appears original and unique. Were "Theodore
Roethke" a chapter in a book with other chapters devoted, perhaps,
to Poe, Emerson, Whitman, Wallace Stevens, and William Carlos
Williams, Parini might make it crucial to see that Roethke stands
in the line of American Romantic poets.

Poetic Method and Technique

Theodore Roethke's Greenhouse poems are achievements in organic
rather than traditional poetic form. It is therefore understandable that references to literary or intellectual backgrounds would

not adequately account for the special impact of the poems or, as Geoffrey Thurley has done in his book, The American Moment, one could dissolve this issue entirely by denying that the Greenhouse poems have much impact at all. Of the poem "Moss-Gathering," for example, Thurley writes, "Roethke does not . . . make us feel what he felt--he tells us what he felt, and implicitly invites us to praise him for his tenderness" (p. 94). Of the Greenhouse poems in general, "description is their medium" Thurley concludes (p. 93). It has become axiomatic in the criticism of the Greenhouse poems, however, that Roethke "endow[s] his brief lyrics with intensity of action," an observation made first by Kenneth Burke in his essay, "The Vegetal Radicalism of Theodore Roethke" (p. 255; Burke's italics). With the exception of Geoffrey Thurley, other critics have sensed that "intensity of action," too, and a rather full explanation of Roethke's greenhouse technique has emerged.

Critical discussion of Roethke's methods in the Greenhouse poems owes a great deal to Kenneth Burke's pioneering essay originally published, it seems incredible now, in 1950. Burke attributes what he calls the "action" of the poems to Roethke's choice of diction and his handling of the individual poem's structure. Roethke's conscious control of diction is the more obvious of the two effects. Burke notes that "you will rarely find in his verse a noun ending in '-ness' or '-ity.' He [Roethke] goes as far as is humanly possible in quest of a speech wholly devoid of abstractions" (pp. 257-58). The density of verse that results is especially evident in Roethke's "Root Cellar," for example:

> Nothing would sleep in that cellar, dank as a ditch,
> Bulbs broke out of boxes hunting for chinks in the
>   dark,
> Shoots dangled and drooped,
> Lolling obscenely from mildewed crates,
> Hung down long yellow evil necks, like tropical snakes.
> And what a congress of stinks!--
> Roots ripe as old bait,
> Pulpy stems, rank, silo-rich,
> Leaf-mold, manure, lime, piled against slippery planks.
> Nothing would give up life:
> Even the dirt kept breathing a small breath.
>   [CP, p. 38]

In dramatic contrast, Burke offers a list of the dozens of abstract words contained in T. S. Eliot's poem, "Burnt Norton," and he concludes that "if Roethke adheres to his present aesthetic, there are more of such expressions in this one Quartet of Eliot's than Roethke's Vegetal Radicalism would require for a whole lifetime of poetizing" (p. 258). Because concrete diction is so fundamental to the Greenhouse poems, Burke objects to the concluding lines of the last poem in the sequence, "Carnations." Words like "coolness" and "eternity" are not "characteristic of Roethke's language," Burke says (p. 257).

Less evidently, though no less importantly, Roethke structures his individual Greenhouse poems so that "no matter how brief the poems are, they progress from stage to stage. Reading them, you have strongly the sense of entering at one place, winding through a series of internal developments, and coming out somewhere else" (p. 255). It is important to recognize that Burke is discussing here the matter of technique that animates the individual lyric, and through those individuals, the sequence as a whole. Burke is referring to a structural, not a thematic effect. He is not suggesting that the Greenhouse poems as a sequence move thematically from life to death or child to adult and so forth. Burke believes such thematic relationships are available in the poems, but in identifying what he calls the "developmental structure" of the poems (p. 256), Burke is pointing to the evolution of a poetic structure. According to Burke, a poem itself grows up in the Greenhouse poems. The Greenhouse poems "have the vigor, and the poetic morality, of action, of form unfolding" (p. 256).

In his book Theodore Roethke: An Introduction to the Poetry, Karl Malkoff reiterates Burke's point about the diction of the Greenhouse poems. Malkoff explains Roethke's shift from the abstract diction of Open House to the concrete diction of the Greenhouse by referring to one of Roethke's own infrequent critical reviews. Roethke does not discuss the poetics of the Greenhouse poems to the degree that he explains and justifies the poetics of the Lost Son narratives. Roethke comments on the Greenhouse poems specifically only in small prefaces to his discussions of his more experimental work, but Malkoff thinks Roethke's favorable description of Roy Fuller's book of poems, A Lost Season, can be applied to the Greenhouse poems. Roethke writes:

> What gives these pieces and others like "Crustaceans" their special power is the feeling that the imagination has been forced to turn to the subhuman to sustain itself. They show, too, that a reliance on the visual image need not produce a poetry of mere surfaces. Intensely seen, image becomes symbol. The visible and invisible meet and reside in the powerfully observed. [SP, p. 122]

After a diatribe at the end of his review against "whole schools of verbalizers, nerveless, slick and often macabre; squeezers of the obvious, vulgar jostlers with words; cerebral gibberers and wild-eyed affirmers; helter-skelter impressionists and frantic improvisers" and so on (SP, p. 123), Roethke reins himself in and hopes for a "poetry of the future" that will be "sensuous but not simple-minded; above all, rooted deeply in life" (SP, p. 124). According to Malkoff, "we recognize here a guiding principle of the greenhouse poems, where experience is presented not as subject to intellectual analysis, but directly in terms of sensory perception" (p. 47).

Roethke's review of Fuller's poems was published in Poetry in January of 1946. George Wolff suggests that another relevant text for understanding Roethke's Greenhouse poetics is his letter to Kenneth Burke, dated February 27, 1945. In that letter, Roethke included a "Statement of General Nature of Project" for a Houghton Mifflin Library Fellowship Award in Poetry in which he said his "first book [Open House] was much too wary, much too gingerly in its approach to experience," and in which he promised, "I am trying to loosen up, to write poems of greater intensity and symbolical depth" (SL, p. 114). By "looseness," Wolff speculates in his book, Theodore Roethke, Roethke "meant the fluctuations in rhythm and line length that accompanied the changes in his own perceptions" (p. 33). Wolff detects those in the Greenhouse poems. Roethke's comment probably better explains the poetic of the Lost Son narratives, however. As he indicates in his broadcast, "An American Poet Introduces Himself and His Poems," Roethke apparently dated his own achievement of a loose and organic poetic form to a time after the writing of the Greenhouse poems. In that broadcast, after quoting the poem "Big Wind," Roethke says that "somewhat later, in 1945, I began a series of longer pieces which try, in their rhythms, to catch the movement of the mind itself" (SP, p. 10). The "longer" pieces, of course, are the Lost Son narratives, not the Greenhouse poems. It is difficult, though, to know exactly what Roethke means by the phrase "movement of the mind itself." Like most other poets and like most critics, Roethke is clearer when he describes the effects of specific devices in specific poems than when he offers generalizations about technique. In a 1960 discussion of "Big Wind" in "Some Remarks on Rhythm," for example, Roethke points out that "participial or verbal forms" are the "formal device giving energy to the piece . . . [they] keep the action going" (SP, p. 83), and that is a technical detail even Kenneth Burke neglected to mention. As the lines from the first part of the poem indicate, Roethke is of course correct:

>Where were the greenhouses going,
>Lunging into the lashing
>Wind driving water
>So far down the river
>All the faucets stopped?--
>So we drained the manure-machine
>For the steam plant,
>Pumping the stale mixture
>Into the rusty boilers,
>Watching the pressure gauge
>Waver over to red,
>As the seams hissed

And the live steam
Drove to the far
End of the rose-house,
Where the worst wind was,
Creaking the cypress window-frames,
Cracking so much thin glass
We stayed all night,
Stuffing the holes with burlap. . . .
                                     [SP, p. 41]

In observing that structure and diction are the important aspects of Roethke's Greenhouse technique, Kenneth Burke set the agenda for the two best studies of that issue to follow his.   In "Texture and Form in Theodore Roethke's Greenhouse Poems," John D. Boyd argues that "organization generates its own dynamism" in the Greenhouse poems, and he credits Kenneth Burke alone for having noticed that (p. 414).   Roethke created the Greenhouse poems out of "unpromising materials," Boyd says, but the poems surmount that because of their formal and structural properties.   Boyd emphasizes the freedom of the Greenhouse poems, their "air of felicitous improvisation" and their "offhand, colloquial idiom," but he focuses especially on the "remarkable inner logic" of the individual poems (p. 413).   His description of that "inner logic" in the Greenhouse poems might in fact be taken as a definition of organic poetic form: "each poem has been allowed to define and shape its own uniquely appropriate formal coherence from within, in accordance with its own subject and theme" (p. 414), he says.   In addition to his extension of Burke's observation of structure in the Greenhouse poems, Boyd goes further with analysis of "Big Wind" and, in a sense, takes up where Burke leaves off.

Boyd's observation of the "inner logic" of the Greenhouse poems can be substantiated in still more detail.   In his book, Theodore Roethke, George Wolff notes that the contraries of "threatening enclosure" and the "counterthrust of perverse life" permeate the Greenhouse poems both structurally and thematically (p. 39).   In "Root Cellar," "grammatical structure enacts an enclosure in which the forces of life are almost evenly matched by the threat of the inanimate" (p. 37), and in biblical poetry, Wolff says, such structure is called the "envelope technique" (p. 38).   Form unfolds in still other recognizable ways in the Greenhouse poems.   Kenneth Burke likens the "developmental structure" of "Big Wind" to the "expository steps . . . of a well-formed argument" (p. 256), but that isolated comparison can be expanded.   A number of the Greenhouse poems exhibit classic rhetorical structures.   The structures of "Cuttings," "Moss-Gathering," and "Flower Dump," for example, emphasize the emergence of the particular out of the general.   In "Cuttings," we move from the plural "sticks-in-a-drowse" to the singular "one nub of growth" (CP, p. 37), and in "Moss-Gathering," we move from a general to a specific aspect of moss-gathering, to the feeling that "something always went out of me" (CP, p. 40). In "Flower Dump," we shift from a vision of "Carnations, verbenas, cosmos,/ Molds, weeds, dead leaves" to "one tulip on top,/ One swaggering head" (CP, p. 43).

Rhetorical organization thus reinforces a theme of individuation out of the many, but Roethke does not structure all of his Greenhouse poems this way. "Forcing House," for example, works exactly in the reverse.

> Vines tougher than wrists
> And rubbery shoots,
> Scums, mildews, smuts along stems,
> Great cannas or delicate cyclamen tips,--
> All pulse with the knocking pipes
> That drip and sweat,
> Sweat and drip,
> Swelling the roots with steam and stench,
> Shooting up lime and dung and ground bones,--
> Fifty summers in motion at once,
> As the live heat billows from pipes and pots.
> [CP, p. 38]

In this poem, the plural subjects and their plural actions are collected by the conclusion in a single noun and verb. The "vines," "shoots," "scums, mildews, smuts" and so forth are gathered into the word "heat," and the "pulse," the "drip and sweat," the "swelling," and "shooting" are combined in the verb "billows." Instead of the individuation of the one out of the many, we have in "Forcing House" the immersion of many identities into the all. The structure of the individual poem reinforces its theme, in other words, and that should be considered in constructing and evaluating thematic overviews of all of the poems.

Where John D. Boyd elaborates on what Burke terms structure, Richard Blessing focuses on what Burke terms diction. Blessing's purpose is to explain how Roethke achieves what Blessing calls a "dynamic vision." In his essay of 1972, "Theodore Roethke: A Celebration," Blessing outlines the various means by which Roethke "manages to transfer the rhythm, the motion, of life from his pulse to the printed page" (p. 180). According to Blessing, these means include "intensification of verbs," "frenetic lists of actions," "energetic rhythms," "associative leaps from image to image," and "playing off of sound against sound, phrase against phrase" (p. 179). Some of these general techniques are more characteristic of the Lost Son narratives, of course, as indicated by Roethke in his essay "Open Letter," but Blessing finds that verbs, participles in particular, are of prime importance in the Greenhouse poems. As Roethke pointed out in discussing "Big Wind," participles "keep the action going," but Blessing observes in his book, Theodore Roethke's Dynamic Vision, that they also give "a sense

of the continuous" (p. 73). Through his "manipulation of point of
view and of verb tenses," Blessing says, Roethke presents "something of the energetic thrusting on of the historical event as it
moves through time and space" (p. 88). For Blessing, such technique serves structurally to reiterate Roethke's thematic bias
toward a "dynamic vision." So complete was Roethke's commitment to an energetic verse, Blessing argues, "the ideal line in
the greenhouse sequence . . . is the line of pure spondee, the
line totally free of unaccented syllables" (p. 72).

The Greenhouse poems of part 1 of The Lost Son and Other Poems
indicate Theodore Roethke's graduation from apprentice to accomplished craftsman. In that respect, a reader might well approach
Roethke's verse as a whole by beginning at the roots of his distinctive vision in the Greenhouse poems. Roethke aspires to larger
things in the Greenhouse poems than he did in the poems of Open
House, and he achieves larger things, too. Roethke's repeated
explorations of the lively world of the family greenhouses create
a poetic vision whose features recur throughout his verse, and as
we have seen, two broadly different views of how the Greenhouse
poems combine to become that coherent vision have emerged since
publication of The Lost Son and Other Poems in 1948. In one view,
the poems record chronologically the growth of a person from childhood to adolescence, while in the other the poems represent cycles
of growth and decay, aspiration and defeat. Both views apply to
the poems, but Roethke's representation of the world of the greenhouse is more comprehensive than either interpretation allows.
Roethke's greenhouse world contains life and death, beauty and
danger, pleasure and pain. Some might think the experiences of
a child in a greenhouse would be of limited relevance in a world
of more sweeping human circumstances, but the greenhouse world
parallels major aspects of the world beyond its confines, and it
is a combination of heaven and hell.
    As might be expected in a place where heaven touches, momentous
things can transpire within the greenhouse when seen from up close
and intensely. Perhaps most notable of these is the unique blending
of the protagonist with the things he perceives, the empathy between human and minimal creature. Some critics have explained that
empathy in distinctively religious language, and have suggested
that the Greenhouse poems show Roethke's mystical sympathies.
Indeed, Roethke's vision of the Greenhouse world forms an important part of any argument about his mystical predilections, but
the poems themselves do not speak in a language of mysticism or
in any traditional philosophical system of discourse. Unlike the
poems of Open House, the Greenhouse poems come primarily from
experience, not from reading. Roethke's Greenhouse vision may
be translated into the language of mysticism or be placed into
the literary and intellectual context of Romanticism, but Roethke's
"vegetal radicalism" creates its own categories and terms. The

extraordinary connection the protagonist of the poems achieves with his Greenhouse world is communicated to a reader's imagination primarily by quiet suggestion.

Roethke's complex perspective in the Greenhouse poems is of considerable import for his and for American poetry; of equal significance is the fact that the Greenhouse poems are technical accomplishments. They are fine poems, perhaps great poems, and are effective because of how and what Roethke says in them, with his choices of diction, and because of how he structures that diction in the individual poem. Roethke fuses content and form in the Greenhouse poems, and he perfects a certain type of lyric poem. Interestingly, the extent of that perfection is indicated by the summary and somehow final tone of some of the critical interpretations of the poems. In reading through that criticism, one can forget that the Greenhouse poems date from an early part of Roethke's career. By accomplishing so well what he set out to do, Roethke appears to have made it redundant, if not impossible, to continue writing Greenhouse poems. That was not a problem for Roethke, however, for he did not waste time by imitating himself as a less ambitious or daring poet might do. As part 4 of The Lost Son and Other Poems shows, Roethke turned his attention from writing dense, short lyrics about a greenhouse to the more expansive landscape offered him by the long narrative poem.

Bibliography

Blessing, Richard A.
1972. "Theodore Roethke: A Celebration," Tulane Studies in English 20, pp. 169-80.
1974. Theodore Roethke's Dynamic Vision. Bloomington: Indiana Univ. Pr.
Boyd, John D.
1971. "Texture and Form in Theodore Roethke's Greenhouse Poems," Modern Language Quarterly 32, 4, pp. 409-24.
Burke, Kenneth
1966. "The Vegetal Radicalism of Theodore Roethke," in Language as Symbolic Action, pp. 254-81. Berkeley: Univ. of California Pr. Appeared in Sewanee Review, pp. 68-108. Winter, 1950. Reprinted in Profile of Theodore Roethke, ed. William Heyen. Columbus: Merrill, 1971.
Dickey, James
1968. "Theodore Roethke," in Babel to Byzantium: Poets and Poetry Now, pp. 147-52. New York: Farrar, Straus, and Giroux. Appeared in Poetry Nov. 1964, pp. 119-122.
Galvin, Brendan
1971. "Kenneth Burke and Theodore Roethke's 'Lost Son' Poems,"

Northwest Review: Theodore Roethke Special Issue Summer, pp. 67-96.
Heyen, William
1968.   "Theodore Roethke's Minimals," Minnesota Review 8, pp. 359-75.
Kunitz, Stanley
1975.   "News of the Root," in A Kind of Order, a Kind of Folly: Essays and Conversations, pp. 83-86. Boston: Little, Brown. Appeared in Poetry Jan. 1949, pp. 222-25.
1975.   "Poet of Transformations," in A Kind of Order, a Kind of Folly: Essays and Conversations, pp. 96-109. Boston: Little, Brown. Appeared in The New Republic Jan. 23, 1965, pp. 23-29. Reprinted in Profile of Theodore Roethke, ed. William Heyen. Columbus: Merrill, 1971.
La Belle, Jenijoy
1976.   The Echoing Wood of Theodore Roethke. Princeton: Princeton Univ. Pr.
Malkoff, Karl
1966.   Theodore Roethke: An Introduction to the Poetry. New York: Columbia Univ. Pr.
Martz, Louis
1965.   "A Greenhouse Eden," in Theodore Roethke: Essays on the Poetry, ed. Arnold Stein, pp. 14-35. Seattle: Univ. of Washington Pr.
Meredith, William
1965.   "A Steady Storm of Correspondences: Theodore Roethke's Long Journey Out of the Self," in Theodore Roethke: Essays on the Poetry, ed. Arnold Stein, pp. 36-53. Seattle: Univ. of Washington Pr.
Mills, Ralph J., Jr.
1963.   Theodore Roethke, Minnesota Pamphlets on American Writers, no. 30. Minneapolis: Univ. of Minnesota Pr.
Molesworth, Charles
1979.   "Songs of the Happy Man: Theodore Roethke and Contemporary Poetry," in The Fierce Embrace. Columbia: Univ. of Missouri Pr.
Parini, Jay
1979.   Theodore Roethke: An American Romantic. Amherst: Univ. of Massachusetts Pr.
Phillips, Robert
1973.   "The Inward Journeys of Theodore Roethke," in The Confessional Poets, pp. 107-27. Carbondale: Southern Illinois Univ. Pr.
Ramsey, Jarold
1972.   "Roethke in the Greenhouse," Western Humanities Review 26, pp. 35-47.
Roethke, Theodore
1961.   Words for the Wind: The Collected Verse of Theodore Roethke. Bloomington: Indiana Univ. Pr.

1965. On the Poet and His Craft: Selected Prose of Theodore Roethke, ed. Ralph J. Mills, Jr. Seattle: Univ. of Washington Pr.
1966. The Collected Poems of Theodore Roethke. Garden City, N.Y.: Doubleday.
1968. Selected Letters of Theodore Roethke, ed. Ralph J. Mills, Jr. Seattle: Univ. of Washington Pr.
Scott, Nathan A., Jr.
1971. "The Example of Theodore Roethke," in The Wild Prayer of Longing: Poetry and the Sacred, pp. 76-118. New Haven: Yale Univ. Pr.
Seager, Allan
1968. The Glass House: The Life of Theodore Roethke. New York: McGraw-Hill.
Spanier, Sandra Whipple
1979. "The Unity of the Greenhouse Sequence: Roethke's Portrait of the Artist," Concerning Poetry 12, 1, pp. 53-60.
Spender, Stephen
1965. "The Objective Ego," in Theodore Roethke: Essays on the Poetry, ed. Arnold Stein, pp. 3-13. Seattle: Univ. of Washington Pr.
Sullivan, Rosemary
1975. Theodore Roethke: The Garden Master. Seattle: Univ. of Washington Pr.
Thurley, Geoffrey
1978. The American Moment: American Poetry in Mid-Century. New York: St. Martin's Pr.
Wolff, George
1981. Theodore Roethke. Boston: Twayne.

Additional Reading

Hall, Donald
1955. "The New Poetry: Notes on the Past Fifteen Years in America," New World Writing Apr., pp. 236-37.
Hoey, Allen
1982. "Some Metrical & Rhythmical Strategies in the Early Poems of Theodore Roethke," Concerning Poetry 15, 1, pp. 49-58.
Maxwell, J. C.
1969. "Notes on Theodore Roethke," Notes and Queries July, pp. 265-66.
Nadel, Alan
1978. "Roethke, Wilbur, and the Vision of the Child: Romantic and Augustan in Modern Verse," The Lion and the Unicorn: A Critical Journal of Children's Literature 2, 1, pp. 94-113.
Parini, Jay
1978. "Theodore Roethke: An American Romantic," Texas Quarterly 21, 4, pp. 99-114.

1980. "Theodore Roethke: The Poetics of Expression," Ball State University Forum 21, 1, pp. 5-11.

Roethke, Theodore
1948. The Lost Son and Other Poems. Garden City, N.Y: Doubleday.

Wolff, George
1971. "Roethke's 'Root Cellar,' " Explicator 29, item 47.
1973. "Syntactical and Imagistic Distortions in Roethke's Greenhouse Poems," Language and Style 6, pp. 281-88.

CHAPTER 3

The Lost Son Narratives

The first four of Theodore Roethke's Lost Son narratives appeared in part 4 of The Lost Son and Other Poems in 1948. Roethke published nine additional narratives in his third book, Praise to the End!, in 1951, and he completed his ongoing narrative project with a fourteenth poem, "O, Thou Opening, O," published in The Waking in 1953. Taken together, the Lost Son narratives tell the story of the Lost Son and what Roethke called his "struggle for spiritual identity" (SP, p. 41). A sense of anonymity, of alienation in its many forms, is the central source of conflict for the poems, and that is not easily or finally overcome. Again and again, the Lost Son works to establish himself, and at various points in the sequence, his desire to be complete is phrased as a wish to unite with minimal creatures, with the father, with the mother, with the woman (or girl) who is the object of his love. These are the ends, ends praised to the end, and most critics acknowledge they are ends the Lost Son variously achieves.

The dramatic landscape of the Lost Son narratives contains the Greenhouse world as a prominent feature, but it extends beyond the confines of that more circumscribed world. The Lost Son ventures, both alone and with others, into the fields, forests, streams, and other areas surrounding the greenhouse itself. These places are, in a sense, extensions of the Greenhouse world, however, because they are additionally complex landscapes that encompass what Roethke earlier termed "heaven and hell." In that respect, the world of the Lost Son is analogous to the Greenhouse world. In the Lost Son narratives, Roethke reiterates but expands the Greenhouse imagery, and extends the range of his poetic of regression to resurrect more dramatically the experience of the child.

The Lost Son narratives record the growth of the protagonist's mind, body, and spirit, but Roethke goes much farther in one direction than did William Wordsworth, for example, in The Prelude or, Growth of a Poet's Mind: An Autobiographical Poem. Through memory, Roethke descends deeply into the past to discover experience of the adolescent, the child, even the infant. In the Greenhouse poems, Roethke would have expressed an infant's experience in the language of an articulate and mature man, but in the Lost Son narratives Roethke frequently eliminates the intermediary. In "Where Knock Is Open Wide," for example, the first of the "infancy narratives," Roethke dares to speak the language of the infant itself:

> A kitten can
> Bite with his feet;
> Papa and Mamma
> Have more teeth.
>
> Sit and play
> Under the rocker
> Until the cows
> All have puppies.
>
> His ears haven't time.
> Sing me a sleep-song, please.
> A real hurt is soft.
>
> Once upon a tree
> I came across a time,
> It wasn't even as
> A ghoulie in a dream.
>
> There was a mooly man
> Who had a rubber hat
> The funnier than that,--
> He kept it in a can.
>
> What's the time, papa-seed?
> Everything has been twice.
> My father is a fish.
>   [CP, pp. 71-72]

The products of such regressions to infancy, it might be expected, are among the most controversial in Roethke's narrative poems.

Individually and collectively, the Lost Son poems are different from and more ambitious in method and scope than any Roethke had before attempted, and in them he takes risks and makes demands of his readers. The individual poems range in length from several dozens of lines to nearly 200 in the longest, most accessible, and best-known narrative, "The Lost Son" itself. These individual narratives are themselves composed of shorter sections, usually numbered, sometimes titled, and those shorter sections are subdivided by verse paragraph or stanza, frequently quatrain or couplet. Within these subdivisions, the individual lines may be metered, may be prose, may be a single telling word. Radical imagery, personal and idiosyncratic language, even nonsense become in the narratives prominent features of Roethke's fully developed and highly varied poetic technique.

At the outset of this chapter, we look at the mixed response Roethke's narrative poems aroused as they appeared, and then consider at some length how Roethke's critics have since placed the completed story of the Lost Son into thematic perspective. Whether they begin with "The Lost Son," the first narrative published, or with "Where Knock Is Open Wide," the poem Roethke eventually placed at the outset of the sequence, the critics do tend to agree that the Lost Son finds himself, but they disagree on how that occurs and what it means. The complex textual problem of the Lost Son narratives is at the root of some of the differences in interpretation of the poems, and in the second part of the chapter we look at what may at first be construed as a merely technical or academic issue. Because Roethke draws so heavily on childhood experience, because a father figures as importantly for the Lost Son as did Otto for Theodore Roethke, and because rises and falls in the Lost Son's progress oddly parallel vacillations in Roethke's own emotional life, some critics have argued that a knowledge of the facts of Roethke's life is indispensable for reading the narrative poems. In the third section of the chapter, we look at such connections perceived between the life of the poet and the story of the Lost Son. Critics have also charted the literary and philosophical backgrounds for Roethke's narratives. Some of those Roethke himself provides; others have been independently discovered, notably the sources for the titles of some of the individual poems, as we will see in the fourth part of this chapter. The originality of purpose and technique is the primary feature of the narrative poems, however. In the fifth and final section, we look at why the language of the Lost Son narratives is thought to be so distinctive, and at how Roethke creates some of his unique effects.

Reviews and Overviews

Harry Williams has observed that differences of opinion are more common than not in criticism of Theodore Roethke, but at the end of his review of that criticism in "The Edge Is What I Have," he concludes that critics agree that the Lost Son narratives are "central" to understanding Roethke's poetry (p. 31). For poet W. D. Snodgrass, the narratives are the "most experimental poetry of the whole period." The voice of these poems is "new and astonishing," Snodgrass says in his essay, " 'That Anguish of Concreteness': Theodore Roethke's Career," published in 1965. The style is "achieved, carrying much meaning, and touching only tangentially other voices we have heard in poetry" (p. 80). In reviewing The Lost Son and Other Poems in 1948, however, critics had but four

of Roethke's narratives to consider; it is thus understandable that
they would be more cautious than Snodgrass. Several reviewers
responded to the technique of the first four narratives, and in
their comments one can infer the milieu of experimentation in poetry into which Roethke's narratives were introduced. Both Robert
Fitzgerald and R. W. Flint were favorably disposed to The Lost
Son and Other Poems, for example, but Flint found Roethke less
innovative and experimental a poet than William Carlos Williams
and Dylan Thomas (pp. 707-8). Peter Viereck counted Roethke
among the "Five Good Poets in a Bad Year" but he thought Roethke's work "too obscure" (p. 95). In his lukewarm review, Howard
Griffin wrote that Roethke is a poet probably not of "great output
or range" (p. 26), but Frederick Morgan singled out the narrative
poems as the most meritorious in the book (pp. 261-62).

   With the publication of thirteen of the narratives in Praise
to the End! in 1951, Roethke's readers could concentrate on his
nearly completed, and completely reorganized, narrative project.
Reviewers again commented on the range of vision Roethke presented in the narratives and on the originality of his poetic
experiment. In reviewing Praise to the End!, William Arrowsmith,
like R. W. Flint before him, cited William Carlos Williams as
a "dangerous Dutch uncle" to Roethke's verse, but he did remark
that Roethke's was "one of the most delightful small poetries of
our time," preferable to Marianne Moore's (p. 620). In an otherwise very complimentary review, Frederick Brantley implied also
that Roethke's was a "small poetry" and predicted that Roethke
would "move to a broader scene and subject in his future poetry"
(p. 477). In her review of 1952, Louise Bogan included Roethke
with poets Horace Gregory, Randall Jarrell, and Richard Eberhart,
all of whom, she said, try "to project feelings of mystery and awe"
(p. 107). Richard Eberhart himself was probably not displeased to
be included by Bogan with Roethke. Eberhart identified Roethke
as one of the "pure poets" in his review (p. 4), and Peter Viereck no longer thought Roethke's poetry "obscure" in his review of
Praise to the End! For Viereck, Roethke's book and Yeats's Collected Poems were the "two most exciting poetry events of 1951"
(p. 81). Viereck predicted that Roethke might "become a great
poet of that same utter exaltation once sung by Rimbaud and Hol-
derlin" (p. 81). Less enthusiastic, less convinced, Rolfe Humphries observed an unevenness to Praise to the End! He anticipated the argument that Roethke's conclusions are forced rather
than organic to the poems and, though he thought that Roethke's
experiment would be widely imitated, he observed that "his jubi-
lates, if no less original, do seem less experienced than his
misereres" (p. 284).

   Despite the variety of response presented by the first reviewers
of the Lost Son narratives, and despite the objections to Roethke's project that are embedded in them, the narrative poems today
are among the least controversial in Roethke's controversial canon.

The narrative poems are no longer the focus of the major charges often leveled at Roethke's work, his narrowness, his imitativeness, his insincerity. Better evidence for those objections, critics argue, exists elsewhere in Roethke's poetry. Thus, the narrative poems themselves have been studied primarily by those who acknowledge the achievement of the poems and who want to explain it.

The reviewers of the Lost Son narratives were at a disadvantage in receiving the poems piecemeal, spread out in three separate volumes and over a period of five years. When the narratives became available as a completed sequence in fourteen titled parts, literary critics were better equipped to put Roethke's project as a whole into perspective. Most critics think the protagonist of the narratives grows and develops in the course of the sequence, but broadly speaking that growth may be perceived in two ways. Some think the Lost Son moves through a series of stages, variously definable in theological, psychological, or mythic terms. Others think the protagonist changes according to a more complicated dynamic, through a dialectical process of progression and regression. Proponents of both views draw similar conclusions about the fate of the Lost Son, however, so in evaluating the two viewpoints, it is helpful to recall how linear and cyclical notions of progress and growth in the Greenhouse poems were equally and not exclusively applicable.

Since they provide the simplest overview of the poems, it is probably best to begin with those critics who think the Lost Son passes through broad and definable stages. In his 1965 essay, "The Monocle of My Sea-Faced Uncle," for example, John Wain sees the protagonist of the poems progressing from an Inferno to a Paradiso. Wain locates the Inferno in "The Lost Son" and the Paradiso in "Praise to the End!" but finds no Purgatorio, "no trace of a region of suffering which purifies and strengthens" (p. 65). George Wolff takes the theological categories of John Wain to a certain extreme in his book, Theodore Roethke. Wolff argues that the imagery in the narrative sequence represents a "confrontation of birth and death" (p. 99). The major themes of the sequence are contained in the title poem, "The Lost Son," according to Wolff, and they include alienation from the father and from God, the philosophy of naturalism, and faith in divine creation and eternal life (p. 51). The themes are explored in imagery of "threatening enclosures," "protective enclosures," and birth, he says (p. 51). Again like John Wain, who thinks the protagonist moves from Inferno to Paradiso, Wolff sees a progress in "The Lost Son" from threatening enclosure, even imprisonment, to protective enclosure, and, in "The Return," the fourth part of the poem, the Lost Son achieves vision (p. 57). "It was beginning winter," the final section of "The Lost Son," is the culmination of the sequence for Wolff. This section "raises the father-son reunion in memory to a higher spiritual significance, making it in-

to something like the state that mystics call 'illumination' . . .
the direct emotional and sensuous awareness of God's closeness,
and it can be worked toward through self-abnegating discipline"
(p. 57). Wolff's sense that the Lost Son achieves some kind
of reconciliation with himself and his memories is widely shared,
but depicting the protagonist as someone who would think the
"essence of the mystic's discipline is trying to make his own
spirit match the stillness of the Father's spirit" too narrowly
represents the Lost Son as an otherworldly mystic (p. 57).

Karl Malkoff charts the growth of the protagonist according to
psychoanalytic theory in his 1966 book, Theodore Roethke: An
Introduction to the Poetry. Malkoff's is the most widely cited
psychoanalytic interpretation of Roethke's narrative poems, though
he is indebted for his point of departure to Kenneth Burke's essay of 1950, "The Vegetal Radicalism of Theodore Roethke." Like
Burke, Malkoff thinks the lyric poem "Night Crow" is a useful
entry into the Lost Son narratives. Malkoff builds his argument
upon the psychoanalytic implications of the poem:

> When I saw that clumsy crow
> Flap from a wasted tree,
> A shape in the mind rose up:
> Over the gulfs of dream
> Flew a tremendous bird
> Further and further away
> Into a moonless black,
> Deep in the brain, far back.
> [CP, p. 49]

According to Malkoff, psychoanalyst Carl Jung would find in the
poem a "reactivated archetype." Such "primordial images," Jung
says, are "called to life by the primitive, analogical mode of
thinking peculiar to dreams" (p. 59). For Malkoff, "Night Crow"
establishes Roethke's interest in and use of archetypal images
drawn from the "collective unconscious, the racial memory held in
common by all humanity" (p. 59). After grounding his discussion
in the terminology of Carl Jung, Malkoff moves to the Lost Son
narratives. There, Malkoff finds that Roethke again avails himself of several archetypal images, but the major image he uses to
structure his narratives Jung calls "the process of individuation"
(p. 64). Drawing his conclusions from Roethke's own observations
in "Open Letter" (SP, pp. 36-43), Malkoff observes that "the
earlier poems deal with the formation of the individual in a fundamental, psychological sense; while the later poems recapitulate
much of this material, they emphasize not the struggle for mere
existence, but rather the struggle for a significant existence"
(p. 84; Malkoff's italics).

Malkoff prefaces his psychoanalytic discussion of the narratives
with the disclaimer that we should not "identify Roethke with

those who arbitrarily seed their poems with established Freudian symbols. . . . Roethke's poetry is deeply rooted in life. The value of a symbol is never imposed upon it from without; the symbol is rather the experience itself--it means itself" (p. 48). In concluding his book, Malkoff reiterates the point that Roethke used psychoanalytic theories such as Jung's and Freud's primarily to support and justify his own intuitions (p. 220). Though Malkoff frames his interpretation with disclaimers, it is possible to get the impression from his book that Roethke's narrative poems are versified psychoanalytic theory. For example, Malkoff reads "Where Knock Is Open Wide" as the infant stage, "I Need, I Need" as the oral phase, "Give Way, Ye Gates" as the anal-aggressive stage, "Sensibility! O La!" as the Oedipal phase and, Malkoff concludes, "we would expect the next period to be latency, in which the newly developed sexual urges are sublimated and controlled" (pp. 78-83). Where they exist, such connections of Roethke's narrative structure to psychoanalytic theory are interesting and instructive, but Malkoff's distribution of the poems into Freudian stages and categories does seem overly programmatic.

In support of Malkoff's approach, however, Roethke also discusses the development of his protagonist in vaguely psychoanalytic terms. For example, he tells us that "I Need, I Need" "opens with very oral imagery, the child's world of sucking and licking" (SP, p. 10). In what Roethke calls "subsequent poems," the protagonist is the "young adolescent, half a child, then the randy young man boasting and caterwauling" (SP, p. 12). In "The Flight," the first part of "The Lost Son," Roethke says "the protagonist [is] so geared-up, so over-alive that he is hunting, like a primitive, for some animistic suggestion, some clue to existence from the subhuman. . . . He goes in and out of rationality; he hangs in the balance between the human and the animal" (SP, p. 38). "The Pit," the second part of "The Lost Son," Roethke says "is a slowed-down section; a period of physical and psychic exhaustion." "The Gibber," the third part, contains "frenetic activity, then a lapsing back into almost a crooning serenity." "The Return" is a "memory of childhood that comes back almost as in a dream, after the agitation and exhaustion of the earlier actions" (SP, p. 38). In the fifth and last section of "The Lost Son," "It was beginning winter," "the illumination, the coming of light suggested at the end of the last passage occurs again, this time to the nearly-grown man" (SP, p. 39).

Since Roethke describes the growth of the Lost Son in terms reminiscent of psychoanalytic categories, some critics have thought it important to find out how much Roethke himself knew about psychoanalysis and from where he got such knowledge. The issue of the applicability of the psychoanalytic method to the narrative poems surfaced even while Roethke was alive. In a letter to Judith Gerber dated February 28, 1963, Roethke responded to her question about the "influence of Freud's writings or ideas" on his verse:

I can honestly say I have read very little Freud, not even
the basic writings. On the other hand, some of my fancy friends
went through analysis with some of the Viennese people and I dare
say I picked up some notions from their babbling about their
therapy. . . . On the other hand I have known such distinguished
analysts as Eisler of New York and Hoffer of London and much
of their talk has been at least influenced by Freud. But I met
these men a good deal after the writing of the poems that you
would probably consider "Freudian."

I have read part of Jung's Modern Man in Search of a Soul,
but again, rather recently.   Officially I am a Presbyterian,
but a most indifferent one, I'm afraid.   Stanley Kunitz says
I am the best Jewish poet in the language. I am really not
trying to be witty or flippant--all this happens to be the
truth. [SL, p. 260]

Roethke's knowledge of psychoanalytic theory may well have been
as casual as he suggests, for even Karl Malkoff had to admit in
a footnote in his book that the "extent and nature" of Roethke's
reading in psychoanalytic literature was simply not easy to
establish (p. 59). However, in his book Theodore Roethke: An
American Romantic, Jay Parini argues at some length that Kenneth Burke tutored Roethke in the use of psychoanalysis in literature and poetry (pp. 55-62). That must be the case, Parini
says, because "Roethke simply did not know enough about psychology
or myth at this point to use them as deftly as he did" in the
narratives (pp. 96-97). In responding to Malkoff's psychoanalytic
interpretation, though, Jenijoy La Belle probably comes closest
to accounting for the nature and origins of Roethke's psychoanalytic insights in her book, The Echoing Wood of Theodore Roethke.
In referring to Maud Bodkin's book, Archetypal Patterns in Poetry,
which Roethke did know, La Belle concludes, "the Jungian archetypes in Roethke's poetry were transmitted to him through Bodkin's
literary study, and refer primarily to psychological patterns
found in literature and only secondarily--or, to be more precise,
only through the medium of a literary tradition--to theories
about the human psyche" (p. 84). Roethke could have discovered
through introspection the patterns psychoanalysis discloses; he
could have picked up ideas in conversations with his friends, as
he mentions in his letter; or, most plausibly, he could have assimilated the inherent patterns he found in his own reading of
literary works. As evidence for La Belle's point it is significant that some of the sources Roethke himself offers for the
narratives in his "Open Letter," folk literature, Mother Goose,
and the Bible, are texts of particular interest to psychologists
of the archetype like Carl Jung.

In his discussion of the Lost Son narratives, Karl Malkoff
emphasizes the psychoanalytic parallels, as we have seen, but
he also believes that Roethke "places as much emphasis on the

spiritual as on the psychological aspects of his quest," and Malkoff notes that the "controlling movement of the poems is certainly from darkness to light" (p. 65). Most readers of the narratives recognize some similar "controlling movement" indicating
the Lost Son's gradual spiritual and psychological progress. In
her 1975 book, Theodore Roethke: The Garden Master, Rosemary
Sullivan parallels Malkoff's sense that the protagonist moves toward affirmation, but she thinks the major changes in the Lost
Son are psychological. She reads the narratives in terms of the
growth of the "mode of consciousness" of the protagonist (p. 60).
After a "crisis of sexual awakening" in the first poems, Sullivan
says, the Lost Son matures and becomes "concerned with the expansion of consciousness and the recovery of innocent vision" (p. 60).
    John Lucas also focuses on the psychological aspects of the Lost
Son's development in his essay, "The Poetry of Theodore Roethke,"
published in 1968. Lucas's reading is especially interesting,
though, because he takes exception to the idea that the first narrative published, "The Lost Son," is structured by imagery of-
growth. Lucas thinks the first three sections of the poem have
a "terrific honesty" and offer "intelligent self-exploration"
(p. 49), but with the concluding lines of "The Gibber," Lucas says
"the poet breaks down completely. He does not manage to cope with
his sense of guilt at discovered sexuality" (p. 49). "The new
calm and sanity" of successive sections results "from a turning
away . . . [it] springs from the poet's retreat from his problems
back to childhood" (pp. 49-50). The remainder of the poems, Lucas
argues, are thus marred by a "fundamental evasiveness" because
Roethke recurrently approaches fearful insights that, ultimately,
he will not reveal (p. 51). Lucas's argument could be countered
by saying that Roethke's poetic method requires periodic regression for authentic progression, but Lucas seems aware of Roethke's
method; he just sounds bored by it. He says the narrative poems
in general engage the truth "up to a point--which is always the
same one, of onanistic guilt, connected with father fear. And
then come the familiar hiatus and the assertion of new maturity"
(p. 51). In his reading of the narratives, Lucas thus reiterates
charges about Roethke's sincerity and limited poetic range raised
in the first reviews, but Lucas does think the Lost Son shows genuine progress in the last poem in the sequence, "O, Thou Opening,
O." That progress Lucas refers to the breakthrough finally achieved
in the Love Poems of The Waking.
    In his book, Theodore Roethke: An American Romantic, Jay Par-
ini identifies two ways in which the psychoanalytic method can
be applied to Roethke's narrative poems. According to Parini,
"an explication of Roethke's difficult sequence requires two points
of reference: the poet's subjective history, or the biographical
elements in the poems, and the larger area of shared experience
represented by myth and archetype" (p. 83). As we shall see in

the third section of this chapter, Parini and others have discussed
the narratives in the terms of the first of these "points of reference"; Parini has used the second reference point to show connections between "The Lost Son" and Joseph Campbell's comments
on the "monomyth" (p. 84), and Mircea Eliade's observations about
the puberty rite. According to Parini, "The Lost Son" might be
read as a "rite of passage" poem because its structure parallels
the three phases of the rite Eliade identifies: separation from
the family, ordeals that may involve symbolic death, and resurrection of the initiate and return to the tribe (p. 85). "The Lost
Son" "recreates the puberty rite in modern terms," Parini says (p.
85), since these three stages are "the exact sequence of events in
'The Lost Son' " (p. 86). Recreation of the myth is necessary for
our day because, Parini writes, echoing T. S. Eliot, "old myths
have been rendered obsolete by science and by the general disin-
tegration of culture" (p. 83). Parini's allusion to Eliot's social
criticism is not appropriate, however. By seeing "The Lost Son"
as a reassertion of Campbell's "monomyth" and Eliade's puberty
rite, Parini suggests that Roethke's narratives contradict Eliot's
argument. Despite Louise Bogan's observations in 1952 that Roethke
"invented a symbolism . . . quite his own" in Praise to the End!,
and that he used "recognizable myth and legend hardly at all" (p.
118), Parini shows the old myths function quite powerfully in Roethke's narrative poems.

Parini shows that Roethke's narrative poems parallel recorded
myths, but Richard Blessing is concerned about how such analogies
can affect interpretations of the poems. In Theodore Roethke's
Dynamic Vision, Blessing writes that "Roethke does not allow his
reader to pin his work to a single and particular myth, to read
the Lost Son Sequence as, say, 'Nothing but' the Oedipus myth or
Christ's story or the dark way of mysticism or of Jungian psycho-
drama" (pp. 88-89). The story of the Lost Son coincides with and
parallels many quests, many rites of passage, and Blessing himself
thinks the narratives are motivated by a "thrust toward the light,
which drives the hero onward" (p. 87). Most would follow Blessing
to that point, but his concept of that hero is unconventional.
For Blessing, the subject of the narratives is "the emerging poem
itself," and the hero of the narratives is "the poetic voice, the
voice that sings itself awake, that creates out of nothing a world
of terror and delight, then comforts us against the terror and
celebrates for us the delight" (p. 92).

While acknowledging in general that the Lost Son grows in the
course of the poems, other critics see his progress as no simple
move from infancy to adolescence or from alienation to reunion.
According to the dialectical interpretation, the Lost Son's growth
occurs only in relationship to other features of his world. For
example, in his book, "The Edge Is What I Have," Harry Williams
reads "The Lost Son" (the only narrative he considers) as a "two-
fold development defined in terms of father and son" (p. 41).

The image of the house symbolizes the father, and the recurrent journeying of the protagonist symbolizes the son. The journey and the house are reconciled, for Williams, in the greenhouse where "the house with all its social ramifications vies with the field with all its vegetal and animal ramifications" (p. 42). According to Williams, the "journey and the house, then, are the two motifs structuring the poem as they echo the house/field equations from their vantage point" (p. 42).

Harry Williams limits his discussion to "The Lost Son," the poem his interpretation most neatly fits, but John Vernon offers a more comprehensive dialectical reading in his essay, "Theodore Roethke's Praise to the End! Poems," published in 1971. Unlike most other critics, Vernon focuses not on "The Lost Son" primarily but on "Where Knock Is Open Wide," which he establishes as the first poem in the sequence. Vernon recapitulates the observation of virtually every commentator that "the emphasis at the beginning of the sequence is upon being lost, and at the end upon embracing the world and being found" but Vernon adds that "the point is that each is also present in the other" (p. 68). Vernon observes that three regressions occur rhythmically in the sequence: regression of the body back to the womb, regression of the world back to slime, and regression of language back to nonsense (p. 61). These regressions, which Vernon says are actually "inseparable," form the first part of the dialectic he sees working in the sequence. In response to these regressions, the Lost Son does not attempt to evolve an identity, as so many critics argue. According to Vernon, the Son "emerges from this primordial confusion and liquid mergence of all things . . . by channeling into the world, into separateness, and carrying the wholeness from which that separateness is descended into every manifestation of it" (p. 61). Thus, confusion and clarity, anonymity and identity, the slime and the light are separate manifestations of a single continuum. Vernon identifies this as Roethke's "world of correspondences" where everything "manifests itself in every other thing, and even--or especially--all opposites exist in and of each other" (p. 78). The Praise to the End! sequence, in other words, implies a monistic rather than dualistic vision of the world, according to Vernon. Inferno inheres in Paradiso and vice versa. As a result, the sequence suggests what Vernon enthusiastically announces is "a total alternative to the dualistic structures of classical Western thought . . . body and world, subject and object, time and space, fantasy and reality, child and man, etc., all exist in a perfect unity, a unity given previous to any reflection" (p. 79). Vernon supports his view by showing how penis imagery (imagery of separateness) and vagina imagery (image of enclosure) eventually are reconciled in the "unity of male and female . . . the perfect image of the unity of separation and wholeness, of discreteness and mergence, which is the final condition of Roethke's world" (p. 64). The dialectic eventually dissolves, according to Vernon, and the Lost Son is found by overcoming an alienated

condition which in reality is only a state of mind. Though he uses
a different approach, Vernon thus arrives at a conclusion similar
to that offered by others who read the narratives according to a
more straightforward notion of the Lost Son's growth.

The Textual Problem

Whether critics see the dynamic of the narrative poems sequen-
tially or dialectically, whether they think the conclusions of the
poems are effective or insincere, they do agree that a growth motif structures the narrative sequence as a whole. Since they are
in accord so infrequently, such agreement on a significant point
is refreshing in the criticism of Theodore Roethke. Like the greenhouse, though, Roethke criticism is a mixture of heaven and hell;
nothing in it is as simple as it seems. The critics' agreement on
the motif of the narratives has its dark side, too, for critics will
not agree on the order of the poems to which they are responding.
    One may read the narrative poems according to the final arrange-
ment Roethke presented in 1958 in Words for the Wind, or according
to the order he wrote them in, the chronological order used in the
Collected Poems. In the Collected Poems, the narratives are arranged as follows:

The Lost Son
1.   The Flight
2.   The Pit
3.   The Gibber
4.   The Return
5.   'It was beginning winter'
The Long Alley
A Field of Light
The Shape of the Fire

Where Knock Is Open Wide
I Need, I Need
Bring the Day!
Give Way, Ye Gates
Sensibility! O La!
O Lull Me, Lull Me

Praise to the End!
Unfold! Unfold!
I Cry, Love! Love!

O, Thou Opening, O

In the Collected Poems, the most widely available version of the

narratives, the only clue provided that Roethke may have intended
another organization is the parenthetical note appended to "The
Shape of the Fire": "This sequence is continued in Praise to
the End!, Part II, and concluded with 'O, Thou Opening, O' in
The Waking" (CP, p. 67). There are no directions about where
to place part 1 of Praise to the End!, which contains six narrative
poems beginning with "Where Knock Is Open Wide" and ending with
"O Lull Me, Lull Me."
   The organization of the narratives in the Collected Poems reflects the order in which Roethke composed and published the
poems, but Roethke himself provided an alternative arrangement
in Praise to the End! (1951) which he then completed in The Waking
(1953). In Praise to the End!, the narrative poems are arranged
in two parts. Part 1 begins with "Where Knock Is Open Wide"
and it concludes with "O Lull Me, Lull Me." Part 2 includes
the four poems from part 4 of The Lost Son and Other Poems and
the three narratives beginning with "Praise to the End!" As
Karl Malkoff has pointed out in his book, in the original version
of Praise to the End!, the sequence concludes with "I Cry,
Love! Love!" (p. 104), but in The Waking Roethke concluded
with "O, Thou Opening, O." The final arrangement that Roethke
came to in the course of The Lost Son and Other Poems, Praise
to the End!, and The Waking is most clearly represented in the
sequence he published in Words for the Wind:

Where Knock Is Open Wide
I Need, I Need
Bring The Day!
Give Way, Ye Gates
Sensibility! O La!
O Lull Me, Lull Me

The Lost Son
1.   The Flight
2.   The Pit
3.   The Gibber
4.   The Return
5.   'It was beginning winter'
The Long Alley
A Field of Light
The Shape of the Fire
Praise to the End!
Unfold! Unfold!
I Cry, Love! Love!
O, Thou Opening, O

   When the Collected Poems first appeared in 1966, Karl Malkoff
knew that this more complete version of Roethke's work would super-
sede Words for the Wind as the standard edition. Unlike Words

for the Wind, the Collected Poems offers a more complete Roethke,
a complete Open House, for example, and more importantly, Roethke's last volume, The Far Field, which appears as Roethke arranged
it. Instead of working with two overlapping editions of Roethke's
verse, Malkoff knew the next generation would pursue study of
Roethke in the Collected Poems, and he therefore registered especially his misgivings about the chronological ordering of the narratives in the Collected Poems in his review of the book in 1967,
"Boundaries of the Self." Given the choice between alternatives,
one would think the critic would select the narrative sequence
the poet himself arranged, of course. As Malkoff feared, that has
not been the case in recent years, however. A growing percentage
of critics use the version of the narratives presented in the Collected Poems.
    The organization of the narratives in the Collected Poems does
offer advantages. Even those who object to the chronological ordering of the narratives will admit, as does Ralph J. Mills, Jr.,
in his 1963 booklet, Theodore Roethke, that "The Lost Son" is
the key poem of the sequence and, as Roethke said himself, the
one with the most obvious narrative construction" (p. 23). From
the point of view of the reader, especially the beginning reader,
entry into the Lost Son narratives is easiest through the title
poem, "The Lost Son." The most accessible of the narratives, it
is also the narrative Roethke wrote and published first. In addition, as J. D. McClatchy points out in his essay, "Sweating Light
from a Stone: Identifying Theodore Roethke," the Lost Son narratives have been "consistently interpreted in the terms the poet
himself outlined in his 'Open Letter' " (p. 8). McClatchy himself
questions that practice because he thinks Roethke's readings of
his own work were probably "dependent on critics' help," notably
W. H. Auden and Kenneth Burke (p. 9), but if "The Lost Son" is
the easiest entrance into the Lost Son narratives, Roethke's detailed discussion of the poem in his "Open Letter" is the easiest
entrance into "The Lost Son."
    Were it not for the nature of Roethke's method in the narrative
poems, the entire textual matter might be simpler. Several critics
have remarked upon ways individual poems in the sequence parallel
one another, structurally. For example, Karl Malkoff observes
that "any attemapt to verify chronological sequence is complicated
by the fact that, according to the theory of regression and progression, each poem begins well before the preceding poem's end"
(p. 70). In Theodore Roethke's Dynamic Vision, Richard Blessing
implies the same kind of complication when he writes, "each poem
is complete in itself in that in each of them the lost son grows,
changes, or develops in some way. . . . Each poem ends with an
implied beginning" (p. 106). Because of the structural similarities, in other words, one might read the narrative poems in virtually any sequence whatever! No one has yet taken that approach,
but in his essay, "Theodore Roethke's Praise to the End! Poems,"

John Vernon does argue the extreme position that "the sequence represents one long poem, each part of which [that is, each poem] contains and reaffirms that whole" (p. 60). Vernon takes quite seriously his notion that "each poem reflects the whole in Roethke's sequence" (p. 61), and he is the first to account for the narrative poems in terms of the first poem, "Where Knock Is Open Wide." Thus, attention to the poetic method of regression and progression can leave more flexible one's sense of the organization of the sequence, but it should be added that all three of the critics cited above read the poems as they were ordered by Theodore Roethke in The Waking.

Often, those critics who interpret the narrative poems by beginning with "The Lost Son" unwittingly dramatize the value of beginning with "Where Knock Is Open Wide." They begin with "The Lost Son," it sometimes appears, because they do not particularly like or even appreciate the other narrative poems. When they leave "The Lost Son" and its three attendants, "The Long Alley," "A Field of Light," and "The Shape of the Fire" for the infancy narratives, impatience, even resentment, is evident in their prose. For example, in describing the centrality of "The Lost Son" in his book, Theodore Roethke: An American Romantic, Jay Parini argues that "all his other poems must be interpreted in its light, with attention to the key symbols as they appear in this poem" (p.96). For Parini, "the other poems in the sequence repeat, less grandly, the same heroic journey or dwell on some particular phase of it" (p. 96). When Parini then opens his analysis of "Where Knock Is Open Wide," he sounds less than enthusiastic about it: "fathers, mothers, pets, and the usual nursery rhymes are here" (p. 109). A similar deflated tone emerges in Rosemary Sullivan's analysis in her book, Theodore Roethke: The Garden Master. Within the space of just three pages, Sullivan observes in "Where Knock Is Open Wide" the child-protagonist's "long and arduous effort" (p. 60), his "arduous evolution of moral conscience" (p. 61), and his "long arduous process of self-definition" (p. 62). Indeed, the child-protagonist engages in a protracted struggle, but it is not all that hard. Or arduous.

It makes sense that the move from "The Lost Son" to "Where Knock Is Open Wide" would be deflating, though, because "The Shape of the Fire," the last poem in part 4 of The Lost Son and Other Poems, closes so dramatically, as Susan R. Van Dyne has discussed in detail in her essay, "Self-Poesis in Roethke's 'The Shape of the Fire.' " That drama is reflected in Parini's text where he himself reaches a resounding conclusion after discussing the final image in that poem. Parini writes, "this paradisiacal image appropriately completes The Lost Son, which is his most essential writing, the center of his work, and the book that informs the poetry which follows in the next fifteen years" (p. 107). In her book, Rosemary Sullivan writes (she even rhymes), "the image describes a world of unity and containment in which

the pulse of sun energy, like water in a vase, fills the whole of
space" (p. 53).   That elevated moment is effectively tempered,
if not overpowered, however, not by the beginning of "Where Knock
is Open Wide," but by the inevitable regression that opens "Praise
to the End!," the poem Roethke intended should follow "The Lost
Son." If one moves from "The Shape of the Fire" to "Where Knock
Is Open Wide," however, as both Parini and Sullivan do, the anti-
climax cannot be contained.   Roethke, of course, never meant for
it to occur.
     Rosemary Sullivan is aware of the textual problem, however.
In a note in her book, she defends her approach by saying, "As
I am interested in the development of Roethke's poetry, I have
preferred to study them [the Lost Son poems] in their original
order of composition as they appear in the Collected Poems" (p.
38).   Earlier in her discussion, however, Sullivan observes that
"after Open House Roethke was always meticulous about the order
and arrangement of poems within each book" (p. 26), and she bases
her view on Roethke's comment in "Theodore Roethke Writes . . ."
that "a book should reveal . . . some kind of coherent whole that
is recognizable to the careful reader. This means that some poems will sometimes support other poems, either by being comple-
ments to them, or by providing contrasts" (SP, pp. 57-58).   At
first glance, Sullivan's defense of the chronological version of
the narrative poems seems reasonable, but if she wants to study
Roethke's development, it would be better to chart any and all
changes be made over time in the order of poems in the sequence.
Those changes are also part of his development.
     In his book, "The Edge Is What I Have," Harry Williams admits
from the outset that he will limit himself to what he calls Roethke's "three long poems" (p. 32).   He identifies ""Meditations of an
Old Woman" and, of course, the "North American Sequence" as "sequence" poems, and he discusses all of the parts of those sequences.
Of Roethke's longest sequence, however, the Lost Son narratives,
Williams isolates only "The Lost Son" for analysis because it is
the longest single poem in that sequence. Williams himself recognizes the inconsistency of his method, but he avoids the other narratives in the sequence for an interesting reason indeed: "Some
of the poems, or portions thereof, are opaque to analysis, taken
up with the idea of psychic regression by means of the child's ir-
rational expressions of his surroundings, expressions that Roethke
abandoned after this volume" (p. 45). In fact, "The Lost Son" is
more clear, more "rational" than any of the other narratives, but
that does not necessarily privilege the poem in the sequence. In
a sense, opacity and irrationality are fundamental to the Lost
Son narratives. In them, Roethke appeals to things other than the
understanding.   "Read them aloud!" he says of the narratives at
the end of his "Open Letter" (SP, p. 43). "And I wish to be read
aloud," he says at the end of "Theodore Roethke Writes . . .,"
his comment on Words for the Wind (SP, p. 60). Focusing only on

or primarily on that poem that at first makes the "most sense" limits aims Roethke had for the sequence. As is apparent from Roethke's later arrangement, "sense" is something the Lost Son (and the reader) grow toward and earn. It is not given from the outset, as those who single out "The Lost Son" apparently demand.

While the reasons for settling for the version of the Lost Son sequence contained in the Collected Poems have a certain logic, a more cynical person might think they reduce, eventually, to the matter of critical convenience. One uses the Collected Poems because it makes all the poems readily available, one starts with "The Lost Son" because it is the easiest narrative to read, and one starts with "The Lost Son" because Roethke himself talked about how to read it. One cannot ignore Roethke's discussion of "The Lost Son" in his "Open Letter," but it is not correct to think the poet directs us to that poem exclusively. It should be added that Roethke discussed other, more difficult narrative poems in his essays "An American Poet Introduces Himself and His Poems" and "Some Remarks on Rhythm." The beginning reader may at first profit from reading the narratives as presented in the Collected Poems. Without doubt, that is the way to get acclimated to Roethke's poetic language and to his associative method. After that, however, the best way to appreciate Roethke's narrative purpose in the poems is to begin with the child-protagonist of "Where Knock Is Open Wide." By virtue of his reorganization of the sequence of the poems in Praise to the End!, and by virtue of his verifying that organizaion in The Waking and then a third time in Words for the Wind, it is clear that Roethke directs us to begin with "Where Knock Is Open Wide."

The Biographical Backgrounds

It is clear from his essays on the narratives that Theodore Roethke did not want his readers to make central any of the connections evident between the protagonist in and the author of the Lost Son narratives. In his BBC broadcast of 1953,"An American Poet Introduces Himself and His Poems," he writes that his purpose in the narrative poems is "to trace the spiritual history of a protagonist (not 'I' personally but of all haunted and harried men)" (SP, p. 10). In other essays, in "Open Letter," "An American Poet Introduces Himself and His Poems," and "Some Remarks on Rhythm," Roethke is careful to speak of the Lost Son, the "I" of the narrative poems, in the third person. Usually he refers to the Lost Son as the "protagonist" (SP, p. 40; SP, p.75), but he also calls him the "speaker" (SP, p. 41). (In one instance Roethke blurs the distinction. In "On 'Identity,' " he remarks, "in calling upon the snail [in "The Lost Son"], I am calling, in a sense, upon God" [SP, p. 25].) In his essays, Roethke emphasized the difference between the Lost Son and himself because he wanted his narra-

tives to be more than private and personal. They were to have "a
true and not arbitrary order" (SP, p. 10) so that, as Ralph J.
Mills, Jr., puts it in Theodore Roethke, the Lost Son's "struggle" could symbolize "a more general body of human experience"
(p. 16). Despite Roethke's care in distinguishing between the
Lost Son and himself in his essays, however, most critics think it
useful to note a parallel between the father of the Lost Son narratives and Roethke's own father, Otto, and a parallel between the
Lost Son's progressions toward and regressions from his goals, notably reunification with the father, and the dynamic of the symptoms of Roethke's own manic-depressive illness.

Though, as we have seen, John Vernon stresses equally imagery
of the penis and the vagina, the masculine and the feminine, the
father and the mother in the Lost Son narratives, most critics
think the recurrent references to the father earn him special attention. Whether one starts reading Roethke's narrative poems
with "Where Knock Is Open Wide" or with "The Lost Son," the reason
for the "lostness" of the Lost One is his father's death. In
"Where Knock Is Open Wide," the father's death is described according to the child's perspective: "Kisses come back,/ I said
to Papa;/ He was all whitey bones/ And skin like paper" (CP, p. 73).
In "The Lost Son," the older boy represents the father's death
more obliquely: "At Woodlawn I heard the dead cry" (CP, p. 53). (As
Allan Seager has pointed out [p. 473], Roethke's own father was
buried in Oakwood Cemetery, yet another indication of how Roethke
wished to shift attention from his own biography.) Just as "Where
Knock Is Open Wide" and "The Lost Son" begin with the father,
the final narrative of the sequence ends with veiled reference to
him. As Kenneth Burke notices in "The Vegetal Radicalism of Theodore Roethke," the Lost Son's appeal, "God, give me a near" in
"Where Knock Is Open Wide" (CP, p. 73), is answered in the final
poem, "O, Thou Opening, O," with an indication of the son's reconciliation, "I'm near" (CP, p. 99).

Separation from the father has a special impact on the Lost Son
because of the enormity of his feeling for the man. Throughout
the narratives, that feeling, and the motive for the son's remorse
and his quest, are emphasized again and again by descriptions of
the father drawn from the son's memory. In "The Return," for example, the fourth part of "The Lost Son," the son recalls the way
the greenhouse responds to his father's entering it:

> Once I stayed all night.
> The light in the morning came slowly over the white
> Snow.
> There were many kinds of cool
> Air.
> Then came steam.
>
> Pipe-knock.

Scurry of warm over small plants.
Ordnung! ordnung!
Papa is coming!

A fine haze moved off the leaves;
Frost melted on far panes;
The rose, the chrysanthemum turned toward the light.
Even the hushed forms, the bent yellow weeds.
Moved in a slow up-sway.
[CP, p. 57]

The son's description is a mixture of love and fear and, as Karl
Malkoff has correctly noted in Theodore Roethke: An Introduction to the Poetry, such depictions of the father "always convey
a sense of awesome, godlike power" (p. 3). Malkoff thinks that
the "father as a symbol of God is more than an artificially conceived literary image" in Roethke's verse; "it is charged with
experience" (p. 3). Roethke's complex vision of the father appears
elsewhere in his poetry, as we have already seen in chapter one's
discussion of "My Papa's Waltz." That poem points up "the duality
of Roethke's relationship with his father" because the waltz is
at once a "happy and terrifying activity," William V. Davis observes in his essay, "Fishing an Old Wound: Theodore Roethke's
Search for Sonship" (p. 33). Davis sees Roethke's entire career
as an attempt to deal with the "spectral figure of the father"
(p. 29) in fact, and he interprets Roethke's poems in terms of that
"single obsession" (p. 30).

Another important portrait of the father appears in Roethke's
last book, The Far Field. In "Otto," Roethke does not stand
behind the mask of the Lost Son, however. He addresses his father
as the son, Theodore Roethke, but Roethke's description of Otto
has the same features as does that of the Lost Son. As elsewhere,
Roethke communicates his love for his father in "Otto," but the
son's ambivalence does emerge in lines such as "He potted plants
as if he hated them./ What root of his ever denied its stem?/
When flowers grew, their bloom extended him" (CP, p. 224). Roethke also makes a good deal of how closely his father lived to violence in "Otto." In two of the four stanzas of the poem, Otto
carries a gun. In both cases his aim is frightfully unerring.

Because of the similarity between Roethke's view of his father
and the Lost Son's view of his father, most critics dissolve the
distinction between Roethke and the Lost Son. Allan Seager's biography of Roethke has made that procedure relatively easy. In
The Glass House, Seager is more interested in the man than in the
poetry, but his analysis of Roethke's attitude toward his father
might be applied to that of the Lost Son. Under the gaze of a
father such as Roethke describes in "My Papa's Waltz," the Lost
Son narratives, and "Otto," most youngsters would probably either

conform to his wishes or rebel against them. According to Allan
Seager, Roethke's concept of his father was complicated by the
fact that he had the chance to do neither:

> Ted once wrote in a letter that he had had "murderous" feelings
> toward his father. Many boys wish their fathers dead, not nec-
> essarily because of any Oepidal involutions, merely in a resent-
> ful flare-up after they have been slapped or beaten, but few have
> their fathers die with what must have seemed a dreadful prompt-
> ness afterward.   Ted would still have been enough of a boy at
> thirteen to fear that he had obscurely caused his death, and, even
> if he hadn't, the juxtaposition in his life of the wish and the
> dying would have been enough to make him guilty forever. [p. 104]

(In his discussion of "Where Knock Is Open Wide," Karl Malkoff
emphasizes precisely the "Oedipal involutions" Seager tries to
dismiss, but Malkoff is discussing the Lost Son's psychology, not
Theodore Roethke's: "the child, aware to some extent of his par-
ents' sexual activities, and, according to Freud, inevitably desiring his mother and fearing his father's retribution, assumes the
guilt for his father's death" [p. 76].) In Seager's view, Roethke's
career as a poet was to some extent a reaction, an "act of defiance,
the poet as criminal, defying the hobbles of bourgeois custom, denying the ghostly expectations of his father and his family, these
acts eliciting simultaneously a stupendous energy and God knows how
much guilt" (p. 104). At the same time, Roethke's career ambitions
were an attempt to please his father, Seager says. Since Otto
Roethke died when Roethke was thirteen, however, Roethke could
never know what his father would have thought about his work. According to Seager, the father could only be "wistfully appealed
to"; he "could give no answer, render no decisions" (p. 104).
Thus, Roethke was compelled eternally to ask himself, "which was
he, the disobedient son or the triumphant prize winner?" (p. 105).
Seager believes that "Otto Roethke seems to have been a lifelong
presence in his son's mind" (p. 104), but he thinks that Roethke
began to resolve his conflict toward the end of his life, and he
thinks the last poetry has forgiven everyone everything, demolished
its hatreds, and solved all its discords" (p. 251).

Seager is more comfortable in dealing with the man than with
the poetry, however. When in his conclusion he comes near to
suggesting that Roethke "strives toward a mystical union with his
Father" in his last poems, he immediately qualifies the remark
with "but this was unconscious" (p. 251). George Wolff makes no
such qualification in his discussion in Theodore Roethke. According to Wolff, the "two key emotional sources for most of the
themes in Roethke's poetry" are Roethke's manic-depressive illness
and the death of Otto Roethke (p. 22). Wolff thinks Roethke

translated those experiences into his poetry wholesale: "the loss of his father becomes the loss of God, and the uncontrollable plunges from sanity into wild elation or utter despair take on the semblance of the mystic's successes and failures in the struggle to achieve union with God" (p. 23).

The impact of Otto's death upon Theodore was enormous, and Roethke appears to have sought replacements for his father throughout his life. For example, there is significance in the fact that Roethke frequently addressed his older friend Kenneth Burke in his letters as "Pa," and in the letter of May 2, 1946, he uses "O Critical Parent" (SL, p. 118). Along with the playfulness, Roethke no doubt also intended respect. Roethke's interest in God, if one must phrase it as Wolff does, may also have functioned as a kind of replacement. The image of Otto Roethke does come to mind when, in "On 'Identity,' " Roethke writes, "God for me still remains someone to be confronted, to be dueled with" (SP, p. 26). The father is thus central in the Lost Son narratives and elsewhere in Roethke's poetry, and Otto Roethke was the significant figure in Theodore Roethke's life. Neither father is alone a sufficient point of reference to explain either the narrative poems or the life, however. We need to recall that the Lost Son also finds important in his quest the minimal things of nature, his mother, and a girl he begins to love. We need also to remember that along with the Lost Son narratives and "The Dying Man," Theodore Roethke wrote the Greenhouse poems, "Old Lady's Winter Words," "Meditations of an Old Woman," and a number of Love Poems in which, of course, a woman, not a father, figures most prominently.

In his essay "The Vegetal Radicalism of Theodore Roethke," Kenneth Burke observes that the Lost Son narratives are an "alternating of two motives: repression, and a nearly lost, but never quite relinquished, expectancy that leads to varying degrees of fulfillment" (p. 266). The "alternation" Burke describes leads to the second biographical reference used to illuminate Roethke's narratives. As Karl Malkoff puts it in Theodore Roethke: An Introduction to the Poetry, "throughout his adult life, Roethke was subject to periodic breakdowns within a broader cycle of manic-depressive behavior" (p. 6). The nature of Roethke's illness is not exactly understood, but there is evidence that Roethke himself made an effort, at least earlier in his career, to use his illness as an opportunity in his verse. While reference to Roethke's illness has been used to explain different emphases in his poetry, notably the mystical element, it is probably most valuable in highlighting the major structural dynamic of the Lost Son narratives, the ebbs and the flows.

The fullest description of Roethke's manic-depressive illness appears in Allan Seager's 1968 biography of the poet, The Glass

House. In fact, under the entry "Roethke, Theodore" in Seager's index, there are more references to "mental illness" than to anything else. In "Trouble," chapter 7 of the book, Seager recounts the events leading up to Roethke's first breakdown, which occurred while he was teaching in the English Department at Michigan State College in 1935 (pp. 86-109). According to Seager,

> Ted was drinking a great deal. He had started almost as soon as the semester began, not only whisky and beer--he hardly ever drank gin--but dozens of cups of coffee and cokes every day. He also was taking aspirin tablets by the handful. He seemed to reach that happy drunkard's state where it took only a few drinks every day to keep him affable. He did not miss any classes. He kept himself well in hand most of the time but both [John] Clark and [Peter] De Vries thought his behavior unusual for a man in a new position, especially when the students circulated a story that Ted had climbed up on top of a desk, crouched, and went "Ah-ah-ah-ah-ah!" as if he were mowing them down with a Tommy gun. Catherine De Vries went walking with Ted in the country once or twice. He said to her, "I could throttle you and stick you under a culvert and they wouldn't find you for weeks." Mrs. De Vries is not a large woman and she says she had sense enough not to act scared. His friends could feel something preparing, rushing to a crisis, but what it was, they didn't know. [p. 90]

On the night of November 11 Roethke's breakdown occurred, and during it he had what Seager terms a "mystical experience with a tree" (p. 90). Neal Bowers has more to say about the significance of this bizarre incident in Theodore Roethke: The Journey from I to Otherwise and in an essay distilled from that book, "Theodore Roethke: The Manic Vision."
Seager devotes much space in his sad but illuminating chapter to documenting the official academic investigation of Roethke that ended in his termination at Michigan State. Seager paints a dark picture of the behavior of Department Head W. W. Johnston and also of Dean Lloyd Emmons. He presents a convincing case for judging their reaction to Roethke's misfortunes as "inhumane" (p. 100). Ned O'Gorman, one reviewer of the biography, found Seager's account so repellent that he concluded that Roethke's emotional instability should be attributed, in general, to the numbing environment is which he had to live and work (pp. 34-36). That is not Seager's view, however. He mentions that Roethke was diagnosed, variously and throughout his life, as a " 'manic-depressive neurotic, but not typical,' as a 'manic-depressive psychotic, but not typical,' and as a 'paranoid schizophrenic' . . . [the] psychiatrists told me [Seager] that one of the characteristics of manic-depressive patients was their insistence that they brought their attacks on themselves" (p. 101). The last comment helps to explain Seager's

THE LOST SON NARRATIVES   93

conviction that he was "personally quite willing to believe that
the episode at Michigan State Ted brought on himself" (p. 105).
Theodore Roethke adds support to Seager's notion that the poet
himself had some control over his illness. In the symposium on
the later poem, "In a Dark Time," in Anthony Ostroff's The Contemporary Poet as Artist and Critic, Roethke writes that "there
are those who believe the true artist is impelled by forces outside
himself. . . . But the conscious will can be a factor, I have found,
in either a rise or a fall of a cyclic phase. The danger to the
human condition lies in excessive acceleration, either way. The
way up and the way down may be the same, but the pace often varies,
sometimes disastrously" (pp. 49-50). Of course, there are precedents for a poet's willfully disorienting the senses in the service
of art. Both Stepen Spender and Jerome Mazzaro have compared to
Roethke's the poetic principle of the French surrealist poet, Arthur Rimbaud, who called for a "systematic derangement of the
senses." In fact, Roethke echoes Rimbaud in his "Open Letter"
when he says of the Lost Son that his "disassociation often precedes
a new state of clarity" (SP, p. 41).
Roethke's friend, Stanley Kunitz, also thinks that Roethke en-
couraged the extremity of mental states he was prone to. As he
remarks in his reminiscence, "Remembering Roethke," "eventually, he [Roethke] more than half believed that the springs of his
disorder, his manic-depressive cycles, were inseparable from the
sources of his art, and he could brag of belonging to the brother-
hood of mad poets that includes William Blake, John Clare, and
Christopher Smart, with each of whom he was able to identify himself as 'lost' " (p. 80). Roethke's wife, Beatrice, however, believes that her husband held such a view more lightly. Her remarks
conclude Allan Seager's biography: "When Ted and I were first mar-
ried he thought it [mental illness] might be a requisite, but over
a period of years he revised his thinking about this, I believe.
What are generally thought of as his best poems were written when
he was well and out of the hospital" (p. 290). In the end, Allan
Seager admits to being uncertain about the origins of Roethke's
illness. "But all these [psychiatric] conjectures may be false,"
he says. "The source may have lain in the chemistries of his blood
and nerves" (p. 109), but he does think Roethke's manic-depression
important in reading the narratives especially (see Seager's appen-
dix to chapter 9, pp. 287-90).
Though in fact Roethke's illness and his breakdowns were a source
of pain, embarrassment, and fear to himself and those who loved
him, some critics have suggested that manic-depression offered
Roethke special opportunity as a poet. In his book, Karl Malkoff
advances that point:

If insanity involves more acute as well as distorted perceptions
of reality, then, in certain areas, the insane man holds a priv-

ileged position; he is in the forefront of human consciousness
partly by virtue of his insanity, and, if he can control the tools
of language, he can write the poetry of prophecy, he can give to
the rest of mankind the insight necessary to change one's life so
that it will be more in accord with reality than our mind-dulling
society allows. [p. 8]

That is a great deal to imply for anyone, sane or otherwise, but
Neal Bowers makes a similar connection and a similar large claim
in his recent book, Theodore Roethke: The Journey from I to
Otherwise (1982).   The mystical quality of Roethke's verse and
experience is Bowers's main theme, and in his discussion of it
Roethke's manic-depression figures prominently.   Bowers thinks
the Lost Son narratives, for example, are "largely the product of
Roethke's manic experience."   Roethke knew his illness could give
rise to poems, Bowers says, "and that is why he took such chances
by courting his illness, virtually wishing it upon himself" (p. 97).
To support those conclusions, Bowers shows that Roethke had read
numerous books about mystical experience earlier in his career than
was previously suspected, and he also reprints an extraordinary account of Roethke's "mystical experience with a tree" that Allan
Seager mentions occurred during Roethke's stay at Michigan State.
According to Bowers, the essence of that experience, what he calls
"contemplation" and what Roethke calls "long looking," becomes in
Roethke's poetry both method and content.   Bowers argues that "contemplation he employed to discover poetic material seems to have
become the poetry itself . . . the struggle and the poetic account
of that struggle fused" (p. 19).   Though Bowers acknowledges that
the narratives set up wider and mystical reference with the move
from darkness to light, from lost son to found "sun," in his view
it is manic-depression that accounts for the "back-and-forth movement in the sequence" (p. 118).

Bowers provides a good discussion of how knowledge of Roethke's
manic-depressive psychosis can illuminate the method and content
of the narratives, but his argument is not completely consistent.
At the outset of his book, Bowers argues that manic-depression and
mysticism are closely related.   Because of his illness, Bowers
says, Roethke had a "propensity for mystical insight" (p. vii).
According to Bowers, the cyclical emotional phases characteristic
of manic-depression correspond to the "periods of expansion and
contraction of consciousness characteristic of natural or affective
mysticism" (p. vii).   Roethke knew of the similarity between mystical
experience and the symptoms of manic-depression, Bowers says, and
"if it is a mistake to relate the manic-depressive symptoms to the
mystic's perceptions, then it is a mistake Roethke himself made"
(p. 16).   Toward the end of his book, however, Bowers says, "I do
not believe Roethke ever considered himself a mystic" (p. 205).
"More than likely," Bowers writes, "he believed that, through some

accident of chemistry or biology, he had been granted a comparable perception, had been admitted through some back or side door into the world of the mystics" (p. 207). Thus, Roethke was somewhat of a mystic but not a "genuine mystic" (p. 203). Since Roethke, as a man, could not finally release himself from "the bonds of 'I-hood,' " he had to achieve that release in his poetry (p. 203). Bowers supports that qualification by appealing to Northrop Frye's notion that there are some poets "who have a heightened sense of the Absolute but whose ultimate loyalty is to the artistic creation rather than to the perception which inspires it'" (p. 201). That conclusion does correspond to the assertion Bowers begins with: "While Roethke may not have been a mystic, his poetry is unquestionably mystical" (p. 17).

It has been suggested that Roethke's narratives owe their origins to what Karl Malkoff terms "insanity"; it has been suggested also that the narratives functioned for Roethke as therapy for that insanity. The regressions and the progressions of the Lost Son are inherently, perhaps unconsciously, therapeutic, Karl Malkoff says in Theodore Roethke: An Introduction to the Poetry. He explains the alternating structure of the Lost Son's quest by reiterating Carl Jung's observation that "when a man encounters an obstacle with which he cannot cope, he regresses to childhood, or even to the time before childhood--that is, to the collective unconscious--to find a new way of dealing with his current situation" (pp. 60-61). Jung's comment can decribe the method of the protagonist in the poems, and the method of the poet who constructed the protagonist and the poems, so the narratives are doubly therapeutic, apparently. In his book, Theodore Roethke: An American Romantic, Jay Parini does not make that distinction so clearly as does Malkoff, however. Parini simplifies the issue by noting that "one must not overlook the therapeutic effect of these poems on the developing artist; they became, in effect, a psychic autobiography in which the poet recovered, in a Freudian sense, his own lost past" (p. 123). No doubt writing the Lost Son narratives was psychologically useful to Theodore Roethke, as writing The Waste Land was psychologically useful to T. S. Eliot, as writing itself is often therapeutically useful for any writer. The act of writing explains us to ourselves. The composition of the Lost Son narratives was probably thus similarly illuminating to Theodore Roethke, but Roethke does not talk about the narratives as if any therapeutic effect, aside from that which the Lost Son achieves, were important for understanding the poems. In his letter to Selden Rodman on June 23, 1947, he speaks quite dispassionately about the narratives. He is referring to "The Lost Son," "The Long Alley," and "The Shape of the Fire":

> Let me say once more how pleased I am that you like those pieces. I thought I went far beyond the early work, and that's what W.H.A. [W. H. Auden] and L.[ouise] Bogan, Wms. [William

Carlos Williams], etc. tell me, too.   It's odd: I can feel very
impersonal about them, for they seem to come from a tapping of
an older memory--something that dribbled out of the unconscious,
as it were, the racial memory or whatever it's called.   Hence,
my unabashedness about them--which may be tiresome and naive.
[SL, p. 130]

Because Roethke's narrative poems are challenging, it makes
sense that critics would avail themselves of any biographical
information that could make the poems more accessible.   But there
is danger in emphasizing such correspondence.   Connecting the
poems too closely to the biographical data inevitably opens the
narratives to the kind of criticism Geoffrey Thurley advances in
his book, The American Moment: American Poetry in Mid-Century.
Thurley thinks the narratives cannot stand by themselves.   They
require the reader to know too much about Roethke's biography.
In citing the lines from "The Lost Son," "Snail, snail, glister
me forward,/ Bird, soft-sigh me home,/ Worm, be with me./ This
is my hard time" (CP, p. 53), Thurley comments, "in trying to
bring out the inner skeleton of Roethke's work, one seems driven
to talk about the personal life of the man . . . in describing
the first, one is perforce referring to the second" (p. 95).   It
is interesting that Roethke's own comment on these lines is the
sole instance in his prose where he himself forgets the distinction between protagonist and poet.
     Despite what Thurley says, and despite the useful parallels that
can be drawn between Roethke's life and the narrative poems, the
narratives can stand on their own.   Roethke provides within the
poems all that is necessary for understanding them.   When Jay
Parini observes, correctly, that the Lost Son narratives are "cen-
tered on an autobiographical myth" (p. 16), we should not therefore
be too easily misled about which I is I.   The first person perspective, not Theodore Roethke, is the landscape on which that myth
takes place.   We can go elsewhere to discover that Roethke's father,
Otto, figures as importantly in the son's life as does the father
of the Lost Son, and we can read in Roethke's medical history a
blueprint for behaviors of the Lost Son.   Such connections only
illuminate what Roethke emphasizes in the poems themselves, however.
In describing the growth and trial of the "I" in his narratives,
Roethke does not rely on a system of referencing or alluding to
the facts of his own life as confessional poets like Robert Lowell,
Anne Sexton, and Sylvia Plath do. To no similar degree does he
direct us beyond the narrative poems themselves.

Literary Backgrounds and Sources

With the exception of one passage, the originality of Theodore

THE LOST SON NARRATIVES 97

Roethke's Lost Son narratives has not been questioned to large
degree. After these poems, John Ciardi remarks in his review,
literature has a "subject, a rhythm, and a kind of perception that
are specifically Roethkean" (p. 410). At the same time, the Lost
Son poems are not aboriginal, are not without origins entirely. We
have seen that Roethke wants to locate those origins in a "collective unconscious" or, as he calls it, a "racial memory." In his
"Open Letter," he says that "in this kind of poem, the poet, in
order to be true to what is most universal in himself, should not
rely on allusion" (SP, p. 42). As a result of such indications,
perhaps, the mythic and biographical rather than the literary backgrounds and sources have been most widely cited in discussion of
the Lost Son narratives. However, it should be added that Roethke
indicates also that the narratives have other and specifically literary antecedents, what repeatedly Roethke calls "ancestors" (SP,
p. 41).

The first accounting of the literary sources for the Lost Son
narratives comes from Roethke's "Open Letter" published in 1950
after he had written eight of the narratives and had the ninth in
mind. In a parenthetical remark in that essay, Roethke directs
us to "German and English Folk literature, particularly Mother
Goose; Elizabethan and Jacobean drama, especially the songs and
rants; the Bible; Blake and Traherne; Durer" (SP, p. 41). Though
the list is incomplete, one can still get a sense of the world of
the Lost Son from these sources, George Wolff says in Theodore
Roethke. The realm of the narrative poems will be "childlike,
violent, and religious" (p. 47), Wolff argues, but he probably
mistakes Roethke's intent in listing the Bible among his sources.
As M. L. Lewandowski points out in "The Words of Their Roaring:
Roethke's Use of the Psalms of David," Roethke used the Bible
as he did other literary sources. He responded to its language
and distinctive technique, and from the Bible he borrowed psalmic
rhetorical patterns like the invocation (p. 157) and parallelismus
membrorum, a concise pattern of repetition (p. 159).

The sources Roethke acknowledges figure in any discussion of
literary antecedents of the narrative poems, but more attention
has been directed to authors Roethke did not identify. Among
these, the names of Romantic poets and writers, notably that of
William Wordsworth, most frequently appear, but Walt Whitman
and T. S. Eliot are also cited. In "Theodore Roethke and the
Landscape of American Poetry," C. W. Truesdale refers Roethke's
narratives to the American Romantic tradition, particularly to
the works of Walt Whitman. (In his essay of 1960, "Some Remarks
on Rhythm," Roethke also acknowledges Whitman as an influence on
his poetry, notably "Elegy for Jane" [SP, pp. 82-83].) Truesdale
draws parallels between Walt Whitman's practice of revising, re-
arranging, and reprinting the poems in his masterpiece, Leaves of
Grass, and Roethke's similar practice in composing and reorganiz-
ing the Lost Son narratives, though Truesdale notes that Roethke's

poems are considerably smaller in scope (p. 351). Nonetheless, Truesdale believes Roethke achieves more than Whitman, for Roethke was "untroubled by the grandiose and megalomaniac aspects of nineteenth century Romanticism"; he "never seems to have yielded to the temptation that very nearly ruins Whitman's work . . . the temptation toward bardic chauvinism" (p. 351).

Not everyone would agree that Whitman comes out on the short side of a comparison to Roethke, of course, but in Theodore Roethke: An American Romantic Jay Parini reiterates Truesdale's point that American Romantic writers, especially Emerson, Thoreau, and Whitman, must be added to the list of Roethke's sources (p. 5). While Parini wants in particular to show that Roethke is an American Romantic poet, he thinks the roots of Roethke's narratives go deeper into Western tradition. In that it recapitulates the essential structure of the quest romance, "the journey toward home, the hero's necessary pilgrimage," Parini sees Roethke's poetic project as "Romantic in essence," and he thinks Homer's Odyssey is the prototype of Roethke's narrative poems (p. 10). Roethke's quest motif need not be taken so far back into history, however, and William Wordsworth is more usually cited as the parent of Roethke's voyage in and out of the self. As early as 1954, Hilton Kramer observed in "The Poetry of Theodore Roethke" that Roethke's subject in the narratives is Wordsworth's subject, "the spirit's education in the world of nature, and the recovery of human feeling" (p. 134). Kramer thinks that Roethke takes Wordsworth's subject further, though, "into sources more primeval," and he uses a language not characterized by the "serenity and philosophic discretion of Wordsworth's language" (p. 134).

In his book, The American Moment, Geoffrey Thurley argues that there is "something suspect in his [Roethke's] recourse to procedures which Wordsworth, some 150 years before, inaugurated with such impressive authenticity and power" (p. 96), but Jenijoy La Belle disagrees. In The Echoing Wood of Theodore Roethke, she shows that Roethke does not simply reiterate Wordsworthian philosophy. Indeed, there are undeniable similarities, and La Belle notes parallels between the two poets' depictions of the child, paticularly in that both "bring into their poems not only the delights but also the terrors of childhood" (p. 45), and she notices also that both poets stress "spiritual and visionary illumination" (p. 47), what Wordsworth calls "spots of time" and what Roethke calls "heightening and awareness of one's self" (SP, p. 25). There are differences, however. According to La Belle, Roethke's journey in the Lost Son narratives is as much a literary as a psychological and spiritual journey. She argues that Roethke examines and evaluates Wordsworthian responses to nature, for example, especially in "Bring the Day!" (pp. 67-69). Roethke differs from Wordsworth in that "the necessary precondition for this journey from unity to division to re-unification is the widening of Roethke's own sensi-

bilities to construct and encompass a literary tradition character-
ized by similar cycles of self and other" (p. 83). The journey of
William Wordsworth in The Prelude is, in other words, but a leg of
Roethke's own journey.

La Belle illustrates her point by showing how Roethke revisits
and revises famous Wordsworthian images. Her most compelling
example comes from the final lines of "The Shape of the Fire,"
lines famous in their own right. Before the distinctively vegetal
and thus Roethkean image at the end of the poem, La Belle says,
Roethke rouses Wordsworth:

> To see cyclamen veins become clearer in early sunlight,
> And mist lifting out of the brown cat-tails;
> To stare into the after-light, the glitter left on
> the lake's surface,
> When the sun has fallen behind a wooded island;
> To follow the drops sliding from a lifted oar,
> Held up, while the rower breathes, and the small
> boat drifts quietly shoreward;
> To know that light falls and fills, often without our
> knowing,
> As an opaque vase fills to the brim from a quick
> pouring,
> Fills and trembles at the edge yet does not flow over,
> Still holding and feeding the stem of the contained
> flower.
>
> [CP, p. 67]

Before the "light falls and fills," La Belle indicates, Roethke
echoes the boat-stealing incident from book 1 of The Prelude.
Thus, we should notice in the conclusion of Roethke's poem "both
the interaction between the poet's mind and those objects described
in the poem and the interaction between Roethke and Wordsworth"
(p. 48). La Belle is willing to push the point still further:
"what we and Roethke are finally observing here [at the end of
"The Shape of the Fire"] is not just the natural world, but also
Wordsworth's poem" (p. 48).

La Belle draws a distinction between Roethke's use of literary
sources in the first narratives he published, the four in The
Lost Son and Other Poems, and those he added later in Praise to
the End! and The Waking. In his first narratives, Roethke uses
other poets somewhat less explicitly than he does in later narratives. He relies primarily on his "perception of archetypes" rather than on allusion or quotation (p. 88). From Blake's The Four
Zoas, The Book of Thel, and "The Little Boy Lost" and "The Little
Boy Found" from The Songs of Innocence and Experience, for example, Roethke has recovered "the underlying archetypal patterns of
innocence and experience, of being lost and found . . . that are

basic to Blake's thought" (p. 100). La Belle thinks Roethke
found many specific archetypal images in his reading, and he used
many in his poetry. These archetypes could be traced extensively,
she says, and she demonstrates by charting the archetypal image
of "slime" through Nietzsche, Blake, and Coleridge (pp. 88-95).

The first four narratives published differ also in that Roethke
used material from within those poems for the names "The Lost
Son," "The Long Alley," "A Field of Light," and "The Shape of
the Fire." He did not reach back into the literary tradition for
the titles of these poems. Roethke did otherwise in titling the
ten other narrative poems, La Belle points out. The title for the
sequence itself, Praise to the End!, Roethke took from Wordsworth's The Prelude (p. 43). "Where Knock Is Open Wide," the
title of the first poem in the sequence, Roethke borrowed from
eighteenth-century poet Christopher Smart's poem, "A Song to
David" (p. 51). The title of the second poem, "I Need, I Need,"
La Belle finds is "similar to [William] Blake's inscription 'I
Want! I Want!' for the ninth design in his series For Children:
The Gates of Paradise" (p. 56). "Bring the Day!" comes from the
fourth book of Wordsworth's long poem, The Excursion (p. 67). La
Belle traces the title of the fourth poem, "Give Way, Ye Gates,"
to the first line of "The Wassaile," a poem by seventeenth-century
love poet Robert Herrick (p. 72). She finds the title "Sensibility! O La!" in a nineteenth-century Mother Goose rhyme (pp. 76-
77), and the title of the sixth and last poem in the first section
of the sequence, "O Lull me, Lull me," is from "In Commendation
of Musick" by seventeenth-century poet William Strode (p. 80).
The titles of poems in the second section of the sequence come,
similarly, from metaphysical and Romantic poets. As we have
seen, "Praise to the End!" comes from Wordsworth. "Unfold! Unfold!" is from the first words of the seventeenth-century poem,
"The Revival," by Henry Vaughan (p. 104). "I Cry, Love! Love!"
derives from William Blake's poem Visions of the Daughters of
Albion (p. 90), and the title of the last poem in the sequence,
"O, Thou Opening, O," La Belle tracks to a love poem by the Scot-
tish Romantic, Robert Burns (p. 107).

In his otherwise innovative narrative poems, why would Roethke
decide to borrow language for his titles? In the instance of the
first narrative, "Where Knock Is Open Wide," La Belle says that
Roethke's appropriation of Christopher Smart's words helps to
show how the two poems are connected thematically. Both poets
"image a psychic state where the usual disjunction between desire
and gratification does not occur" (p. 53). That state "exists
for the man of prayer" in Smart's work; "for Roethke, it exists
for the child" (p. 53). Roethke could have found other poets in
literature with whom he felt that particular philosophical affinity, La Belle says, but he chose Smart because he wanted also to
ground his own departure from more conventional poetic practices

by aligning himself with Smart's previous break with traditional
modes. "By consciously choosing Smart's line as the title for his
poem," La Belle writes, Roethke "directs the reader to see even
his break with tradition as itself part of a tradition" (p. 56).

Bernard Heringman draws a similar conclusion about the rationale
of Roethke's literary borrowing in his essay, " 'How to Write
like Somebody Else,' " but he does so in the context of discussing
Roethke's use of William Blake. Heringman thinks Blake offered
Roethke an "encouraging precedent for extreme expression of a radical vision . . . his prophetic works also provided more specific
precedents: frequent exclamations and exhortations, sudden shifts
of subject and tone, questions and aphorisms in series" (p. 33).
Though La Belle's and Heringman's arguments coincide, La Belle
disagrees with Heringman's interpretation of Roethke's specific
uses of Blake. Roethke referred to Blake with the title of his
second poem, "I Need, I Need," because both poets use the "same
movement from union to disunion, from harmony to disharmony, to
describe and symbolize the growth of the child," she says (p. 58).
La Belle concludes that "by consciously relating himself to Blake,
Roethke places himself within a tradition of poetry notable for its
conceptual complexity in spite of the simplicity of its diction"
(p. 58).

Jenijoy La Belle's argument in The Echoing Wood of Theodore
Roethke is a carefully conceived and meticulously researched response to the various charges that Roethke was overwhelmed by
other poets' voices. In his use of "underlying archetypal patterns" in the first narratives published and in his use of direct
quotations as titles of the ten narratives that followed, La Belle
stresses that Roethke was conscious of what he was doing and why.
In the Lost Son narratives as well as elsewhere in his verse, La
Belle says, Roethke is "continually referring the reader to a heritage of poetry that at once defines the cultural ambiance in which
the work must be understood and aids the poet in moving beyond 'solitary experience' to the creation of transpersonal experience" (p. 4).

Even before Jenijoy La Belle discovered and systematized so many
of the details of Roethke's use of sources in his narrative poems,
one echo in one passage had already become prominent and controversial. Some thought it damaged irreparably the conclusion of the
pivotal poem. In the final lines of the fifth section of "The Lost
Son," the protagonist asks:

> Was it light?
> Was it light within?
> Was it light within light?
> Stillness becoming alive,
> Yet still?
>
> A lively understandable spirit
> Once entertained you.

It will come again.
Be still.
Wait.

[CP, p. 58]

Though there is disagreement about whether Roethke echoes "Ash
Wednesday," "Burnt Norton," "Little Gidding," or "East Coker"
with these lines, it is agreed that the poet echoed is T. S. Eliot.
Some readers think Roethke thus puts his poem and his poetic vision into direct competition with T. S. Eliot, and according to
Geoffrey Thurley, for example, such competition serves "only to
emphasize Roethke's limitations" (p. 98), for Eliot's vision is
much broader and more profound (p. 97). Thurley bases his conclusions on an examination of the question and answer technique common to both poets. For Thurley, "Eliot reveals his stature when
he answers his own disturbing questions with his own profound
answer" (p. 97). When Roethke asks such a question, he "falls
into a flip 'enigmatic' manner" in his answering (p. 97). Thurley
thinks spiritual matters are simply beyond Roethke's reach. His
"experienced reality is, to put it baldly, simply more confined"
than is T. S. Eliot's (p. 97).

In that both explore the self and attempt to come up with "spiritual order," Ralph J. Mills, Jr., notes similarities between
Eliot's Four Quartets and Roethke's "The Lost Son" in his book
Theodore Roethke. Mills is right to emphasize the key differences,
though. T. S. Eliot does not reach into "prerational areas" nor
does Roethke "step into religious orthodoxy" (p. 28). Babette
Deutsch comes to similar conclusions about "The Lost Son" in her
book, Poetry in Our Time. She observes that "not even Eliot has
so fully communicated the 'terror and dismay' of the dark night
of the soul" (p. 200). Deutsch thinks Roethke's poem is not
overwhelmed by Eliot's precedent, but "The Lost Son" is "a remarkable example of his method" (p. 198), a point Rosemary Sullivan also makes in her book, Theodore Roethke: The Garden Master
(p. 87). As might be expected, Jenijoy La Belle believes that
Roethke is in complete control of the reverberations of his echo
of Eliot. Roethke boldly rouses Eliot in a prominent place in
a prominent poem in order to highlight the essential difference
in their poetic visions. For the Eliot of the Four Quartets,
"waiting is continual--a waiting based on hopelessness"; for the
Roethke of the Lost Son narratives, La Belle says, "Waiting is
conditional--a waiting with hope for regeneration" (p. 102). In
evaluating Roethke's echo of the most famous poet of the century,
La Belle's distinction is worth considering, as is the fact also
that Roethke again alludes explicitly to T. S. Eliot in the "North
American Sequence" for similar purpose and with similarly controversial effect.

Poetic Method and Technique

Discussions of sources for Roethke's narrative poems are certainly useful, but referring the narratives only to biographical or
literary backgrounds misses the essentially experimental quality
of the poems. After all, the Lost Son poems are not important primarily because they illuminate Theodore Roethke or his reading.
They are known for themselves as poems, as language coordinated
and calculated to create particular and unusual effects. To that
end, they contain an array of techniques, poetic and otherwise:
proverbs, questions and responses, snatches of prose, little songs
in rhyme, musings and meditations, authorial asides and commentary, nonsense, neologisms, and throughout, of course, a narrative
line of the Lost Son's quest for identity. The effects of such
devices are not inevitably available to all readers, though. In
reviewing Roethke's poetry in Agenda, for example, Ian Hamilton
offered praise for the Greenhouse poems, but he was positively
enraged by the narratives of Praise to the End! "To get anything
out of the book," he wrote, "one has to be as swamped by its obsessive gesturing, its psalming hysteria, as the poet himself
seems to be" (p. 7). Daunted by the poems, and in an effort to
make sense out of them, Hamilton resorted to an obsessive method
himself. He counted the number of times Roethke names an animal
in the poems (he found 165), he counted the exclamation points
(there are 45), and counted the number of question marks (there
are 80). In fact, this raw data can lead to some useful conclusions about Roethke's poetic technique, but Hamilton is unable to
determine anything other than that Praise to the End! is a "very
bad book" (p. 7). Though Charlotte Lee attempts a more sympathetic and significant kind of empirical analysis in her essay,
"The Line as a Rhythmic Unit in the Poetry of Theodore Roethke,"
for the most part, the methods by which Roethke creates effects
in the Lost Son narratives are best illuminated by other means.
    The critical analysis of the methods and techniques Roethke
uses in the Lost Son narratives might be broken into two areas
of emphasis. Some critics have focused in general terms on the
nature of Roethke's poetic language in the narratives, on what
makes it distinctive and sometimes difficult and frustrating to
understand, on how Roethke tries to make an "actuality" out of
his words. Roethke's own poetry can provide a point of contrast
in this respect because in addition to the experimental Lost
Son narratives, Roethke also speaks a more conventional poetic
discourse. Other readers have concentrated on detailing the
discernible means Roethke uses within the context of his innovative poetic to provide order and coherence in the narratives.
Roethke has himself provided some guidance for both of these efforts. Toward the end of his "Open Letter," Theodore Roethke
outlines the technical criteria he kept before him when composing
the narrative poems:

Rhythmically, it's the spring and rush of the child I'm after--
and Gammer Gurton's concision: <u>mutterkin's</u> wisdom. Most of the
time the material seems to demand a varied short line. I believe
that, in this kind of poem, the poet . . . must scorn being "mysterious" or loosely oracular, but be willing to face up to genuine
mystery. His language must be compelling and immediate: he must
create an actuality. He must be able to telescope image and symbol, if necessary, without relying on the obvious connectives:
to speak in a kind of psychic shorthand when his protagonist is
under great stress. He must be able to shift his rhythms rapidly,
the "tension." . . . If intensity has compressed the language
so it seems, on early reading, obscure, this obscurity should
break open suddenly for the serious reader who can hear the language: the "meaning" itself should come as a dramatic revelation,
an excitement. The clues will be scattered richly--as life scat-
ters them; the symbols will mean what they usually mean--and sometimes something more. [SP, pp. 41-42]

If they do feel it, most critics have tried to describe the impact
of Roethke's language by detailing how the language of the narratives
functions differently from more ordinary and from other poetic languages. Kenneth Burke was the first to indicate such a distinction
in his essay, "The Vegetal Radicalism of Theodore Roethke" (pp.
257-58). In an effort to pinpoint the unique features of the narrative language, subsequent discussions assume the difference Burke
describes. As early as 1954, Hilton Kramer commented on Roethke's
innovative use of language in the narratives. He noted that in
the Lost Son poems, "drama has really <u>become</u> words. . . . It is
indeed a poetry of words, words passionately wedded to their objects
but totally divorced from telling any 'anecdote' in the conventional way" (p. 136; Kramer's italics). In "The Power of Sympathy,"
Roy Harvey Pearce focuses on how the language of Roethke's narratives makes demands of the reader. Echoing Kenneth Burke's quip
that Roethke writes "pre-verse," Pearce says the narratives are
"pre-poems," and the reader as "protopoet most actively . . . completes them" (p. 180). Implying that Roethke is not concerned
with referentiality or meaning in the conventional sense, Pearce
says the reader "can only try to talk through them--which perhaps
is a way, a way we too much neglect, of learning, all over again,
to talk" (p. 180). By departing from conventional patterns, however, Roethke has not resorted to randomness or chaos, according
to Pearce. Pearce sees the "paradigm" of the poems as "violence
transformed into power through order" (p. 169).
    Order, yes, but reason, no, says William Meredith in "A Steady
Storm of Correspondences: Theodore Roethke's Long Journey Out of
the Self." Meredith sees the Lost Son sequence as an achievement
in organic poetic form but it is an achievement perpetually threatened by the fear that "an order inimical to man's spirit might be
discovered, or no order at all" (p. 41). According to Meredith,

Roethke assumes in his narratives that "knowledge is felt," not
discovered and articulated (p. 45; Meredith's italics). Meredith
reads Roethke's little "mock-aphorisms" that stud the narratives
as "calling into question the whole project: can knowledge be
worded, once it has been felt?" (p. 47). Not only is the language
of the infancy poems nonreferential, as other critics note, but
for Meredith, it results in poems that are a "continuous feeling
out of the structure of existence in contempt, or near contempt,
of reason" (p. 45).

   In "Theodore Roethke and the Landscape of American Poetry,"
C. W. Truesdale argues also that language does not have references
in the usual way in the narrative poems. Whereas language is ordinarily used to refer to a world outside of itself, in Roethke's
narratives language "becomes the means or instrument for the res-
toration of primary nature, for the re-immersion of the sensibility in primary experience" (p. 355). Truesdale sees a connection
between Roethke's "nonsense" and the nonsense of the fool in King
Lear; each is a "measure of our disturbing distance from nature
and ourselves" (p. 355). In "Theodore Roethke's Praise to the
End! Poems," John Vernon does not emphasize in his discussion of
"Where Knock Is Open Wide" the social or cultural criticism that
Truesdale thinks the narratives imply, however. Rather, he sees
Roethke's use of language as the way of indicating the protagonist's gradual involvement in the world. The language of "Where
Knock Is Open Wide" is "language at its most silent because it
is language with little reference outside of itself. It is language
as almost pure gesture, as a mouth, where the condition of all
the body is that of a mouth" (p. 62). At times within the first
poem, Vernon notes, "the hard edge of 'reality' is beginning to
impinge upon the soft primordial wholeness of the child's world"
(p. 63). Unlike Truesdale, though, Vernon sees such intrusions
of the world as necessary for the development of the child.

   The best evidence for such assertions, of course, lies in a reader's experience of the poems. If the reader does not sense the
differences these critics point out, it is hard to believe their
commentary can persuade otherwise. However, Roethke's narrative
technique can be more precisely, if less comprehensively, described
by making distinctions about the language of the narratives themselves, and by looking more closely at individual technical features
of the poems. Perhaps the first observation to make is the one
any reader will feel who follows the order of the narratives as
published in the Collected Poems. Moving from the elegant conclusion of "The Shape of the Fire" to the first lines of "Where
Knock Is Open Wide" will register as a linguistic shock (a shock
eliminated, of course, by the version of the narratives published
in Words for the Wind). In "Where Knock Is Open Wide," we confront lines such as these: "We went by the river./ Water birds
went ching. Went ching./ Stepped in wet. Over stones./ One,
his nose had a frog,/ But he slipped out" (CP, p. 73). The first

lines of "The Flight," the first section of "The Lost Son," have
different impact:

> At Woodlawn I heard the dead cry:
> I was lulled by the slamming of iron,
> A slow drip over stones,
> Toads brooding (in) wells.
> All the leaves stuck out their tongues;
> I shook the softening chalk of my bones,
> Saying,
> Snail, snail, glister me forward,
> Bird, soft-sigh me home,
> Worm, be with me.
> This is my hard time.
>
> [CP, p. 53]

(Since the fourth line of this passage is so frequently misquoted,
it is worth pausing for a correction.   In Words for the Wind,
the line appears as "Toads brooding in wells" [WW, p. 79], and
Roethke uses that phrasing on his recording, Theodore Roethke
Reads His Poetry.   Even in the absence of such authority, this
version of the fourth line is preferable to the one presented
in the Collected Poems.   The verb "brood" may be used transitively   or   intransitively.   If used transitively, as the Collected
Poems suggests, the toads are brooding wells as if to hatch them.
If used intransitively, the toads are at once brooding in wells
as if to hatch something, and they are also sulking moodily.
"Sulking moodily," of course, parallels the protagonist's emotional
state; the version in Words for the Wind is thus doubly preferable.)
    Clearly, the perceptions expressed and the language used by the
voice of "The Flight" reflect a speaker older than that of "Where
Knock Is Open Wide."   The voice of "The Flight" is the voice of
the Greenhouse poems.   That voice reincarnates the child who en-
treats snail, bird, and worm.   In "Where Knock Is Open Wide,"
however, the child is there from the very beginning.   In this respect, an index of the protagonist's maturity is intelligibility
itself.   The more readily intelligible the discourse, the more
mature the Lost Son.   Naturally, then, the poems that present the
older protagonist are more popular ones, for on the surface Roethke
seems in less control of his language in the narratives depicting
the protagonist as infant or small child.   Roethke recognized that
problem, but he wanted the infancy narratives "written entirely
from the viewpoint of a very small child: all interior drama; no
comment; no interpretation.   To keep the rhythms, the language
'right,' i.e., consistent with what a child would say or at least
to create the 'as if' of the child's world, was very difficult technically. . . .   The rhythms are very slow; there is no cutesy prat-
tle; it is not a suite in goo-goo" (SP, p. 41).   Roethke's challenge was more than to mimic or reproduce the child's speech; par-

adoxically, he needed to carefully control a kind of unreason. Louise Bogan recognized that need in her review of The Lost Son and Other Poems (1948). She pointed out that though Roethke is rendered "almost inarticulate by the fears and pressures in which he has submerged himself," he controls such experience by ordering it with "the language of the adage, the proverb, the incantation, and the nonsense rhyme" (p. 118), an orderliness, a "rigorous artistic control," that Rosemary Sullivan also observes in her book of 1975, Theodore Roethke: The Garden Master (p. 86).

In his essay, "Theodore Roethke's Proverbs," Brendan Galvin analyzes one of the distinctive techniques that Roethke embeds in his narratives. Examples include these proverbs from the middle of "The Shape of the Fire":

> The wasp waits.
> The edge cannot eat the center.
> The grape glistens.
> The path tells little to the serpent.
> An eye comes out of the wave.
> The journey from flesh is longest.
> A rose sways least.
> The redeemer comes a dark way.
> [CP, p. 66]

And these from "O, Thou Opening, O," the final poem in the sequence:

> The Depth calls to the Height
> --Neither knows it.
> Those close to the Ground
> --Only stay out of the Wind.
> [CP, p. 97]

> Who reads in bed
> --Fornicates on the stove.
> An old dog
> --Should sleep on his paws.
> [CP, p. 99]

According to Galvin, such proverbs have two major functions in the narratives. They serve to organize and order the poems as a whole; they are "strategies to keep Roethke's protagonist moving in his perpetual quest for higher levels of being" (p. 46). In addition, Galvin says, the proverbs contribute important content to the reader, and thus fulfill the traditional function of the proverb, that of instruction (p. 38).

Richard Blessing offers a different explanation for the proverbs in his book, Theodore Roethke's Dynamic Vision. Blessing's is probably the single most detailed discussion of Roethke's poetic technique. According to Blessing, the proverbs are not particularly sagacious; in fact, they are intentionally disorienting and essentially antirational. For Blessing, the proverbs and aphorisms in the narratives encourage the suppression of reason as a way of ordering the world. Roethke presents the proverbs quickly, repetitively, and "our inability to grasp one proverb before we are hit by another," Blessing writes, "our sense of being overwhelmed by sheer speed--these sensations become a kind of revelation in themselves, a sudden excitement that crowds us toward . . . the madman's insight and the child's dignity" (p. 104).

Blessing argues that Roethke's question and answer technique also disables rationality. When we are confronted with questions such as "Tell me:/ Which is the way I take;/ Out of what door do I go,/ Where and to whom?" and then are given answers like "Dark hollows said, lee to the wind,/ The moon said, back of an eel,/ The salt said, look by the sea" (CP, p. 54), Blessing says we are forced "to confess our ignorance, to acknowledge the mysteriousness of things and the inadequacy of reason as a way of knowing" because the answers are "often more puzzling than the questions which occasioned them" (p. 102). Roethke thus confounds our ability to reason but not gratuitously, Blessing says. He does it for a reason. Roethke wants us to forego reason so that we might go back to where language "grows naturally out of the vigorous rhythms of the human body, that special 'knowing' of muscle and blood and nerve and bone" (p. 94). In other words, Roethke's proverbs and aphorisms and his questions and answers are designed to return us to the sensibility of the child, a point John Wain makes also in "The Monocle of My Sea-Faced Uncle" (p. 71). In his essay, "Roethke and Merwin: Two Voices and the Technique of Nonsense," T. R. Hummer contributes a similar explanation for Roethke's use of nonsense. Hummer distinguishes two kinds of nonsense Roethke uses in the narratives, the nonsense of the prerational consciousness and the nonsense of the postrational visionary. Roethke uses both kinds of nonsense for the same reason, though. He wants to make the reader break conventional patterns of thought and thus experience something not brought to the poem (pp. 273-77).

In addition to showing how Roethke's poetic technique undermines a rational bias, Richard Blessing observes that diction in and of itself is one of Roethke's means of heightening what Blessing terms the "dynamism" of his poems. According to Blessing, "the word, the right word, was one way to plunge into the intensity of one's childhood, into the 'imagination of the race' " (p. 64). That view comes directly from Roethke's own comments about diction in "Some Remarks on Rhythm": "We all know that poetry is shot through with appeals to the unconsciousness, to the fears and desires that go far back into our childhood, into the imagination of the race. And we know that some words, like <u>hill</u>, <u>plow</u>, <u>mother</u>, <u>window</u>, <u>bird</u>, <u>fish</u>, are so drenched with human association, they sometimes can make even bad poems evocative" (SP, p. 80).

Blessing's view derives from Roethke, but it also has antecedents in Kenneth Burke's observation in "The Vegetal Radicalism of Theodore Roethke" of the prevalence of intuitions over ideas in Roethke's poetry. Jerome Mazzaro reiterates that point in "Theodore Roethke and the Failures of Language," originally published in 1970. As noted in chapter 1, Mazzaro accounts for Roethke's diction by discerning two kinds of language, the Brahmin and the primal. The diction of the narratives is essentially primal and symbolic, Mazzaro says, and it represents a dramatic shift from the educated, normalizing Brahmin diction Roethke uses in Open House (p. 69).

In The Echoing Wood of Theodore Roethke, Jenijoy La Belle detects two kinds of diction within the context of the narratives themselves. The diction of the child is typically "monosyllabic, familiar, concrete, naive, and active," La Belle says, while the language of the "speaker not in innocence" is typically "polysyllabic" and "Latinate" (p. 60). An instance of the latter voice is the ironic prose passage in "O, Thou Opening, O":

And now are we to have that pelludious Jesus-shimmer over all things, the animal's candid gaze, a shade less than feathers, light's broken speech revived, a ghostly going of tame bears, a bright moon on gleaming skin, a thing you cannot say to whisper and equal a Wound?

. . . . Where's the great rage of a rocking heart, the high rare true dangerous indignation? Let me persuade more slowly. . . .
[CP, p. 98]

La Belle does not limit her discussion to the matter of diction alone, however. Roethke's poems require the reader to resurrect the experience of the child, she says, but part of that experience comes from one's "own knowledge of the tradition of poetry from which Roethke's lines spring" (p. 64). In other words, in reading Roethke we are bringing to his text our experience of nursery rhymes as children. Most critics trace Roethke's use of nursery-rhyme technique to William Blake, but La Belle capably argues that Blake himself was influenced by the nursery rhymes of Mother Goose, a source Roethke also acknowledges. Nursery rhyme techniques common to Blake and Roethke that La Belle detects include "sprung" rhythm, the short line, internal rhyme, the command (pp. 62-63), and what Roethke calls "repetition in word and phrase and in idea" (SP, p. 77). La Belle concludes that the diction Blake and Roethke use is also "consistent with what a child would say," as Roethke puts it (SP, p. 41) and, one might add, consistent with how a child would speak.

In addition to the proverbs, the questions and answers, the nursery rhymes, the distinguishable dictions, it should be mentioned also that Roethke measures out his lines quite purposively, especially in concluding his narrative poems. Most of the narratives

close emphatically, frequently with a resoundingly final series of
last lines. Roethke indicates his awareness of the technique,
but in another context. In discussing the conclusion of "Elegy
for Jane" in "Some Remarks on Rhythm," Roethke observes in the
poem "a successive shortening of the line length, an effect I have
become inordinately fond of, I'm afraid" (SP, p. 82). Roethke
was enamored of the technique even earlier, though, as these concluding verse paragraphs from three narratives indicate:

> (from "I Need, I Need")
>
> I know another fire.
> Has roots.
>   [CP, p. 76]
>
> (from "Bring the Day!")
>
> O small bird wakening,
> Light as a hand among blossoms,
> Hardly any old angels are around any more.
> The air's quiet under the small leaves.
> The dust, the long dust, stays.
> The spiders sail into summer.
> It's time to begin!
> To begin!
>   [CP, p. 78]
>
> (from "O, Thou Opening, O")
>
> I keep dreaming of bees.
> This flesh has airy bones.
> Going is knowing.
> I see; I seek;
> I'm near.
> Be true,
> Skin.
>   [CP, p. 99]

Experience and reason tell us poems end. Roethke usually satisfies that rational expectation at the ends of his narratives, but
the effect of the diminishing lines in the second example is especially noteworthy in this respect. While the lines slim down
to one word, graphically, thus creating a sense that the poem
ends, the content of the lines directs us forward optimistically.
In other words, Roethke has it both ways in this instance. He
concludes the poem but he does not end. In the context of the
passage, that is in keeping with the overall alternating motion
of progression and regression that Roethke uses to structure the

narratives. Thus, Roethke could work at the implicitly conclusive points in his sequence to sustain that motion at all costs or, as the third example indicates, he could simply stop it.

Theodore Roethke's Lost Son narratives depict their protagonist's flight into and out of alienation. Critics have read this flight in theological terms, as a quest for salvation, in psychoanalytic terms, as a quest for identity and sexual maturity, and in archetypal terms, as a quest recapitulating the major features of timeless Western myths. Still other critics think that aspects of heaven and hell appear in each narrative, and no matter the Lost Son's progress, they say, he must repeatedly reconstruct himself at each new stage of growth. Such dialectical interpretations emphasize the oppositions in the poems, and the Lost Son's alternation between flight and security, between lost and found. Despite major differences in perspective, however, nearly all critics agree that the Lost Son grows in the poems--he ages and matures--and most think also, in the end, that he realizes his goal. He is "near" (CP, p. 99). Critics might agree on more than that point, however, were the text of the poems better established. In addition to occasional differences in the details of the two versions of the narratives available, the actual sequence of the narratives is disputed. That disagreement has affected critical perspectives of Roethke's narrative project as a whole.

Interpretation of the poems has been supplemented first by Roethke's own prose statements on his methods and intentions. In addition, considerable attention has been devoted to the parallels between Roethke's own life and the history of the Lost Son. The absence of the father in the life of the Lost Son has been connected to Roethke's own early loss of his father, Otto, and Roethke's manic-depressive illness has been connected to the way the Lost Son seeks his goal through a series of resounding successes and terrible trials and failures. Those who use the biographical backgrounds imply that Roethke wrote the narratives out of his experience, but additional backgrounds for the narratives have been discerned in literary and philosophical traditions, notably the Romantic tradition. Roethke directs us to certain literary sources with the titles of his later narrative poems, and he lists influences in his prose essays. Though such references are indeed useful, few overestimate their impact on the poems as a whole. Roethke's originality of voice and vision is not significantly in question in the narrative poems, though some have suggested he limits himself too much to the relatively narrow subject matter of the growth of the poet's mind and body.

Some of the most useful and interesting discussions of Roethke's Lost Son narratives concern the variety of poetic techniques he employs in them and to what effects. The narratives contain poetry in many forms, a little prose, much sense and some nonsense, all gauged to make the reader's experience of the Lost Son's quest a rich and compelling one. Literary critics of Roethke's own day had gone some distance in articulating such experience. Subsequent ones, of course, have pressed the matter still further. To some degree, however, that ongoing interpretive effort was interrupted by the appearance in 1953 of the poems in Roethke's Pulitzer Prize-winning book, The Waking. Many readers anticipated that Roethke would, in his next work, develop along the lines of his innovative narrative poems, but it was a disappointment to some of them that the last poems in The Waking showed Theodore Roethke had turned toward a style and subject matter more familiar than dangerously new.

Bibliography

Arrowsmith, William
1952. "Five Poets," Hudson Review Winter, pp. 619-20.
Blessing, Richard A.
1974. Theodore Roethke's Dynamic Vision. Bloomington: Indiana Univ. Pr.
Bogan, Louise
1948. New Yorker May 15, p. 118.
1952. New Yorker Feb. 16, pp. 107-8.
Bowers, Neal
1982. Theodore Roethke: The Journey from I to Otherwise. Columbia: Univ. of Missouri Pr.
1982. "Theodore Roethke: The Manic Vision," Modern Poetry Studies pp. 152-63.
Brantley, Frederick
1952. "Poets and Their Worlds," Yale Review Spring, pp. 476-77.
Burke, Kenneth
1966. "The Vegetal Radicalism of Theodore Roethke," in Language as Symbolic Action, pp. 254-81. Berkeley: Univ. of California Pr. Appeared in Sewanee Review, pp. 68-108. Winter, 1950. Reprinted in Profile of Theodore Roethke, ed. William Heyen. Columbus: Merrill, 1971.
Ciardi, John
1953. "Poets of the Inner Landscape," Nation Nov. 14, p. 410.
Davis, William V.
1974. "Fishing an Old Wound: Theodore Roethke's Search for Sonship," Antigonish Review 20, pp. 29-41.
Deutsch, Babette
1963. Poetry in Our Time. Garden City, N.Y.: Anchor.
Eberhart, Richard
1951. "Deep Lyrical Feelings," New York Times Book Review Dec. 16, p. 4.

Fitzgerald, Robert
1959. "Patter, Distraction, and Poetry," New Republic Aug. 8, p. 17.
Flint, R. W.
1950. "Ten Poets," Kenyon Review Autumn, pp. 707-8.
Galvin, Brendan
1972. "Theodore Roethke's Proverbs," Concerning Poetry 5, pp. 35-47.
Griffin, Howard
1948. "Exciting Low Voices," Saturday Review July 10, p. 26.
Hamilton, Ian
1964. "Theodore Roethke," Agenda Apr. 7, pp. 5-10.
Heringman, Bernard
1972. " 'How to Write like Somebody Else,' " Modern Poetry Studies 3, pp. 31-39.
Hummer, T. R.
1979. "Roethke and Merwin: Two Voices and the Technique of Nonsense," Western Humanities Review 33, pp. 273-80.
Humphries, Rolfe
1952. "Verse Chronicle," Nation Mar. 22, p. 284.
Kramer, Hilton
1954. "The Poetry of Theodore Roethke," Western Review Winter, pp. 131-46.
Kunitz, Stanley
1975. "Remembering Roethke (1908-1963)," in A Kind of Order, a Kind of Folly: Essays and Conversations, pp. 77-82. Boston: Little, Brown.
La Belle, Jenijoy
1976. The Echoing Wood of Theodore Roethke. Princeton: Princeton Univ. Pr.
Lee, Charlotte
1963. "The Line as a Rhythmic Unit in the Poetry of Theodore Roethke," Speech Monographs Mar. pp. 15-22.
Lewandowski, M. L.
1980. "The Words of Their Roaring: Roethke's Use of the Psalms of David," in The David Myth in Western Literature, eds. Raymond-Jean Frontain and Jan Wojcik. West Lafayette, Ind.: Purdue Univ. Pr.
Lucas, John
1968. "The Poetry of Theodore Roethke," Oxford Review 8, pp. 39-64.
Malkoff, Karl
1966. Theodore Roethke: An Introduction to the Poetry. New York: Columbia Univ. Pr.
1967. "Boundaries of the Self," Sewanee Review Summer, pp. 540-42.
Mazzaro, Jerome
1980. Postmodern American Poetry. Urbana: Univ. of Illinois Pr., pp. 59-84. Appeared as "Theodore Roethke and the Fail-

ures of Language," Modern Poetry Studies, pp. 73-96. July, 1970.
McClatchy, J. D.
1972. "Sweating Light from a Stone: Identifying Theodore Roethke," Modern Poetry Studies, pp. 1-24.
Meredith, William
1965. "A Steady Storm of Correspondences: Theodore Roethke's Long Journey Out of the Self," in Theodore Roethke: Essays on the Poetry, ed. Arnold Stein, pp. 36-53.   Seattle: Univ. of Washington Pr.
Mills, Ralph J., Jr.
1963. Theodore Roethke.   Minnesota Pamphlets on American Writers, no. 30.   Minneapolis: Univ. of Minnesota Pr.
Morgan, Frederick
1948. "Recent Verse," Hudson Review Summer, pp. 261-62.
O'Gorman, Ned
1969. "Theodore Roethke and Paddy Flynn," Columbia Forum, pp. 34-36.
Ostroff, Anthony, ed.
1964. The Contemporary Poet as Artist and Critic: Eight Symposia.   Boston: Little, Brown.
Parini, Jay
1979. Theodore Roethke: An American Romantic.   Amherst: Univ. of Massachusetts Pr.
Pearce, Roy Harvey
1965. "The Power of Sympathy," in Theodore Roethke: Essays on the Poetry, ed. Arnold Stein, pp. 167-99.   Seattle: Univ. of Washington Pr.   Reprinted in Historicism Once More.   Princeton: Princeton Univ. Pr., 1969.
Roethke, Theodore
1961. Words for the Wind: The Collected Verse of Theodore Roethke.   Bloomington: Indiana Univ. Pr.
1964. "On 'In a Dark Time,' " in The Contemporary Poet as Artist and Critic: Eight Symposia, ed. Anthony Ostroff, pp. 49-53.   Boston: Little, Brown.   Originally appeared as "The Poet & His Critics," ed. Anthony Ostroff, in New World Writing 19, pp. 189-219, 1961.
1965. On the Poet and His Craft: Selected Prose of Theodore Roethke, ed. Ralph J. Mills, Jr.   Seattle: Univ. of Washington Pr.
1966. The Collected Poems of Theodore Roethke.   Garden City, N.Y.: Doubleday.
1968. Selected Letters of Theodore Roethke, ed. Ralph J. Mills, Jr.   Seattle: Univ. of Washington Pr.
1972. Theodore Roethke Reads His Poetry.   New York: Caedmon Records TC 1351.
Seager, Allan
1968. The Glass House: The Life of Theodore Roethke.   New York: McGraw-Hill.

Snodgrass, W. D.
1965. " 'That Anguish of Concreteness' ": Theodore Roethke's Career," in Theodore Roethke: Essays on the Poetry, ed. Arnold Stein, pp. 78-93. Seattle: Univ. of Washington Pr.
Spender, Stephen
1965. "The Objective Ego," in Theodore Roethke: Essays on the Poetry, ed. Arnold Stein, pp. 3-13. Seattle: Univ. of Washington Pr.
Sullivan, Rosemary
1975. Theodore Roethke: The Garden Master. Seattle: Univ. of Washington Pr.
Thurley, Geoffrey
1978. The American Moment: American Poetry in Mid-Century. New York: St. Martin's Pr.
Truesdale, C. W.
1968. "Theodore Roethke and the Landscape of American Poetry," Minnesota Review, pp. 345-58.
Van Dyne, Susan R.
1981. "Self-Poesis in Roethke's 'The Shape of the Fire,' " Modern Poetry Studies 10, pp. 121-36.
Vernon, John
1971. "Theodore Roethke's Praise to the End! Poems," Iowa Review Fall, pp. 60-79. Reprinted in The Garden and the Map: Schizophrenia in Twentieth Century Literature and Culture, pp. 159-90. Urbana: Univ. of Illinois Pr., 1973.
Viereck, Peter
1948. "Five Good Poets in a Bad Year," Atlantic Nov., p. 95.
1952. "Techniques and Inspiration," Atlantic Jan., p. 81.
Wain, John
1965. "The Monocle of My Sea-Faced Uncle," in Theodore Roethke: Essays on the Poetry, ed. Arnold Stein, pp. 54-77. Seattle: Univ. of Washington Pr. Appeared as "Theodore Roethke," in Critical Quarterly, pp. 322-38. Winter, 1964.
Williams, Harry
1977. "The Edge Is What I Have." Lewisburg: Bucknell Univ. Pr.
Wolff, George
1981. Theodore Roethke. Boston: Twayne.

Additional Reading

Callahan, Margaret B.
1952. "Seattle's Surrealist Poet," Seattle Times Magazine Mar. 16, p. 7.
Chang, Diana
1952. "The Modern Idiom," Voices May-Aug., pp. 42-43.
Davidson, Eugene
1948. "Poet's Shelf," Yale Review Summer, p. 747.

Deutsch, Babette
1948. "Fusing Word with Image," New York Herald Tribune Book Review July 25, p. 4.
Ferril, Thomas
1948. San Francisco Chronicle Magazine, June 13, p. 18.
Gibb, Hugh
1948. "Symbols of Spiritual Growth," New York Times Book Review Aug. 1, p. 14.
Hall, Donald
1953. "American Poets Since the War," World Review Jan., pp. 48-49.
Hall, James
1948. "Between Two Worlds," Voices Summer, pp. 57-58.
McLeod, James R.
1971. "Bibliographic Notes on the Creative Process and Sources of Roethke's 'The Lost Son' Sequence," Northwest Review: Theodore Roethke Special Issue Summer, pp. 97-111.
Mowrer, Deane
1948. "Reviews of Some Current Poetry," New Mexico Quarterly Summer, pp. 225-26.
Parkinson, Thomas
1950. "Some Recent Pacific Coast Poetry," Pacific Coast Spectator Summer, pp. 290-305.
Reichertz, Ronald
1967. "Where Knock Is Open Wide, Part 1," Explicator Dec., item 34.
Rodman, Selden
1951. "Intuitive Poet," New York Herald Tribune Book Review Dec. 2, p. 32.
Roethke, Theodore
1948. The Lost Son and Other Poems. Garden City, N.Y.: Doubleday.
1950. "Open Letter," in Mid-Century Poets, ed. John Ciardi, pp. 67-72. New York: Twayne.
1951. Praise to the End! Garden City, N.Y.: Doubleday.
Sawyer, Kenneth B.
1952. "Praises and Crutches," Hopkins Review Summer, pp. 131-32.
Schutz, Fred C.
1975. "Antecedents of Roethke's 'The Lost Son' in an Unpublished Poem," Notes on Contemporary Literature 5, 3, pp. 4-6.
Shapiro, Harvey
1952. Furioso Fall, pp. 56-58.
Vasakas, Bryon
1952. "Eleven Contemporary Poets," New Mexico Quarterly Summer, pp. 224-25.

CHAPTER 4

The New Poems of Words for the Wind

After Praise to the End! (1951), Theodore Roethke published two more volumes of poetry in the 1950s, The Waking and Words for the Wind. The new poems in these two volumes are significantly different from the Greenhouse poems and the Lost Son narratives. Both The Waking and Words for the Wind contain much that is not new, however. The Waking presents Roethke's generous selection of the poems he wrote before 1953, and Words for the Wind is subtitled "The Collected Verse of Theodore Roethke"; it includes the poems Roethke wished to preserve up to 1957, and contains The Waking in its entirety. In fact, after The Lost Son and Other Poems, the only book Roethke published that did not reach back into the past to bring forward poems from previous volumes was his last collection, The Far Field. Roethke added only eight new poems to The Waking, and two of those he added to existing sequences, "Frau Bauman, Frau Schmidt, and Frau Schwartze" to the Greenhouse poems, and "O, Thou Opening, O" to the Lost Son narratives. Taken together, however, the thirty-five "New Poems" Roethke published in part two of Words for the Wind amount in length and scope to a separate volume.

Though there were indications of where Roethke was heading with the new poems of his Pulitzer Prize-winning book, The Waking, published in 1953, the extent of the change at work in Roethke's verse was not fully evident until the publication in 1958 of Words for the Wind. As the reviews cited in the first part of this chapter indicate, many readers objected to the poems that resulted from that change. Where the Greenhouse poems and the Lost Son narratives are slanted toward energy, vitality, desire, and the things of this world, in the new poems of The Waking and Words for the Wind Roethke shifts toward the opposing pole in the dialectic that animates his verse. In the new poems Roethke relies again, as he did in Open House, on categories drawn from neo-Platonic philosophy. To correspond with his resuscitated philosophical bias toward the spirit, Roethke broadens his poetic vision in the new poems to include the subjects of love and death.

Roethke's interest in love is evident in The Waking in the highly formal and philosophical poem, "Four for Sir John Davies," and in Words for the Wind it emerges in the section called "Love Poems." Roethke addresses the spectre of approaching death in "Old Lady's Winter Words" in The Waking and in the two long poems that conclude Words for the Wind, "The Dying Man, In Memoriam: W. B. Yeats" and "Meditations of an Old Woman."

Roethke's experience of love and death provides the background for his neo-Platonic explorations in the new poems, but he has an additional motive in treating these subjects that complicates the poems and evaluations of them. Roethke left the greenhouse for the more abstract and philosophical landscape of love and death in order to respond to the charge that his verse was too limited in range and too subjective in perspective. The Lost Son narratives concern the self, the individual "I," almost to the exclusion of other concerns; Roethke intends for the new poems of The Waking and Words for the Wind to represent a move in the opposite direction entirely. In the Love Poems, in particular, Roethke wants to break the shell of the self he had consolidated so completely in earlier poems. His Love Poems are his first major and extended attempt to make a person other than himself come alive in his verse. As we will see in the second part of this chapter, even those who are otherwise committed to Roethke's work express reservations about the success of his effort to "personalize" his poetry.

As in the poems of Open House, Roethke is again uneasy in the new poems of the 1950s about losing his identity, a loss it appears he thinks love, like death, necessitates. As a result, the kind of love Roethke seems most comfortable with involves a kind of safe distance. At the same time, Roethke is not a "mineral man," as he says in "Words for the Wind" (CP, p. 124). He responds to his desires, and paradoxically he is most drawn to the woman of the Love Poems when she is least human, most animal. Discussion in the third part of this chapter shows that Roethke resolves this conflict, at times, if resolution it is, by trying to limit and control his passion and by setting a spiritualized love above the physical.

With the thematic bias toward a reasoned and philosophical outlook on the world comes a more serious voice in the poems of the 1950s. Where the voice speaking in the Lost Son narratives was, variously, an adolescent, a boy, a child, in some of the new poems Roethke speaks from the perspective of an elderly person, an old man in "The Dying Man," and an old woman in "Old Lady's Winter Words" and in "Meditations of an Old Woman." In the Love Poems, Roethke speaks as a mature man, usually without an explicit mask, and he resorts to no nonsense. The nonsense and irrationality so prominent in the Lost Son narratives are absent from the major poems of Words for the Wind; they have been banished entirely from the serious work and, like so many disorderly children,

are relegated to their own place in the book, a section titled
"Lighter Pieces and Poems for Children."
Some of Roethke's critics have referred these changes in his
voice to the influence on Roethke of the great Irish poet, William
Butler Yeats. Roethke explicitly acknowledges his indebtedness
to Yeats in both poems and prose, acknowledgments that are at
once a source of and evidence for one of the major charges leveled
against Roethke's later poetry. On the issue of poetic influence,
it must be said, Theodore Roethke is probably his own worst enemy,
but he acknowledges influences because he wants to align himself
with or distinguish himself from literary figures and traditions.
In that respect, his use of literary ancestors has elements of loyalty and competitiveness, of respect and challenge. As we shall
see, the charge of "undue influence" in Roethke's later verse will
not easily be put to rest. It is used usually to demote Roethke's
verse as a whole in comparing it to works of other poets, but it
can also be employed to illuminate his literary sources and the
features of his later poetic technique, as discussion in the
fourth part of this chapter suggests.

In comparison to the Lost Son narratives, the new poems of The
Waking and Words for the Wind indicate Roethke's greater interest
in and command of conventional poetic forms. Roethke's reversion
to traditional forms, to stanzas, rhymes, and meters, has been, in
an era of experimentation, extremely controversial, but it does
seem compatible with the more rational, studied, occasionally
even academic, outlook on the world he presents in the new poems.
In addition, Roethke's handling of conventional poetic form is
considerably more varied and impressive than his apprentice work
in Open House. Among the outstanding individual achievements in
the new poems of the 1950s are "I Knew a Woman" and "The Waking,"
the latter one of the finest renditions in the twentieth century
of the complex poetic form, the villanelle.

Reviews

The Waking, published in 1953, is what today we would call "selected" poems. In it, Roethke included seventeen poems from Open
House, all thirteen of the Greenhouse poems (plus the poem, "Frau
Bauman, Frau Schmidt, and Frau Schwartze"), eight of the twelve
poems in parts 2 and 3 of The Lost Son and Other Poems, the fourteen Lost Son narratives organized to begin with "Where Knock
Is Open Wide," and a section of pieces called "New Poems" (later
titled in Words for the Wind "Shorter Poems, 1951-1953"). In
this last section appear some indications of Roethke's later
love poems ("Four for Sir John Davies," "The Visitant," "A Light
Breather," "Elegy for Jane"), of his poems in what might be called
the Yeatsian mode (again, "Four for Sir John Davies"), and of

his return to traditional poetic form ("The Waking"). It is not surprising that the section of "New Poems" received less attention than it might have were it published separately from Roethke's other poems. For the first time, in The Waking, the Lost Son narratives appeared in final form, completed by the poem, "O, Thou Opening, O." Some reviewers of The Waking directed their comments to the poet of the Lost Son narratives, therefore, and he continued to receive mixed response for his narrative project. Writing in the New York Times Book Review, Hayden Carruth credited Roethke for being the only original and really experimental poet on the landscape on the basis of his Lost Son poems (p. 14), but Joseph Bennett declared Roethke was among the "least impersonal of our poets," a man of "pure untethered originality" to be sure, but a poet of "extremely small range" (p. 305). The new poems of The Waking suggested to Gerald Previn Meyer, however, that Roethke was "working out of this sort of thing [the narrative experiments] into a more conscious and formal art" (p. 19).

Questions about Roethke's subjectivity and the range of his poetry, of course, had been raised before and would be raised again, but after publication of The Waking, and after Roethke began to receive major national awards, such questioning took on an insistent, even virulent tone. From his stinging review of The Waking in the Black Mountain Review, one would not suspect that Martin Seymour-Smith was discussing the work of the Pulitzer poet of the year. Seymour-Smith has harsh things to say about virtually every facet of Roethke's verse. He singles out the poems of Open House as especially insignificant ones "because the form was thought of first" (p. 43), and he thinks the first two-thirds of The Waking are about terror but a terror Roethke never adequately explores. Of the lines, "The half grown chrysanthemums staring up like accusers" and "And everyone, everyone pointing up and shouting" from the Greenhouse poem, "Child on Top of a Greenhouse," Seymour-Smith asks "Why?" (p. 44-45). Of "The Lost Son" he asks, "What, exactly, is the matter? What is this unease?" (p. 45). Of that poem as a whole, he concludes by answering his own question: "What impact can it make on us besides puzzlement?" (p. 46).

For one area of the country, at least, Seymour-Smith's review drew a clear line between those who applauded The Waking and those who condemned it. As a result of the review, poet and critic Kenneth Rexroth resigned from the editorial board of the projectivist journal, Black Mountain Review. In his subsequent "Comment" on Rexroth's resignation, poet Robert Creeley supported and then enlarged upon Seymour-Smith's position. "Certainly, it is not Roethke's fault," Creeley wrote, "that those very characteristics in his work which are most lamentable, e.g., diffusion, generality, and a completely adolescent address to the world in which he finds himself, should be the ones on which his reputation

is maintained" (p. 64). Of course, an "adolescent address" is the
fundamental vantage-point of the protagonist in several of the
Lost Son narratives, but Creeley's criticism goes farther than that.
He suggests that Roethke is constitutionally unable to respond
like an adult, even in those poems where a mature protagonist is
speaking.

The language, if not the substance, of Creeley's criticism may
have originated in Kenneth Burke's essay, "The Vegetal Radicalism of Theodore Roethke." Burke is trying to specify the essential
subject matter of Roethke's verse: "With 'prowess in arms' (virtus)
he is not concerned. The long poems . . . are engrossed with problems of welfare (salus), though of a kind attainable rather by
persistent dreamlike yielding than by moralistic 'guidance of the
will.' As for venus, in Roethke's verse it would seem addressed
most directly to a phase of adolescence" (p. 263). Burke's meaning,
it should be clear, is different from Creeley's view that Roethke
presents love in his poetry like an adolescent. Nonetheless, by
the time that Words for the Wind appeared in 1958, part of the
substance and much of the tone of the negative response to Roethke's
poetry was established. Supporters of the new Roethke were less
ready in shaping a defense, but Roethke received the National Book
Award for Words for the Wind, recognition at once defense in itself and, to opponents, repetition of the Pulitzer offense.

Words for the Wind made available once again the full range
of Roethke's verse: with its selections from Open House, The
Lost Son and Other Poems, and Praise to the End!, The Waking
appears in its entirety again as part 1 of the volume, but in
part 2, the dozens of "New Poems" present a different Theodore
Roethke. Part 2 contains seven children's or nonsense poems
in a section entitled "Lighter Pieces and Poems for Children"
and subtitled "An Interlude," sixteen "Love Poems" for which
there is little precedent in Roethke's verse, ten poems ranked
under the title "Voices and Creatures," most of which might be
described as poems addressed to minimal creatures ("Snake," "Slug,"
"The Siskins"), and two long poems, "The Dying Man," subtitled
"In Memoriam: W. B. Yeats," and "Meditations of an Old Woman,"
a poem in five parts. In reviews of Words for the Wind, Roethke
received the usual comments about the "excesses" or the "originality" of the Lost Son narratives, but the most telling responses
to Roethke's book concerned the poems of part 2, and, retrospec-
tively, some of the "Shorter Poems, 1951-1953" printed earlier
at the end of The Waking.

In addition to a certain amount of appreciative response due
an award winner, of course, the appearance of Words for the Wind
crystallized two objections to the new trend of Roethke's poetry.
Roethke published a sizable section of Love Poems in Words for
the Wind (he published another in his last volume, The Far Field),
and he wrote these poems to prove that his poetic vision was

larger than before expected. After examination of the new poems
of Words for the Wind, however, some critics argued that, despite
his efforts, Roethke had not written compellingly of things beyond
the self. Because he had not done that, it became increasingly
evident that Roethke had not addressed other issues beyond the
self, notably social and political matters. He had ignored the
vast and turbulent world outside a Lost Son's experience in a
greenhouse environment, critics argued, and they concluded that
Roethke's poetic vision was narrow and limited in comparison to
those of other poets of his and previous generations. The second
and somewhat more pervasive criticism of Roethke's poetry of the
1950s concerned his return to the formal lyric and his development
of a "philosophical" voice and style. In trying to speak in the
manner of Yeats in the second part of Words for the Wind, critics
said, Roethke stepped out of his element (and out of his class),
and he subordinated his authentic poetic voice to that of a more
potent other. Roethke's voice may once have been original, but
it ceased to be so when Roethke overreached himself by trying
to outdo William Butler Yeats. From the grave the Irish poet's
magisterial voice overpowered Theodore Roethke's.
    These objections appeared in various guises and to varying de-
grees in many of the reviews of Words for the Wind. Writing in
the Spectator, Robert Conquest remarked favorably upon Roethke's
Love Poems, but he noted also that "Roethke in many ways resembles a Yeats with a blunter cutting edge and a less strongly
organised mind" (p. 211). In the Hudson Review, W. D. Snodgrass
found much to like in Words for the Wind, notably the "prosier"
poems like "Slug" and "Meditations of an Old Woman," but he also
expressed misgivings about the intrusion of Yeats's voice in the
Love Poems and "The Dying Man" (pp. 114-17). John Wain prefaced
his remarks in Encounter with the refreshing observation that
Roethke is fun to read (p. 82). In noting that Roethke had two
voices, however, the "fun" voice of the Lost Son narratives and
the "ventriloquial" voice of the lyric poems, Wain concluded that
Roethke lacked the thing necessary for a great poet--"an unmis-
takeable identity" (p. 82). Where John Wain heard two voices,
poet Thom Gunn heard three. In "Poets English and American" in
the Yale Review, Gunn noted that Words for the Wind sounded as
if it were "written by three different men" (p. 623). He observed
the influence of Louise Bogan and Yvor Winters in the poems of
Open House, he thought the "not very good nonsense poems" of
Praise to the End! revealed a Roethke "completely concealing"
his purposes (p. 624), and he found that when Roethke's verse
finally turned "rational," it showed the "pernicious influence of
Yeats" (p. 624).
    In his review entitled "Creative Splendor" for the New York
Times Book Review, Richard Eberhart saw Roethke's use of Yeats's
voice in a different light. The change in style signaled by
Roethke's Yeatsian mode, Eberhart said, showed his need for more

control after the poems of Praise to the End! It was a necessary move for Roethke in order to achieve a "unified sensibility"
(p. 34). Nearly ten years later, Eberhart reasserted his position
in "On Theodore Roethke's Poetry." He stressed Roethke's originality, his independence, his realization that "what is called fash-
ionable or current today will be outmoded tomorrow" (p. 619), but
he also conceded the point other reviewers had made against Words
for the Wind: since Roethke's poetry is "highly subjective rather
than objective in the large sense of depicting the conflicts of
people . . . his limitation would not let him sympathize with char-
acters as such, to the point of communicable projection" (p. 620).

The Problem of Personalization

Most critics would agree that Roethke wrote convincingly about
the minimal creatures and about himself, but when he tried to
depict another human being, particularly a woman, in his poetry,
many would say he experienced difficulty. The root of such criticism of Roethke's handling of his subject matter in the new poems of Words for the Wind may be found once again and again, perhaps surprisingly, in Kenneth Burke's "The Vegetal Radicalism of
Theodore Roethke," one of the best and most appreciative readings
of Roethke's earlier verse. After drawing attention to the considerable strengths of the Greenhouse poems and the Lost Son narratives, Burke concludes his essay by drawing a distinction between personification and what he calls "personalization." In
"The Lost Son," Burke observes that Roethke uses the technique
of personification: his "imagism merges into symbolism, his flowers and fishes become Woman in the Absolute" (p. 281). Burke
thinks Roethke is capable of more sophisticated technique than
that because he had already demonstrated command of personalization in his poem, "Elegy for Jane." Burke warns Roethke against
his tendency toward the philosophical, and he recommends that
Roethke lean toward what Burke calls the historical. In that way,
Burke says, Roethke can better "personalize" his poetry through
an "individualizing of human relations" (p. 281; Burke's italics).

Burke's advice had an effect on Roethke, and it established a
goal that he wanted to meet. In his letter to Burke in January
of 1952, Roethke mentions the issue of "personalization" specifically. He is referring to the poem, "Old Lady's Winter Words":
"take a look at the current Kenyon. There's a piece (by me) that
may bear out your prophecy: about a person that is" (SL, p. 171).
To Kenneth Burke, it might be said, we owe the new poems of Words
for the Wind or, at least, as Rosemary Sullivan concludes from
Roethke's letter in her book, Theodore Roethke: The Garden Master, "clearly, he [Roethke] felt more than is generally supposed
the pressures toward a poetry of social concern" (p. 91). Roethke

recognized the relative absence of other persons in his verse before he undertook to rectify that situation in the new poems of
Words for the Wind, however, though it is true he seems to have
thought referring to few humans in the Lost Son narratives was
important for his purposes.

In his comment on the conclusion of "Praise to the End!" in
his "Open Letter," for example, Roethke writes, "but--and this is
the point--in this passage the protagonist, for all his joy, is
still 'alone,' and only one line mentions anything human: 'I've
crawled from the mire, alert as a saint or a dog.' Except for
the saint, everything else is dog, fish, minnow, birds, etc. . . ."
(SP, p. 40). References to other human beings are more prevalent
in the narratives than Roethke suggests, however. "I'm cold all
over," the protagonist says in "The Lost Son." "Rub me in father
and mother" (CP, p. 56). And while "Mother Mildew" and "Father
Fear" of the same poem are not human beings (CP, pp. 55-56), the
"Papa" of "The Return" assuredly is. Earlier in the "Open Letter,"
Roethke refers to the man as "the florist" (SP, p. 39). Roethke
thus overstates the point about the scarcity of human beings in
the narrative poems, but the fact that he makes the point itself
remains significant. The narratives entertain the existence of
other human beings, ourselves included, primarily by implication.
In his BBC Broadcast in 1953, "An American Poet Introduces Himself and His Poems," Roethke said the purpose of the narratives
was to "trace the spiritual history of a protagonist (not 'I'
personally but of all haunted and harried men)" (SP, p. 10). We
are all Lost Sons and Lost Daughters, Roethke suggests. Our
struggle to be found is an essentially solitary business.

However, it is not inconsistent with the essentially solo performance of the Lost Son that, toward the end of the narratives,
he begins to see the value of other persons. In her book, The
Echoing Wood of Theodore Roethke, Jenijoy La Belle finds it especially significant that the titles of the concluding narratives,
"I Cry, Love! Love!" and "O, Thou Opening, O," come from love
poems, and with the lines, "A dry cry comes from my own desert;/
The bones are lonely . . ./ . . . We never enter/ Alone" ("I Cry,
Love! Love!," CP, p. 93), La Belle says that "Roethke states
his desire to join with another and thereby to increase the range
of his poetry" (p. 107). There is thus some evidence for seeing
the new poems of Words for the Wind, especially the Love Poems,
as outgrowths of a vision that Roethke arrived at toward the end
of the narrative poems.

Ralph J. Mills, Jr., is perhaps foremost among critics who have
argued that the new poems of Words for the Wind figure importantly in the evolution of Roethke's poetic vision, but he mentions
some key differences between the new poems and the Lost Son narratives in his essay of 1962, "The Lyric of the Self." Mills notes
that the Love Poems in particular represent a "sharp departure

from self-contemplation" and a "change from consideration of self
to fascination with the other"; through the mediation of the woman, however, the speaker of the poems experiences a "rapport with
creation," Mills says (pp. 16-17). Mills thinks this immersion
in nature is a major goal of all of Roethke's verse, and in his
1963 booklet, Theodore Roethke, he argues that the Love Poems
bring "to a certain measure of fulfillment the evolution of the
self begun with the childhood and adolescence poems" (p. 34). According to Mills, the woman of the poems plays an important role
in this development. In the poem, "Words for the Wind," for example, Mills finds that the woman "merges with flowers, the wind,
a stone, the moon, and so she appears to be present in almost every living thing, in objects or the elements" (p. 35). While she
is represented as "frankly physical and sexual," Mills says, she is,
more significantly, a "creature of spiritual and mythological proportions" (p. 36). Since she appears in so many guises, however,
the woman of the Love Poems might be considered what Kenneth
Burke has earlier termed "Woman in the Absolute" (p. 281). In
Burke's view, such personification is a deficiency in Roethke's
poetry, of course, but in Mills's reading the various "personifi-
cations" coalesce in what he calls a "constant image within the
poet himself, the archetypal female principle dwelling in man
which Jung called the anima" (p. 36). Through love of the woman,
the protagonist can achieve a "harmony with the cosmos" and a psychological, "an internal balance too," Mills says (p. 36). In
Theodore Roethke George Wolff draws a similar conclusion in his
discussions of other Love Poems, "The Dream," "Words for the
Wind," "I Knew a Woman," and "The Voice" (p. 81). In these poems,
Wolff says, Roethke resolves the "earlier opposition between love
of nature and love of woman" by forging a "new union--the woman
and nature become one" (p. 75).
      In Theodore Roethke: An Introduction to the Poetry, Karl Mal-
koff agrees with Mills that the love poetry represents a step forward for Roethke's poetic vision. H agrees also that the woman
of the poems of the 1950s is "an image of woman in general"; in
the "Shorter Poems, 1951-1953" of The Waking, Malkoff sees her as
"personification of the spirit, student, mother, and (in "Four for
Sir John Davies") both the sensual partner and figure of [Dante's]
Beatrice" (p. 112). Malkoff finds somewhat less harmony in Roethke's love poetry than Mills suggests, however. Malkoff argues
that love for Roethke is a "tension-filled yoking together of opposites rather than their complete resolution" (p. 128). These
opposites are evident, according to Malkoff, in the archetypal imagery that Mills points out. Malkoff views the "Shorter Poems,
1951-1953" of The Waking, in particular, as essentially antithet-
ical to the Lost Son narratives. Where Mills thinks these poems
mark another stage in an evolution of the self, Malkoff believes
they are an "invocation of the anima" which should be contrasted

with the Lost Son's "search for the father" in the Lost Son narratives (p. 113). To support this argument about the anima, the feminine element in the psyche of a man, Malkoff shows parallels between psychoanalyst Carl Jung's analysis of the way the anima develops in the male mind and the evolution of Roethke's imagery of the woman in the "Shorter Poems" of The Waking. Roethke represents her as spirit, mother, sexual partner, and benevolent guide or protector, an order that corresponds to Jung's (p. 120). Portrayal of the woman in these guises indicates, according to Malkoff, Roethke's "transformation of love and anxiety into modes of metaphysical exploration" (p. 125).

John Crowe Ransom alludes to certain problems in the new poems of Words for the Wind in his discussion, "On Theodore Roethke's 'In a Dark Time.' " Like Coburn Freer after him, Ransom phrases Roethke's reluctance before love in the language of the Prodigal Son motif: "the grown-up boy must return whether he will or no to the human society, though for the woman as for the man the natural setting is the right place for it" (p. 29). Ransom thinks the Love Poems mark an important stage in Roethke's verse, however. "With the arrival of the grand passion," Ransom writes, Roethke "had come into his artistic as well as his physical maturity; from now on, we say, his characteristic voice is going to meter itself cleanly and beautifully in what we must call the syllabic or high style of this art" (p. 29).

Coburn Freer takes the Prodigal Son motif further in "Theodore Roethke's Love Poetry" and, like Malkoff, he emphasizes also the unresolved conflict Roethke displays in his love poems. In his piece, the only full-length essay devoted to the subject, Freer considers the Love Poems in both Words for the Wind and The Far Field. He thinks the Love Poems of The Far Field are a "very mixed bag," and though he detects a "back-and-forth movement between affirmation and negation" that organizes them, that organization is "dramatically ineffective because the poems differ so greatly in their intents and modes" (p. 60). Freer finds Roethke's earlier love poetry much more compelling. As it is presented in the narrative poems, Freer says, love is characterized by an "easy profligacy," by a "lack of obligation," and he observes that the woman of the narratives is usually sleeping, she never speaks, she is not really an actual woman (p. 44). When this woman of the narratives wakes, so to speak, and becomes a person in the Love Poems of Words for the Wind, the protagonist experiences a significant conflict: when the "sensual and intellectual experience of another person . . . is offered as a gift . . . the gift becomes not a release but a burden and obstruction" (p. 45).

Freer explains the protagonist's uneasy response to a love freely given by suggesting that Roethke invokes the Prodigal Son motif as a means of organizing the Love Poems. "Every poem has its place in the sequence," Freer argues, and he discerns as the structure underlying the sixteen Love Poems the Prodigal's setting out, his wasting of his inheritance, his return, and his resultant guilt (p. 50). By exploring the self in the Lost Son narratives, Freer explains, Theodore Roethke built up a "sense of an unlimited inheritance"; he amassed an "inexhaustibly rich interior" (p. 58). When confronted by a person he loved, that psychological wealth was threatened by the "burden of another's love" (p. 58). Identity and the obligations of love conflict in Roethke's mind, according to Freer, and he believes the conflict is not resolved by the Love Poems. "Either alternative," Freer says, "acceptance of the woman or affirmation of his own separate individuality, will lead the poet very close to spiritual suicide" (p. 58). Freer sees some resolution of the problem in the long poem, "Meditations of an Old Woman," but he notes also that Roethke has resolved his conflict there by stacking the deck: "although the old woman has a fine intelligence she can hardly make sensual gifts to and demands of a man, and that is the crux of the lyrics" (p. 59). Though Freer does not see the Prodigal's conflict solved in the Love Poems, he says we find in them the "kin" of the "divine poems" in the later "Sequence, Sometimes Metaphysical" where "the poet's love for woman and his self-concern as the loved Prodigal take their final religious form" (pp. 65-66).

Richard Blessing thinks the Love Poems are a significant part of Roethke's poetic vision, but unlike other critics Blessing focuses on neither lover nor loved one in his book, <u>Theodore Roethke's Dynamic Vision</u>. Blessing examines the love between them, and he concludes that Roethke is "most moved to love by motion itself"; that inspiration can take the form of a woman, "the leaping of stones, the walking of wind, the rising of the moon, the migration of birds and fish" (p. 172). Thus, according to Blessing, the Love Poems are broader in range and more abstract than previously supposed. "Love and motion are one," he says, and the Love Poems are a "dissertation on love which is, at the same time, a dissertation on motion" (p. 171). The Love Poems are therefore a kind of epistemological quest. For Blessing, "motion answering motion in dance-like give and take . . . forms the intuitive basis for Roethke's mysticism, for his most happy marriages of loving and knowing" (p. 172). In his book, Blessing aims to establish that the "dynamic vision" is fundamental to Roethke's poetry, and it is thus consistent with his argument that motion itself be central to the Love Poems. However, Blessing's reading suggests even more than most others do that Roethke did not "personalize" a woman in his love poetry.

At the end of his survey of the criticism of Theodore Roethke, Harry Williams concludes in "<u>The Edge Is What I Have</u>" that Roethke's critics agreed upon only a few essential points. One was the centrality of the Lost Son narratives, as we have seen; the other was that Roethke's "controlling theme is the journey out of the self" (p. 31), a phrase borrowed from the "North American Sequence" (CP, p. 193). The notion that Roethke successfully in-

corporates another person into his work in the final section of
The Waking, and in the "New Poems" of Words for the Wind, is
fundamental to this prevalent interpretation of Roethke's poetry.
A short summary of the stages of the "journey out of the self"
might go like this: Roethke takes the self as his theme in the
poems of Open House, and he begins to investigate the sources of
identity; he continues in that aim by descending to the level of
the inanimate substances and small beings in the Greenhouse poems;
in the Lost Son narratives, he regresses to infancy in an effort
to find himself, and at the end of these poems he is prepared to
enter his father's world; in the new poems of Words for the Wind,
he makes a concerted effort to involve human beings in his verse
and, coinciding with that move out of the self, he defines his own
voice with the aid of other poets' voices; in The Far Field, and
in the "North American Sequence" in particular, Roethke discovers
the world at large, including his own historical times, in his
fully expanded vision. Some critics think Roethke achieves an all-
encompassing mystical vision in his last poems, a vision that connects finally, as Roethke says, "I to Otherwise, or maybe even to
Thee" (SP, p. 25).

The religious or metaphysical implication is important in most
readings of Roethke's "journey out of the self" because frequently
that journey is perceived as a move from body to soul, from flesh
to spirit. One interpretation that follows those outlines in an
almost literal fashion is James McMichael's essay of 1969, "The
Poetry of Theodore Roethke." McMichael argues that Roethke proceeds on an "avenue to God," motivated by the realization that
"he is irrevocably separate, as long as he is alive, from the
simplicity of God's creation" (p. 8). Roethke's mind informs
him of his separateness, but at the same time it helps him to
"value" the things around him, "to conceive in them the infinite
presence of God" (p. 22). Roethke's project, then, is "to be
purely a soul and at one with his God" (p. 8). In order to accom-
plish that goal, McMichael argues, Roethke must work his way
toward God through the agency of mediators whose value "decreases
according to [their] similarity to the self" (p. 16). McMichael
bases his interpretation on the "North American Sequence," primarily, and he finds that animals, plants, the earth, water, the
air, and light serve as important mediators in that long poem. A
human being ranks rather low in this spirit-making hierarchy, but
it is perhaps more damaging to Roethke's purpose that McMichael
believes people function in his poetry, in his "journey out of
the self," simply as means to a personal spiritual end.

Dennis E. Brown resolves that problem in his analysis of the
"journey out of the self," "Theodore Roethke's 'Self-World' and
the Modernist Position," a statement more philosophical than theological. After grounding his discussion in the works of philos-
ophers F. H. Bradley, William James, and Henri Bergson, Brown
observes that criticism of Roethke's "journey out of the self"

hangs too much on an outmoded notion of the self as the subject term in the traditional subject/object dichotomy. He recommends seeing Roethke's "journey out of the self" (or "self-world," as he awkwardly phrases it) in five stages rather than in terms of flesh and spirit, self and other, man and God. Like McMichael, Brown is careful to point out that Roethke changes directions and uses radically different poetic forms; Brown's five stages "represent foci of interest" rather than a chronological progression because "Roethke's development is by progression and recoil" (p. 1243).

Brown characterizes the first of the five stages as the dramatization in Open House of the entrenched self, "the conventional Western ego at bay" (p. 1244). In the second stage, which Brown locates in the Greenhouse poems, the "embattled" ego of stage 1 begins to crumble; "through the agency . . . of both empathy and revulsion, the two poles of experience--self and not-self--are attracted together into a genuine self-world" (pp. 1245-46). As might be expected, the third stage, the "articulation of the self-world," occurs in the Lost Son narratives. In these poems, "even the cardinal subject-verb-object structure--the grammatical root of the old philosophical dichotomy--becomes, at times, quite abandoned or twisted into new shape. Such writing plunges the reader into the experiential real where things appear to breed language and language appears to invent things" (pp. 1246-47). Brown's fourth stage, the "dialectical realization of self-world in relation to other self-worlds," involves the new poems of Words for the Wind (p. 1243). Brown mentions the emergence of William Butler Yeats's voice in these poems, and, as others had and would do, Brown thinks the echoing of Yeats is but another manifestation of the self's relation to others. He says it creates an "I-Thou relationship in verse" (p. 1250). Whereas McMichael sees preparations for transition to spirit as the end of Roethke's journey, Brown concludes that love is the final permutation or dynamic of the evolving self. In his fifth stage, "the dramatic apotheosis of self-world in a transcendent whole" (p. 1243), Roethke discovers "poised relaxation: the self-world, complete with its properties and relations, may project the innocence of 'immediate experience' into the transcendent Absolute through the mystical power of love" (p. 1252).

Not all critics agree, of course, that the new poems of Words for the Wind advance Roethke's "journey out of the self" appreciably, or that they represent a significant departure from the egocentrism of the Lost Son narratives. Those unpersuaded by Roethke's efforts in the new poems, and in the Love Poems in particular, argue that the woman he represents remains, in the end, an indefinite, a composite, not a "personalized" other. W. D. Snodgrass focuses on that matter in his 1965 essay, " 'That Anguish of Concreteness': Theodore Roethke's Career." Snodgrass thinks Roethke's poetry is a "struggle against his own form," and he observes three major stages in that struggle: Roethke's identification with the smallest living forms (as in "The Minimal"), his regression into animal shapes (sloth, slug, bug), and his love of the woman (p. 86). From the first, Snodgrass was a staunch advocate of Roethke's experimental verse, but he objects especially to Roethke's performance in the last of the three stages he identifies because, he says, "the woman was not affirmed as herself, a person in her own right, but rather as a symbol of all being" (p. 86). That observation, as we have seen, is identical to that made by Mills and Malkoff, for example, but those defenders of Roethke's representation of the woman think it counts as a strength and not a weakness of the poems.

In his essay "Roethke's Broken Music," Denis Donoghue admits that the Love Poems served a useful purpose for Roethke. After the heady experimentation of the Lost Son narratives, the writing of the Love Poems helped to restore in Roethke's work the "principle of order," but Donoghue rejects the vision of love that Roethke discovers: "It never established itself as a relation beyond the bedroom. It never became dialogue, or caritas" (p. 149). The Love Poems are indeed more carnal than critics who want to spiritualize Theodore Roethke's vision will acknowledge, but Donoghue's conclusion that the Love Poems show how "distinctly underpopulated" is Roethke's universe (p. 14) is actually more persuasively argued by John Lucas in his essay, "The Poetry of Theodore Roethke." Lucas, like Donoghue, believes that Roethke does not celebrate humanity, but Lucas attributes that lack to Roethke's "fear of involvement which he saw that love demanded" (p. 54).

Roethke and the new poems come out better in Roy Harvey Pearce's discussion in "The Power of Sympathy." Pearce blames society for Roethke's inability to make the woman of his Love Poems come alive. Roethke's poetic vision encompassed a world which "was first I, then (from the minimal to God) thou--but not yet, as with Blake, he, she, or they," Pearce says (p. 198). Roethke could speak of the self, of creation, and of the cosmos, but he could not bring other persons into his poetry. According to Pearce, Roethke's inability reflects the sad spirit of the age, for "in our time, the world . . . is inhabited by third persons, fearing to be first, therefore unable to reach toward the second" (p. 198). Instead of finding a reason for the weakness of the new poems as Pearce does, Nathan A. Scott, Jr., finds a strength in that weakness in his book, The Wild Prayer of Longing: Poetry and the Sacred. According to Scott, Roethke did not see "high significance in the realm of what Martin Buber calls 'the inter-human.'. . . The ontological mystery was not for him a preeminently human mystery" (p. 106). Roethke's poetry is therefore less social in emphasis, Scott says, but that does not make Roethke's poetry any less profoundly religious.

Aware of the prevalence and persistence of the criticism and aware of how admirers of Roethke's poetry often qualify their appreciation of the new poems of Words for the Wind, James Dickey laments in his 1968 reminiscence of the poet that Roethke never wrote his "prizefighter poems, his gangster poems and tycoon poems" (p. 56). Those poems, Dickey implies, would have shown more dramatically Roethke's feeling for other people. By so saying, of course, Dickey himself admits that that "feeling" for others does not compellingly exist in the published poetry. Though Roethke's success in representing another person in the new poems of Words for the Wind is essential to the view that the "journey out of the self" organizes all of his poetry, we must conclude from their discussions that Roethke's defenders themselves are uneasy about how well Roethke met Kenneth Burke's standard of "personalization." Roethke's opponents, of course, have no such difficulty.

Love's Progress

Though Roethke's ability to "personalize" his poetry of the 1950s remains in doubt, there is little question that the new poems of Words for the Wind represent a change in subject matter for Roethke. In the "Shorter Poems, 1951-1953" at the end of The Waking and in the section of "Love Poems" in Words for the Wind, Roethke lifts his attention from the minimal objects of the physical and natural world; he looks up from the stones, ponds, and moles; he averts his glance from the memories leading him deeply into the residual imagery of his childhood; and finally he explores what it means to love a woman. Beyond the fact that Roethke addresses the subject of love and depicts its sometimes marvelous impact upon himself, he presents no conventional view of love in the new poems of Words for the Wind. Roethke does not take for his source of conflict a lover separated by time or space from his loved one, or prevented by family, social class, or political persuasion from consummating his love. The traditional obstacles to love, and thus the reasons for much love poetry throughout the centuries, do not motivate Roethke's poems. The major source of conflict in Roethke's love poetry is in the lover himself, and love for him is a dynamic emotional continuum.

The Love Poems depict the lover at various stages of that continuum. Love, for Roethke, begins with the woman and desire for her. As Roethke approaches her, as the distance between Roethke and the woman diminishes, however, he often experiences the resulting intimacy as a threat to the self. Thus, love is often represented in the poems as a dying, and the woman who inspires that loss is sometimes figured as death itself. Roethke does not always suffer the loss of self love implies, however. He reacts against what he perceives as a suffocating intimacy in order to protect himself, to save himself, for what he phrases as a higher spiritual goal. In so doing, though, he thwarts his desire which, at some point, will reawaken. Whether he loses himself and loves, or shields himself and does not, desire will begin again. The process will recommence, and Roethke will have to face the point of crisis yet again. Roethke presents his poems so that one gets the sense that all the trouble of love is worth it, but he offers little but a metaphysical release from the closed circle of the emotional continuum of love.

The widely anthologized poem, "I Knew a Woman," is perhaps the best and the best-known of the Love Poems, but it differs from the other fifteen poems in that it depicts a safer, more public, more conventional vision of love. If the other poems express what Roethke means by love, "I Knew a Woman" might better be termed a poem of flirtation. It nonetheless illuminates by virtue of its difference the more personal vision of love Roethke presents in the other poems in the section. "I Knew a Woman" has generated much discussion, particularly in the pages of the Explicator, a journal of close-reading. Virginia Peck offered the first reading of the poem in that journal in 1964. She argues that the poem presents contrasted views of life: the woman symbolizes "disorder, abandonment, vitality" while the man symbolizes "distaste for the banal, the prosaic, the conventional" (item 66). In 1966, Helen Buttel rejected Peck's notion of contrast, and read the poem as an "extravagant eulogy, an exuberant, though serious elegy." She bases her view on the fact that the title is in the past tense. Buttel concludes that the mourning speaker "continues to try to live, or dance, with all the freedom and grace she had taught him" (item 78). In the first of his two readings, Nat Henry suggests that the poem hinges on imagery derived from riding to hounds and from farming rather than from dancing. In his witty discussion of 1969, Henry sees more ribaldry and lustiness in the poem than do Peck or Buttel (item 31).

In his analysis of the poem in American Notes and Queries, Nicholas Ayo looks more closely at literary sources. Ayo acknowledges Henry's discussion of hunting dog imagery, but, aligning himself with Jenijoy La Belle's argument in The Echoing Wood of Theodore Roethke, he says that the source of the terms "Turn," "Counter-Turn," and "Stand" is Ben Jonson's "Pindaric Ode." Ayo identifies Jonson as the poet who "grew up on Greek" (p. 107). In 1979, Nat Henry responded with yet another item in the Explicator. He takes convincing issue with Ayo's and La Belle's view that "Turn," "Counter-Turn," and "Stand" derive from Jonson, and he reasserts his point that Roethke looks to the language of coursing. In the most recent installment on the subject of "I Knew a Woman," found in the pages of the Explicator, Dwight L. McCawley suggests that the woman of the poem is not a real woman but a "personified abstraction" for the Art of Poetry (p. 10).

There seems little reason to insist too much upon the obvious contrast between the man and woman in the poem, as Peck does,

and even less reason to think the poem is elegiac in tone, as Buttel argues. McCawley offers a coherent and consistent reading
to support his view, but he takes all of the fun out of the poem.
We miss much of the point and pleasure of "I Knew a Woman" if we
are blind to the double entendres of lines such as "She was the
sickle; I, poor I, the rake,/ Coming behind her for her pretty
sake/ (But what prodigious mowing we did make)" and "Love likes
a gander, and adores a goose" (CP, p. 127). As much as it echoes
more serious literature, as Ayo and La Belle say, the poem also
echoes popular song ("cheek to cheek"), and its real strength,
for the most part unnoticed, lies in the way Roethke maintains,
so uncharacteristically in a Roethke love poem, a playful but
self-deprecating tone.

Triple rhymes are repeated at the ends of each of the four seven-
line stanzas, and a parenthetical refrain concludes each stanza,
creating an internal chorus in the poem, a way of offering witty
asides: "Of her choice virtues only gods should speak,/ Or English
poets who grew up on Greek/ (I'd have them sing in chorus, cheek
to cheek)" (CP, p. 127). In addition, the speaker is apparently
older than the woman he addresses; some of the humor of the poem
evolves from the fact that the older, wiser one is student to her
beauty. (The poem, in this respect, has much the same context as
the "Elegy for Jane.") However, the speaker accepts his subor-
dinate role as attendant courtier, as trained pet ("I nibbled meek-
ly from her proffered hand" (CP, p. 127). He willingly, even glee-
fully, plays the role in deference to the woman's beauty; he also
knows the role reversal is temporary and part of the game. Thus,
when the poet announces in the concluding stanza, "I'm martyr to
a motion not my own," there is no reason to think he is really
suffering, or perhaps very seriously in love. If he were in any
danger of losing himself to the woman, as we learn in the other
Love Poems, he would not martyr himself so easily.

Unlike "I Knew a Woman," "Words for the Wind," the title poem
of the book, presents love as an emotional continuum. Its four
parts encompass the solitude, desire, point of crisis, and moment
of release more characteristic of Roethke's representation of love
in the section. The poem opens with a reminiscence of the woman's
effect on the man. In the third stanza, we read:

> Motion can keep me still:
> She kissed me out of thought
> As a lovely substance will;
> She wandered; I did not:
> I stayed, and light fell
> Across her pulsing throat;
> I stared, and a garden stone
> Slowly became the moon.
> [CP, p. 123]

In the first part of the poem, Roethke is at ease with his love: "All's even with the odd," he says, "My brother the vine is glad" (CP, p. 123). In the second part of the poem, and in some of the most beautiful writing in the Love Poems, Roethke says, "The sun declares the earth;/ The stones leap in the stream;/ On a wide plain, beyond/ The far stretch of a dream,/ A field breaks like the sea;/ The wind's white with her name,/ And I walk with the wind" (CP, p. 124). These lines are spoken in the absence of the loved one, it is important to note. She is mediated to the poet through nature and through his memory. In this blissful solitude, desire grows: "A fair thing grows more fair;/ The green, the springing green/ Makes an intenser day/ Under the rising moon;/ I smile, no mineral man;/ I bear, but not alone,/ The burden of this joy" (CP, p. 124). In the ambiguous word "burden" we may find both the poetic sense of "refrain" or "song," and the less complimentary sense of "load" or weight."

The calm of the first two parts of "Words for the Wind" is disturbed by the third section. Motivated by his desire, Roethke's emotion swells to an exciting point: "I get a step beyond/ The wind, and there I am,/ I'm odd and full of love." He seems aware that love can be dangerous, but he does not care: "What falls away will fall" (CP, p. 125). Among things to "fall," of course, is the isolation of the self. In the concluding stanza of the fourth section, Roethke meets what, in "I Knew a Woman," he calls the woman of "wanton ways" (CP, p. 127), and what John Keats called "La Belle Dame Sans Merci": "I kiss her moving mouth,/ Her swart hilarious skin;/ She breaks my breath in half;/ She frolicks like a beast" (CP, p. 126). Intensely sexual, partly animal, wholly overpowering, this woman is, in a sense, one-dimensional, a creature only, a desirable and desiring creature but, as Roethke says earlier, only "lovely substance" (CP, p. 123), beautiful material, body alone. She is not haunted by the ambivalence toward love that distresses Roethke. It may appear that Roethke thus dehumanizes and degrades her, but from his point of view he probably does not. By making her less human and more animal, Roethke's desire for her grows. He assimilates her to the intimacies of his Greenhouse worldview, and he can therefore more easily approach her.

There is an intimation of violence, however, of ravishment, which Roethke includes in his description of love. "Words for the Wind" concludes with a hint that Roethke's experience has not been entirely pleasurable: "And I dance round and round,/ A fond and foolish man,/ And see and suffer myself/ In another being, at last" (CP, p. 126). The intentional ambiguity of the word "suffer" requires us to add to its sense of "allow" its more prevalent meaning, "to undergo pain." However, that element does not dominate "Words for the Wind." We are probably to take it that the ease after love of part 1 of the poem will follow naturally after part 4, and thus a perfect circle of desire and love and desire is composed.

Roethke has another reaction to the intimacy of love, however. Love can violate his sense of privacy, his sense of self, and claustrophobia is the result, best illustrated in "The Sensualists." Roethke apparently wants to indicate that this view of love is different from that in the other Love Poems. By using quotation marks, he puts words into other people's mouths, and by naming the poem "The Sensualists," he separates their experience from his own. At the outset of the poem, a woman alludes to the negative aspect of intimacy:

> "There is no place to turn," she said,
> "You have me pinned so close;
> My hair's all tangled on your head,
> My back is just one bruise;
> I feel we're breathing with the dead;
> O angel, let me loose!"
>   [CP, p. 136]

Charles Sanders also notes this discomfort in his discussion of "The Sensualists" in 1980, but his aim is to account for the strange "ghostly figure" watching the couple in their "sensual pen." Basing his reading on Coburn Freer's Prodical Son motif, Sanders thinks this figure, "wrapped in the tattered robe of death," is a muse who "withdraws its 'inspiration.'" The deflating concluding lines, "then each fell back, limp as a sack,/ Into the world of men," signal the "dreaded loss of one's 'inheritance' of poetic inspiration" (p. 10). In the later Love Poem, "The Swan," Sanders thinks the "inheritance" of inspiration is restored to Roethke when " 'father' and 'poet' " are brought together in the line, "I am my father's son, I am John Donne" (p. 10). "The Swan," a poem in the "mature Roethkean mode," Sanders finds a "union with not one, but at least two, possibly three poets," John Donne, William Butler Yeats, and Wallace Stevens, as well as a "union with woman in the flesh" (p. 27).

In her book, Theodore Roethke: The Garden Master, Rosemary Sullivan argues that the excess of intimacy can prepare Roethke for what he calls "the pure fury," the experience she thinks is at the center of the Love Poems (p. 104). The third stanza of "The Pure Fury" displays the essence of the claustrophobic vision:

> How terrible the need for solitude:
> That appetite for life so ravenous
> A man's a beast prowling in his own house,
> A beast with fangs, and out for his own blood
> Until he finds the thing he almost was
> When the pure fury first raged in his head
> And trees came closer with a denser shade.
>   [CP, p. 133]

In addition to his poem devoted to the subject, Roethke describes the "pure fury" in two of his prose pieces. In his essay "On 'Identity' " he says it involves "a very sharp sense of . . . the identity of some other being . . . [it] brings a corresponding heightening and awareness of one's own self, and, even more mysteriously, in some instances, a feeling of the oneness of the universe" (SP, p. 25). According to Roethke's description in his essay "On 'In a Dark Time,' " however, the "pure fury" "is either a total loss of consciousness--symbolical or literal death-- or a quick break into another state, not necessarily serene, but frequently a bright blaze of consciousness" (p. 52). The "pure fury" that can inaugurate love is full of risk, in other words, and Roethke's ambivalence toward that risk permeates the Love Poems of Words for the Wind. This is nowhere clearer than in the concluding stanza of "The Pure Fury" where Roethke equates love with death:

> Dream of a woman, and a dream of death:
> The light air takes my being's breath away;
> I look on white, and it turns into gray--
> When will that creature give me back my breath?
> I live near the abyss. I hope to stay
> Until my eyes look at a brighter sun
> As the thick shade of the long night comes on.
>   [CP, p. 134]

"The Renewal," the poem that follows "The Pure Fury," indicates one of the possible effects of taking the risks of love. Roethke asks, "Will the self, lost, be found again? In form?"; and though he gets no answer in this poem, the alternative of solitude is so intolerable that he ignores his worries about the self's reconstitution:

> Dry bones! Dry bones! I find my loving heart,
> Illumination brought to such a pitch
> I see the rubblestones begin to stretch
> As if reality had split apart
> And the whole motion of the soul lay bare:
> I find that love, and I am everywhere.
>   [CP, p. 135]

"The Renewal" concludes at this point, as well it must to merit its title, but the desire for love must emerge again, inevitably. It is possible that the "pure fury" will then result in the circumstance of "The Sensualists," the poem that follows "The Renewal." According to Roethke, though, that is one of the risks of love.

The success or failure of the Love Poems has commanded much attention in discussions of the new poems of Words for the Wind, as we have seen. Resolution of that issue is complicated by the fact that one of Roethke's points seems to be that we ourselves fail love at least part of the time. Loving another person in the world of these poems is no easy matter, it is clear. In that respect, perhaps Roy Harvey Pearce is right to suggest in "The Power of Sympathy" that Roethke has answered obliquely the charge that the scope of his poetry is insufficiently large. By showing in detail the challenge that love offers, Roethke has made a comment that has implications for other lives. The Love Poems of Theodore Roethke do not present love or a lover as we have come to expect them in poetry, but they honestly depict the risks and rewards of love in an age beset by alienation and self-involvement.

The difficulty of love is taken up elsewhere in the new poems of Words for the Wind, in the surprising context of the section called "Voices and Creatures" that follows the love poetry. This section contains poems addressed to minimal creatures. It does not advance Roethke's attempt to bring other persons into his poetry, but one of the best poems in the section, "Slug," dramatically reiterates the problem of the Love Poems, Roethke's sense of ambivalence before love. In his description of the contents of Words for the Wind, Roethke said that "Slug" is among those poems that depict a "running away" (SP, p. 58). After seeing the way Roethke presents love in the Love Poems, it is consistent that "Slug" concerns "running away" from adulthood and sexuality. With all of the attention devoted to the subject of love in Roethke's poetry, however, "Slug" has not engaged Roethke's critics, with the exception of a brief comment or mention. The poem does share similarities with later poems such as "The Lizard" and "The Meadow Mouse" from The Far Field, with earlier ones such as "The Heron" and "The Bat" of Open House, and with some of the Greenhouse poems. A "minimal" in these instances has inspired extended and detailed description, but such poems are more than representation. They reveal the poet. Frequently his feeling for his subject, as in "The Meadow Mouse," resembles love. In contrast to his responses to other creatures, however, the slug arouses Roethke's anxiety, anger, and disgust.

In the first line of "Slug," Roethke establishes two situations, one past and one present. The poet's introductory address of the slug quickly gives way to a childhood memory:

> How I loved one like you when I was little!--
> With his stripes of silver and his small house on his
>   back,
> Making a slow journey around the well-curb.
> I longed to be like him, and was,
> In my way, close cousin
> To the dirt, my knees scrubbing
> The gravel, my nose wetter than his.
>   [CP, p. 151]

The connection between past and present is not exact, however. The child saw a snail, not a slug, and he liked that snail because of its bright appearance and because of its shell, its "small house." The security it carries on its back has a special appeal for the child; he takes pleasure in identifying with the snail.

The first verb we find in the second paragraph of the poem is "slip": "When I slip, just slightly, in the dark,/ I know it isn't a wet leaf,/ But you, loose toe from the old life" (CP, p. 151). In the second paragraph, Roethke moves from past to present, from child to adult, and from snail to slug, and anxiety begins. Something else has changed: the slug is not an object for childlike wonderment anymore. It is a nuisance, a "cold slime come into being. . . . Eating the heart out of my garden" (CP, p. 151). In paragraph one, the slug was a focus for wonder and envy; in the second paragraph it has focused Roethke's dislike.

The symmetrical contrasts between the first two paragraphs are broken by paragraph three. The first paragraph is childhood past; the second paragraph is adulthood present; the third is a mixture of past, present, and future. To correspond with the disorganization of time, the grammar of the paragraph's sentence is jumbled and indistinct. The language itself is strained, even dismembered, because "you refuse to die decently!--/ Flying upward through the knives of my lawnmower/ Like pieces of smoked eel or raw oyster,/ And I go faster in my rage to get done with it." The poet's rage dominates this portion of the poem until "You shrink to something less,/ A rain-drenched fly or spider" (CP, p. 151).

On its surface, "Slug" presents a contrast between a wide-eyed child and an obsessive adult, but Roethke widens the reference of the poem with a well-known biblical allusion and with a complex of sexual imagery. In so doing, he makes "Slug" both useful and important for understanding his attitude toward love. The slug, of course, might be equated with the biblical serpent that infected the first garden, the Garden of Eden. It then becomes increasingly significant that the contemporary reminder of the biblical serpent, the slug, devils the poet's foot: "Until I'm scraping and scratching at you, on the doormat,/ The small dead pieces sticking under an instep." Such reminder is foretold in God's curse on the serpent in Genesis 3: "he [Adam, man] shall bruise your head, and you shall bruise his heel." While the biblical allusion may be remote, though relevant, it is impossible to miss the phallic imagery in the poem. The "fat, five-inch appendage," the "white skein of spittle" the slug drags, the references to the smoked eel and the aphrodisiac raw oyster, all reinforce an equation of penis and slug. This makes the killing of the slug with the "knives of my lawnmower" all the more terrible, of course. Out of his frustration at being unable to return to his childhood innocence, he resorts to obliterating this symbol of his manhood.

Roethke makes it clear in the conclusion of the poem that his ha-

tred of the slug has little to do with its danger to his garden as
such. Roethke has made peace with other pests:

> With bats, weasels, worms--I rejoice in the kinship.
> Even the caterpillar I can love, and the various
>   vermin.
> But as for you, most odious--
> Would Blake call you holy?

[CP, p. 151]

The poem offers no reconciliation with the slug, however, no indication of Roethke's coming to terms with what it represents. In
the "Proverbs of Hell," Blake wrote that "the cut worm forgives
the plow," so the answer to Roethke's question is yes. It is interesting, though, that Roethke does not provide that answer himself. He does not push his feelings toward a "pure fury." In fact,
to avoid going further to resolve the issue he has raised, Roethke calls upon a poet he would acknowledge as a "father," William
Blake.   Such an appeal is related to Roethke's flight from an
earthly intimacy and his occasional recourse to God in the Love
Poems; in "Slug," it indicates his unwillingness to take on the
risks of adulthood and sex.
    Though the vision of "Words for the Wind" represents Roethke's
comparative ease with the course of love's progress, other poems
in <u>Words for the Wind</u> complicate that view. Love does not always
or only satisfy desire; it encroaches upon the self's privacy, too,
and Roethke reacts against that. As a justification for this response, he suggests that his solitude seeks other ends. In "Plaint,"
for example, he seeks metaphysical release: "Where is the knowledge that/ Could bring me to my God?" (CP, p. 139). Instead of
being a resolution of the problem of love, however, Roethke's
notion that the self must remain intact in order to reach God is
a limitation and a rationalization. It also lessens the value of
loving other human beings, for in the progress toward God, other
people are obstacles. More importantly for Roethke as a poet,
seeking refuge in some spiritual realm creates additional conflict
in an already contentious self. In the love poetry, Roethke's
central desire is for the woman, not for God. The metaphysical
motion that Roethke occasionally offers as relief from that desire,
and that some critics have been persuaded by, actually contorts
and misdirects his poetic vision. It takes him afield from what
he does best, write poems about things of the flesh and the earth.

The Influence of W. B. Yeats

As we have seen, some critics think the theme of love links
the Lost Son narratives to the new poems of <u>Words for the Wind.</u>

The sharp stylistic difference between the two works is more prominent, however, and next to the issue of "personalization," a second
point of contention about the new poems of Words for the Wind is
Roethke's return to a conventional poetic form and his practice,
in so doing, of using the voice and style of William Butler Yeats.
Roethke's choice of Yeats as new "father" to his verse was an un-
welcome surprise to a number of critics. After publication of the
Lost Son narratives, Theodore Roethke was numbered among the most
innovative of poets in American verse, but in 1953, and especially
with the poem "Four for Sir John Davies," he lost that status
and appeared to become a more traditional poet who embraced the
regularities of meter and rhyme. According to a number of critics
and reviewers, Roethke's poems in a "Yeatsian mode" betrayed that
experimental spirit he voiced so dramatically in the narrative poems. Others, however, saw that some return to traditional form
was useful, even necessary, for Theodore Roethke. Defenders of
Roethke's most formal poetry have gone on to show that key differences separate the poetic visions and styles of Yeats and Roethke,
and that Roethke's use of Yeats is an additional result of his effort to "personalize" his poetry.

    Obviously, Roethke could not hide the fact that his new poems
rhymed and were metered, but he could have tried to disguise the
fact that Yeats was the important inspiration behind his new direction. He did not, however, and in fact he clearly acknowledges
his debt to Yeats in both his prose and his poetry. The poem
in which Roethke first names and most exemplifies his use of Yeats
is "The Dance," the first poem in "Four for Sir John Davies,"
published in the section of "Shorter Poems, 1951-1953" at the end
of The Waking. (Additional mention of Yeats appears, of course,
in "The Dying Man," the elegy dedicated to the Irish poet.) In
the third stanza of "The Dance," the speaker says, "I tried to
fling my shadow at the moon,/ The while my blood leaped with a
wordless song./ Though dancing needs a master, I had none/ To
teach my toes to listen to my tongue" (CP, p. 105). In the fourth
and final stanza of "The Dance," Roethke names his dancing-master:

> I take this cadence from a man named Yeats;
> I take it, and I give it back again:
> For other tunes and other wanton beats
> Have tossed my heart and fiddled through my brain.
> Yes, I was dancing-mad, and how
> That came to be the bears and Yeats would know.
>   [CP, p. 105]

In his 1959 essay, "How to Write like Somebody Else," Roethke
quotes "The Dance" as an example of "possibly, an influence sur-
vived" and then he adds, "Oddly enough, the line 'I take this cadence, etc.' is, in a sense, a fib. I had been reading deeply in
Ralegh, and in Sir John Davies; and they rather than Willie are

the true ghosts in that piece" (SP, pp. 68-69). In 1963, in his essay, "On 'Identity,' " Roethke mentions again the names of Ralegh and Davies but, in describing the circumstances behind composition of the poem, he gives compelling reason to credit the influence of Yeats:

> I was in that particular hell of the poet: a longish dry period. It was 1952, I was 44, and I thought I was done. I was living alone in a biggish house in Edmonds, Washington. I had been reading--and re-reading--not Yeats, but Ralegh and Sir John Davies. I had been teaching the five-beat line for weeks--I knew quite a bit about it, but write it myself?--<u>no</u>: so I felt myself a fraud.
>
> Suddenly, in the early evening, the poem "The Dance" started, and finished itself in a very short time--say thirty minutes, maybe in the greater part of an hour, it was all done. I felt, I <u>knew</u>, I had hit it. I walked around, and I wept; and I knelt <u>down</u>--I always do after I've written what I know is a good piece. But at the same time I had, as God is my witness, the actual sense of a Presence--as if Yeats himself were <u>in</u> that room. The experience was in a way terrifying, for it lasted at least half an hour. That house, I repeat, was charged with a psychic presence: the very walls seemed to shimmer. I wept for joy. At last I was somebody again. He, they--the poets dead--were with me.
>
> Now I know there are any number of cynical explanations for this phenomenon: auto-suggestion, the unconscious playing an elaborate trick, and so on, but I accept none of them. It was one of the most profound experiences of my life. [SP, pp. 23-24]

In Roethke's experience of the presence of Yeats, Jerome Mazzaro notes that psychoanalyst Carl Jung would see an "endopsychic automatism." Such "personified thoughts come often in the shapes of sagacious and helpful old men," Mazzaro says, and they "appear in hopeless and desperate situations from which only profound reflection or a lucky idea, compensating the deficiency, can extricate the self" (p. 81). It is interesting that experiences like the one Roethke reports have precedent enough to merit a name; Roethke seems also to have been aware of this. He does not fit his experience into an occult or mystical tradition, however. Rather, he mentions the spectral appearance of Yeats in order to illustrate a theoretical discussion of how to achieve an authentic poetic voice.

As preface to his anecdote about Yeats's ghost, Roethke writes, "in any quest for identity today--or any day--we run up inevitably against this problem: What to do with our ancestors? I mean it as an ambiguity: both the literal or blood, and the spiritual ancestors. Both, as we know, can overwhelm us. The devouring mother, the furious papa. And if we're trying to write, the Supreme Masters" (SP, p. 23). Roethke provides a practical answer to his question in his earlier essay, "How to Write like Somebody Else." There, he observes that "imitation, conscious imitation, is one of the great methods, perhaps the method of learning to write. The ancients, the Elizabethans, knew this, profited by it, and were not disturbed. . . . The final triumph is what the language does, not what the poet can do, or display. The poet's ultimate loyalty . . . is to the poem" (SP, p. 69). In the last lines of his paragraph on imitation, Roethke sounds still more like the T. S. Eliot of the influential essay, "Tradition and the Individual Talent": "If a writer has something to say, it will come through. The very fact he has the support of a tradition, or an older writer, will enable him to be more himself--or more than himself" (SP, p. 69). (Jenijoy La Belle has noticed the connection between Roethke's notion of imitation and Eliot's notion of tradition, and in The Echoing Wood of Theodore Roethke she points out interesting comparisons between Eliot's essay, "The Music of Poetry" and Roethke's "How to Write like Somebody Else" [p. 22].) At the conclusion of "How to Write like Somebody Else," Roethke indicates he realizes his discussion can play into the hands of his opponents. He says, "I should like to think that I have over-acknowledged, in one way and another, my debt to Yeats" (SP, p. 70), and on this point, Roethke is surely correct. Roethke's use of the name and style of Yeats in his poetry and his theoretical defense of that practice are also important evidence for those who think Yeats looms too largely in Roethke's new poetry of the 1950s.

The extent of the reaction against Roethke's "Yeatsian mode" was considerable, as we have seen in some of the reviews of Words for the Wind. In a number of the discussions of these poems, however, sorrow rather than anger or outrage is the dominant tone. That is nowhere more evident than in W. D. Snodgrass's 1965 essay, " 'That Anguish of Concreteness': Theodore Roethke's Career." Snodgrass detected in the "Meditations of an Old Woman" "as much power and authority as any formal verse" (p. 83), and he saw T. S. Eliot, not W. B. Yeats, as the "papa" behind the "Meditations," a long poem that actually bears more resemblance to the later "North American Sequence" than to the "Shorter Poems, 1951-1953" or to the Love Poems of Words for the Wind. Snodgrass conceded also that it was understandable for Roethke to "step back and regather his forces" after the experimentation of the narrative poems, but the new poems of Words for the Wind were a "shock" (p. 81). Snodgrass was distressed that "Roethke, who had invented the most raw and original voice of all our period, was now writing in the voice of another man, and that, perhaps, the most formal and elegant voice of the period" (p. 82). Glauco Cambon's remarks in Recent American Poetry help put Snodgrass's reaction into context. Snodgrass's own poetry is "unashamedly

autobiographical," Cambon says, and he finds it a "gesture of courage in a cultural milieu overshadowed by Eliot's recomendation of
impersonality" (p. 24). Though not the first to have problems
with Roethke's reversion to formal verse, W. D. Snodgrass perhaps
epitomizes the sense of deflation many younger poets and critics
felt upon the appearance of Roethke's "Yeatsian mode." According
to Snodgrass, Roethke "managed to sum up in his work this culture's
war against form and even to advance that attack several steps
further than anyone in his art had previously done. . . . He
also summed up, in his ensuing flight from his own experimental
drive, our peculiar inability to capitalize on our astounding
achievements--our flight from freedom of form, our flight from
the accesses of power which we have released" (p. 78).

In his 1965 essay, "The Monocle of My Sea-Faced Uncle," John
Wain agrees with W. D. Snodgrass's evaluation, but he thinks the
weakness of the new poems of Words for the Wind is attributable
to a quality that at other times is Roethke's major strength.
Roethke had the rare gift of a "spontaneous outflowing of his
imagination into anything he contemplated," Wain says, and that
is evident in the Greenhouse poems and the Lost Son narratives.
At the same time, however, Roethke was always in danger of "becoming" the voice of the poems he admired, and that happened in
his later poetry: "Roethke gave himself utterly to the poems he
loved, and in return they claimed him and exacted their tribute
from his gift" (p. 70). In her book, Theodore Roethke: The Garden Master, Rosemary Sullivan supports Wain's observation. Her
review of Roethke's unpublished notebooks reveals he handcopied
many of the poems that he liked, and this "habit made him peril-
ously susceptible to assimilating the rhythms of other poets,"
Sullivan says (p. 95).

William Meredith believes also that the "rhetorical identity
of Yeats . . . is stronger than the sensible identity, the identity
of sensibility, of Roethke" in the later poems, but he argues that
Roethke's relationship to the "great dead" was not so cordial as
Roethke sometimes suggests in his essays. In his essay, "A Steady
Storm of Correspondences: Theodore Roethke's Long Journey Out
of the Self," Meredith says Roethke competed with William Butler
Yeats, and he finds that incredible, indicative especially of
Roethke's unsettled, competitive spirit, and in the end, his big
mistake. Meredith concludes that "it is hard to think of another
instance where a first-rate poet engages so personally and in maturity a talent greater than his own" (p. 51).

Denis Donoghue stresses also the competition between Roethke
and Yeats in his essay "Roethke's Broken Music." Donoghue agrees
with Meredith that Roethke lost the battle, but more importantly
Donoghue thinks Roethke's need to fight that battle distorted his
poetry. It made him write as he would not have otherwise. For
example, Donoghue says Roethke claimed an "autumnal calm . . .
without really earning it" in "Meditations of an Old Woman" (pp.

140-41). He "tried too hard to be serene"; when that serenity
would not come naturally, he resorted to the resolutions Yeats
(or Wallace Stevens) had come to, and "dressed himself in affirmative robes" (pp. 141-42). Robert Phillips restates Donoghue's
point in a different way in his book, The Confessional Poets: "in
wanting so desperately to achieve . . . an epiphany or illumination, Roethke concludes poem after poem with a description of
a mystic or spiritual event. It is a bit like a whore claiming to
have an orgasm with each new customer" (p. 127). A bit, one wants
to say, but not a lot.

In his book, "The Edge Is What I Have," Harry Williams refers
the problem of the new poems of Words for the Wind to a more general difficulty in Roethke's work. Williams argues that Roethke's
poetry suffers when he commits himself to any established form at
all. Williams thinks Roethke's strength is in the more spontaneous
approach to experience that open verse affords; he likes especially those poems that present the "unfolding of an idea or mood"
(p. 135). For that reason, the "seeming lack of argument and
definition of character" in "Meditations of an Old Woman" is its
major "achievement, its success" because it helps "dramatize the
woman's animistic sensibility" (p. 76). In the less successful
Yeatsian poems, however, Roethke loses his spontaneity in the pre-
established form and he "states more than dramatizes the argument"
(p. 139). In fact, however, Williams's objections and preferences
are not based entirely on formal matters alone, for he finds the
proverbs and aphorisms of "The Lost Son" very effective. The
diminution of impact he detects in some of the later poems, therefore, cannot be attributed only to Roethke's use of established
forms.

Other critics who are in general favorably disposed to Roethke's
return to the formal poem have suggested that Roethke's turning
to predictable and thus more manageable meter and rhyme may have
been a means of gaining control over language he had daringly and
dangerously liberated in the narrative poems. In "News of the
Root," his review of The Lost Son and Other Poems, Stanley Kunitz actually predicted such a return by saying, "it would seem that
Roethke has reached the limits of exploration in this direction,
that the next step beyond must be either silence or gibberish" (p.
86). The two choices Kunitz offered did not exhaust the possibi-
ities, of course. Roethke published the infancy narratives in 1951,
but Kunitz did sense rightly that the energy of Roethke's "experimental drive," to use W. D. Snodgrass's phrase, could not last indefinitely.

Ralph J. Mills, Jr., reiterates Kunitz's rationale for Roethke's
use of Yeats in his 1963 book, Theodore Roethke. "With his sequence finished," Mills says, Roethke "could no longer exercise
the devices he employed there: that vein was thoroughly mined and
could only be kept open at the risk of repetition, boredom, and
stultification" (p. 30). Like Babette Deutsche (p. 199) and

John Crowe Ransom (p. 29), Mills is less convinced than some others that Roethke's own voice is overpowered by that of Yeats. He admits that Roethke's "use of cadences" in "Four for Sir John Davies" and in "The Dying Man" is "somewhat reminiscent of those in the poetry of Yeats," but he thinks "these are intentional effects on Roethke's part" (p. 30).

In his essay in the <u>Hudson Review</u>, "Poetry's Debt to Poetry," poet Richard Wilbur cites three specific things that Roethke got from Yeats: the "muscular" pentameter line, a "ruggedly vatic style in which such words as 'soul' could sound convincing and modern," and a "physical mysticism of the dancing body and of the marriage-bed" (p. 280). (At the end of his essay, "How to Write like Somebody Else," Roethke observed that "in the pentameter, I end-stop almost every line"; he says this is "an important technical difference" between his work and that of Yeats [SP, p. 70].) Such borrowings were justifiable in Wilbur's opinion, however, because Roethke's use of Yeats "kept him talking . . . limbered, emboldened and extended him, so that he became capable of those last poems which are better than ever and so much more his own" (p. 280).

There are indeed important stylistic and thematic differences between Roethke and the poets he echoes in his new poems of the 1950s. Though he argues that the influence of Yeats and Eliot damaged Roethke's new poems, poet John Berryman helps identify Roethke's uniqueness by contrasting his work with that of Robert Lowell. In "From the Middle and Senior Generations," his review of <u>Words for the Wind</u>, Berryman finds Lowell to be "Latinate, formal, rhetorical, massive, historical, religious, impersonal" while he finds Roethke "Teutonic, irregular, colloquial, delicate, botanical and psychological, irreligious, personal"; Lowell is a "poet of completed states" while Roethke is a "poet of process" (p. 384). Berryman does not make the connection, but most of the adjectives he applies to Lowell would fit T. S. Eliot, and some of them would fit W. B. Yeats.

According to poet Delmore Schwartz, Roethke appropriated Yeats's manner "to guard against the deadly habit of self-imitation which has paralyzed some of the best poets in English" (p. 204). Roethke is not only different from himself but different from Yeats, Schwartz says in his review of <u>Words for the Wind</u>. By comparing Roethke's "The Pure Fury" to Yeats's "Among School Children," Schwartz concludes that Yeats is "full of a <u>contemptus mundi</u>, a scorn of nature, a detestation of history" while Roethke is "capable of far greater affirmation" (p. 205), a point Frederick Hoffman picks up in his essay, "Theodore Roethke: The Poetic Shape of Death." Hoffman notes that the speaker of "The Dying Man" "sees dying as a continual becoming" and "thus Roethke is a poet who finds it unimaginable to rest with any large denial of life" (pp. 108-9). Daniel Liberthson pushes this distinction between Roethke and Yeats a little further in his book, <u>The Quest</u>

for Being: Theodore Roethke, W. S. Merwin, and Ted Hughes. Roethke refuses to reject the world of nature, Liberthson says, while
Yeats does reject the "natural tumult," the "mackerel-crowded
seas." For Liberthson, Roethke's "The Dying Man" "is an acceptance of 'death's possibilities,' while 'Sailing to Byzantium'
denies them" (p. 36).

In his discussion, "The Yeats Influence: Roethke's Formal Lyrics
of the Fifties," William Heyen makes still more distinctions between and observations about Roethke and Yeats. He notes that
Roethke shows most interest in the later Yeats, not the Yeats of
the Celtic Twilight (p. 20); he says that Roethke did not have a
native folklore or myth or a pressing political circumstance to
rely on (the latter is a point some critics would vehemently dis-
pute) (p. 21); he notes that Yeats turned toward the social sphere
while Roethke turned inward (p. 24); and he concludes that Roethke
is essentially a happier and more affirmative poet than Yeats on
the whole, but "Roethke's joy, when finally attained, is less complicated, less philosophical" (p. 28). Despite the differences he
can find between Roethke and Yeats, however, and the potential
they afford for a defense of Roethke's later poems, William Heyen
concludes that "the greatest number of Roethke's formal lyrics are
forced" (p. 55). He accounts for what he calls Roethke's occasional successes in that mode by suggesting, rather weakly, that they
are "literally, inspired performances" (p. 55).

The most comprehensive and detailed discussion of poetic influence
in Roethke's poetry, and the most extended defense of Roethke's
use of literary predecessors in the new poems of the 1950s, appears
in Jenijoy La Belle's book, The Echoing Wood of Theodore Roethke. According to La Belle, the Love Poems in particular indicate
Roethke's attempt to break the limitations of the isolated self,
and in this respect they are an important part of his "journey out
of the self." In La Belle's opinion, that journey is a successful venture because in the Love Poems Roethke's "response to the
woman he loves is simultaneously a response to the poets he loves"
(p. 117). Thus, La Belle concedes that the Love Poems do not succeed as love poetry in any conventional sense. She admits that
the woman of the poems is not rendered as a significant other;
Roethke does "personalize" his poetry, however, in that the persons he brings into his love poetry are other poets: "the significant creative 'lover' is the poet (or poets) with whom Roethke
has joined" (p. 125).

La Belle supports her view with an exhaustive examination of
sources of and allusions in specific poems. For example, in the
poem Roethke addresses to the sixteenth-century poet Sir John
Davies, contemporary of Shakespeare and author of two philosophical poems, Orchestra and Nosce Teipsum, La Belle finds connections to Davies and Yeats, of course, but also to Shakespeare,
Dante, and Pope (pp. 109-17). These poets were important for
Roethke, La Belle says, because they embody a "tradition of poe-

try in which contraries are harmonized" (p. 116), and that is the essential theme of the poem itself (p. 110). In fact, the poem is more than an anthology of voices, La Belle takes pains to point out; it is "at once a poem and a concept of tradition" (p. 116). Using similar method, La Belle shows that the sources of the poem "I Knew a Woman" may include authors as diverse as St. Augustine, Donne, Drummond, Jonson, Marvell, D. H. Lawrence, and Yeats. As in "Four for Sir John Davies," according to La Belle, Roethke "functions as both critic and poet" (p. 125). "I Knew a Woman" is Roethke's own "continuation of metaphysical wit." He orchestrates a selected group of poets, a personal literary tradition of sorts, whose voices in the poem actually "sing in chorus, cheek to cheek" (p. 125).

Throughout The Echoing Wood of Theodore Roethke, La Belle stresses that Roethke is aware of how and why he uses his literary ancestors. She insists on the point in discussing Roethke's use of quoted material in the titles for some of his Lost. Son narratives, for example, and she does so again in discussing his construction of a tradition in the new poems of Words for the Wind. At the same time, however, La Belle wants to preserve the intuitive qualities of Roethke's methods; she does not want to represent him as an allusive poet. Roethke himself rejected the allusive method quite explicitly in his "Open Letter," as we have seen, and in "How to Write like Somebody Else," Roethke dismissed what he called the "referential poem, or less charitably, the poem which is an anthology of other men's effects" (SP, p. 62). Indeed, Roethke alludes to other poets sparingly. Some of the titles of his infancy narrative poems allude to other poets, he mentions the name of poet John Davies in "Four for Sir John Davies," he names Yeats in that same poem, he mentions Whitman in the "North American Sequence," and he wants to rank himself with Blake, Christopher Smart, and John Clare in the poem, "Heard in a Violent Ward." But one would not call Roethke an allusive poet in the sense that T. S. Eliot and Ezra Pound were allusive poets, nor was Roethke an academic poet, one who "polishes the surface of old conventions," as Ralph J. Mills, Jr., puts it in Theodore Roethke (p. 6).

Later in her book, however, La Belle argues that Roethke's conscious use of literary sources eventually became "virtually subconscious" (p. 165). In his later poetry, especially in his major sequences, La Belle thinks that "the techniques and images learned over many years of reading became as much a part of his memory as his personal non-literary experience, so that eventually there was no division in his mind between the two" (p. 165). Though an arguable point, and one that could doubtless be made about anyone, La Belle here plays into the hands of Roethke's opponents. Since he could not tell differences between the voices of others and his own, it might be said, Roethke was all the more susceptible to being overpowered by those unheard, remembered voices, because his own voice was, in comparison to theirs, less forceful. La Belle does

not lend weight to her view by citing Roethke's experience of
Yeats's presence while he was writing "The Dance," nor does adding
that Roethke's "sense of tradition was an emotional attitude in-
volving his whole psychological condition" strengthen her argument
(p. 166). Though the point is probably only partially true, La
Belle is strongest in arguing that Roethke's use of his literary
predecessors was systematic, an act of criticism, utterly conscious.

La Belle's analysis is a worthy response to much discussion of
influences in Roethke's poetry that amounts to little more than
assertion and counter-assertion, but one of her own assertions requires clarification. La Belle writes that "for Roethke, writing
poetry was like making love: it was an activity requiring a partner.
All of his poems are literary love-children, the issue of a union
between Roethke's own vision and the work of other poets whom he
admired" (p. 117). Other critics, of course, have disagreed with
that vision of Roethke's relation to other poets. In his essay,
"Poet of Transformation," Stanley Kunitz notes Roethke's "arro-
gant usurpation of the Yeatsian beat" (p. 103), and Roethke himself says in "How to Write like Somebody Else" that an inevitable
result of the imitative method is that "One dares to stand up to
a great style, to compete with papa" (SP, p. 70). Oddly enough,
La Belle agrees: "Roethke not only draws upon the poets in his
tradition for images and themes, he also continually struggles to
outdo these other poets" (p. 120). Thus, she herself denies that
Roethke's relationship to his literary predecessors was a matter
of love exclusively. He honored his ancestors, yes, but he competed with them also.

Richard Blessing focuses on the ambivalent quality of Roethke's
relationship with his literary predecessors in his book, Theodore
Roethke's Dynamic Vision, and he accounts for it by distinguishing between what he calls "mother" and "father" form. Blessing
argues that form functioned as "mother" for Roethke in Open House,
as a "comforting womb-like space capable of bearing imaginative
life which he could not otherwise have conceived" (p. 157). He
observes also that the "predominantly feminine forms" Roethke
used in Open House were perfected by "poetic mothers," by Dickinson, Wylie, Bogan, and Adams (p. 157). In his later poetry,
Blessing says, Roethke "no longer conceals his use of the technical devices of others; indeed, he insists that his reader be aware
of them, that the reader be the judge of whether or not he has
given back more than he has taken . . . while working within the
framework of a stanzaic form and metrical pattern that once be-
longed to Papa" (pp. 158-59). Where Roethke's early use of forms
is a matter of love, his later appropriation of form is a matter
of hate, according to Blessing, "a defiant act and a courageous
one" (p. 158).

Concealment and disclosure do distinguish Roethke's uses of
poetic forms in Open House and in the new poems of Words for
the Wind, and Blessing is also correct that the references in

"Four for Sir John Davies" and in "The Dying Man" direct us to
Papa Yeats. The forms of those poems can direct us elsewhere,
however, as Blessing himself shows. Roethke does achieve "enormous compression" by using repetition in the Love Poems, and he
does increase velocity of lines in those poems by using monosyllabic
rather than polysyllabic words (pp. 177-79), but Blessing also convincingly argues that the poems of Open House and the Love Poems
of Words for the Wind share the three-beat line (p. 176). In that
significant respect, then, the Yeatsian poems and the poems of
Open House are formally similar. A mother and a father form, therefore, are not so clearly distinguishable, but Blessing is correct
to show Roethke uses his literary predecessors more confidently in
his later than in his earlier poetry.
    Despite the number, reputation, and effort of those who have ral-
lied to defense of the new poems of Words for the Wind, the argument that Roethke made a mistake in turning to the traditional lyric and the voice of Yeats has remained prominent in discussions
of these poems and in criticism of Theodore Roethke. In fact,
Harry Williams observes in "The Edge Is What I Have," that the
contributors to Arnold Stein's useful collection, Theodore Roethke:
Essays on the Poetry, might be categorized according to their stance
on the issue (p. 22). The beginnings of such a divided reaction to
his most formal poetry troubled Roethke, it is clear, and affected
him in a way different from the less focused objection to his Lost
Son narratives. In response, Roethke presented uncharacteristically theoretical defenses of his imitative method. His frustration
and anger at needing to do so comes through his prose. In "How to
Write like Somebody Else," for example, a defiant, even condes-
cending, tone contradicts Roethke's call for quiet at the beginning
of the passage:

> A little humility may be in order. Let us say that some people
> --often inarticulate simple types--can hear a poem, can recognize
> the real thing; far fewer know what a line is; and fewer yet, I
> suspect, are equipped to determine finally whether a writer has
> achieved his own tone, or whether he has been unduly influenced
> by another; for such a judgment involves a truly intimate knowl-
> edge not only of the particular writers concerned, but also the
> whole tradition of the language; a very exact medium sense; and a
> delicate and perceptive ear. I suggest that the central critical
> problem remains: whether a real poem has been created. If it has,
> the matter of influence becomes irrelevant. [SP, p. 62]

Roethke is right that the "problem remains," and it persists because
enough readers believe the new poems of Words for the Wind do not
consistently or sufficiently measure up to the standard Roethke
himself establishes, and that he had already shown he was very capable of meeting.

Some of Theodore Roethke's finest and most memorable poems appear in the new poems of Words for the Wind, but the strength of these individual efforts has been overshadowed by criticisms leveled at the entire direction of Roethke's poetry of the 1950s. The first reviews of The Waking and of Words for the Wind contain the essence of the two major objections that have been reiterated in various ways in the past three decades: Roethke's poetic vision does not extend beyond the self, and Roethke's poetic voice is easily smothered by the poets with whom he chooses to compete. Any argument that Theodore Roethke ranks among the great American poets of this century needs to deal in some way with these matters. To a degree, such challenge has been met, but defenders of Roethke's poetry of the 1950s have given as much as they have gotten, it must be said. There is thus little reason to believe disagreement over the poems of Words for the Wind will soon end.

It is clear that in the Love Poems of Words for the Wind Roethke wanted to take his poetry beyond the self he had explored so deeply in the Lost Son narratives. Roethke's supporters have largely conceded that the woman Roethke depicts in these poems is not a "personalized" individual, however, but a generalized representation of a person Roethke sometimes loves. His response to this woman is uneasy, and the Love Poems are unconventional, because Roethke experiences love as both attraction and threat. Roethke's ambivalence toward love helps the section of poems cohere, thematically, but that theme places the "I" of the poems, rather than the other person, at center stage. Thus, Roethke's vision in the new poems of Words for the Wind has not significantly enlarged, one can argue, and that damages a prevalent view that an ongoing "journey out of the self" informs all of Roethke's poetry.

Roethke's defenders have fared somewhat better on the issue of poetic influences in the new poems of Words for the Wind. Roethke's return to a formal poetry and his use of Yeats have been explained by suggesting that Roethke needed to stabilize himself after the various disorientations of the Lost Son narratives, by arguing that echoing other poets was a means of "personalizing" his verse, and by advocating, as Roethke himself does, the virtues of the imitative method. All are worthy points in defense, but the most compelling arguments on the matter of poetic influence emphasize the crucial differences between Roethke and Yeats. Roethke may have borrowed Yeats's cadence, but Roethke does not see as Yeats sees. In the end, Yeats denies the world while Roethke affirms it. Indeed, Roethke's own statement of a desire for God, for pure spirit, emerges yet again in his last volume, The Far Field, in the formal poems of the "Sequence, Sometimes Metaphysical," but the more earthbound Theodore Roethke begins to return in the long and loosened lines of the "North American Sequence."

Bibliography

Ayo, Nicholas
1975. "Jonson's Greek Ode in Roethke," American Notes and Queries 13, p. 107.
Bennett, Joseph
1954. "Recent Verse," Hudson Review Summer, p. 305.
Berryman, John
1959. "From the Middle and Senior Generations," American Scholar Summer, pp. 384-90.
Blessing, Richard A.
1974. Theodore Roethke's Dynamic Vision. Bloomington: Indiana Univ. Pr.
Brown, Dennis E.
1974. "Theodore Roethke's 'Self-World' and the Modernist Position," Journal of Modern Literature July, pp. 1239-54.
Burke, Kenneth
1966. "The Vegetal Radicalism of Theodore Roethke," in Language as Symbolic Action, pp. 254-81. Berkeley: Univ. of California Pr. Appeared in Sewanee Review, pp. 68-108. Winter, 1950. Reprinted in Profile of Theodore Roethke, ed. William Heyen. Columbus: Merrill, 1971.
Buttel, Helen T.
1966. "Roethke's 'I Knew a Woman,' " Explicator 24, item 78.
Cambon, Glauco
1962. Recent American Poetry. Minnesota Pamphlets on American Writers, no. 16. Minneapolis: Univ. of Minnesota Pr.
Carruth, Hayden
1953. "The Idiom Is Personal," New York Times Book Review Sept. 13, p. 14.
Conquest, Robert
1958. "The Language of Men," Spectator Feb. 14, pp. 210-11.
Creeley, Robert
1954. "Comment," Black Mountain Review Fall, p. 64.
Deutsch, Babette
1963. Poetry in Our Time. Garden City, N.Y.: Anchor.
Dickey, James
1968. "The Greatest American Poet," Atlantic Nov., pp. 53-58. Reprinted in Sorties. New York: Doubleday, 1971.
Donoghue, Denis
1965. "Roethke's Broken Music," in Theodore Roethke: Essays on the Poetry, ed. Arnold Stein, pp. 136-66. Seattle: Univ. of Washington Pr. Reprinted in Connoisseurs of Chaos: Ideas of Order in Modern American Poetry. London: Faber and Faber, 1965.
Eberhart, Richard
1958. "Creative Splendor," New York Times Book Review Nov. 9, p. 34.

1965. "On Theodore Roethke's Poetry," Southern Review Summer, pp. 612-20.
Freer, Coburn
1971. "Theodore Roethke's Love Poetry," Northwest Review: Theodore Roethke Special Issue 11, pp. 42-66.
Gunn, Thom
1959. "Poets English and American," Yale Review June, pp. 623-26.
Henry, Nat
1969 "Roethke's 'I Knew a Woman,' " Explicator 27, item 31.
1979. "Roethke's 'I Knew a Woman,' " Explicator 38, pp. 16-18.
Heyen, William
1977. "The Yeats Influence: Roethke's Formal Lyrics of the Fifties," John Berryman Studies 3, pp. 17-63.
Hoffman, Frederick
1965. "Theodore Roethke: The Poetic Shape of Death," in Theodore Roethke: Essays on the Poetry, ed. Arnold Stein, pp. 94-114. Seattle: Univ. of Washington Pr.
Kunitz, Stanley
1975. "News of the Root," in A Kind of Order, a Kind of Folly: Essays and Conversations, pp. 83-86. Boston: Little, Brown.
1975. "Poet of Transformations," in A Kind of Order, a Kind of Folly: Essays and Conversations, pp. 96-109. Boston: Little, Brown. Originally appeared in The New Republic, pp. 23-29, Jan. 23, 1965.
La Belle, Jenijoy
1976. The Echoing Wood of Theodore Roethke. Princeton: Princeton Univ. Pr.
Liberthson, Daniel
1977. The Quest for Being: Theodore Roethke, W. S. Merwin, and Ted Hughes. New York: Gordon.
Lucas, John
1968. "The Poetry of Theodore Roethke," Oxford Review 8, pp. 39-64.
Malkoff, Karl
1966. Theodore Roethke: An Introduction to the Poetry. New York: Columbia Univ. Pr.
Mazzaro, Jerome
1980. Postmodern American Poetry, pp. 59-84. Urbana: Univ. of Illinois Pr. Appeared as "Theodore Roethke and the Failures of Language," Modern Poetry Studies, pp. 73-96. July, 1970.
McCawley, Dwight L.
1979. "Roethke's 'I Knew a Woman,' " Explicator Spring, pp. 9-11.
McMichael, James
1969. "The Poetry of Theodore Roethke," Southern Review Winter, pp. 4-25. Reprinted in Profile of Theodore Roethke, ed. William Heyen. Columbus: Merrill, 1971.

Meredith, William
1965. "A Steady Storm of Correspondences: Theodore Roethke's Long Journey Out of the Self," in <u>Theodore Roethke: Essays on the Poetry</u>, ed. Arnold Stein, pp. 36-53. Seattle: Univ. of Washington Pr.
Meyer, Gerald Previn
1954. "Logic of the North," <u>Saturday Review</u> Jan. 16, pp. 18-19.
Mills, Ralph J., Jr.
1962. "Theodore Roethke: The Lyric of the Self," in <u>Poets in Progress: Critical Prefaces to Ten Contemporary Poets</u>, ed. Edward Hungerford, pp. 3-23. Evanston: Northwestern Univ. Pr.
1963. Theodore Roethke. Minnesota Pamphlets on American Writers, no. 30. Minneapolis: Univ. of Minnesota Pr.
Pearce, Roy Harvey
1965. "The Power of Sympathy," in <u>Theodore Roethke: Essays on the Poetry</u>, ed. Arnold Stein, pp. 167-99. Seattle: Univ. of Washington Pr. Reprinted in <u>Historicism Once More</u>. Princeton: Princeton Univ. Pr., 1969.
Peck, Virginia
1964. "Roethke's 'I Knew a Woman,' " <u>Explicator</u> 22, item 66.
Phillips, Robert
1973. "The Inward Journeys of Theodore Roethke," in <u>The Confessional Poets</u>, pp. 107-27. Carbondale: Southern Illinois Univ. Pr.
Ransom, John Crowe
1964. "On Theodore Roethke's 'In a Dark Time,' " in <u>The Contemporary Poet as Artist and Critic: Eight Symposia</u>, ed. Anthony Ostroff, pp. 26-35. Boston: Little, Brown.
Roethke, Theodore
1961. <u>Words for the Wind: The Collected Verse of Theodore Roethke</u>. Bloomington: Indiana Univ. Pr.
1964. "On 'In a Dark Time,' " in <u>The Contemporary Poet as Artist and Critic: Eight Symposia</u>, ed. Anthony Ostroff, pp. 49-53. Boston: Little, Brown. Originally appeared as "The Poet & His Critics," ed. Anthony Ostroff, in <u>New World Writing</u> 19, pp. 189-219, 1961.
1965. <u>On the Poet and His Craft: Selected Prose of Theodore Roethke</u>, ed. Ralph J. Mills, Jr. Seattle: Univ. of Washington Pr.
1966. <u>The Collected Poems of Theodore Roethke</u>. Garden City, N.Y.: Doubleday.
1968. <u>Selected Letters of Theodore Roethke</u>, ed. Ralph J. Mills, Jr. Seattle: Univ. of Washington Pr.
Sanders, Charles
1980. "Roethke's 'The Swan,' " <u>Explicator</u> 38, 3, pp. 26-28.
1980. "Roethke's 'The Sensualists,' " <u>Explicator</u> 38, 4, pp. 9-10.

Schwartz, Delmore
1959. "Cunning and Craft of the Unconscious and the Precon-
scious," Poetry June, pp. 203-5.
Scott, Nathan A., Jr.
1971. "The Example of Theodore Roethke," in The Wild Prayer
of Longing: Poetry and the Sacred, pp. 76-118. New Haven:
Yale Univ. Pr.
Seymour-Smith, Martin
1954. "Where Is Mr. Roethke?," Black Mountain Review Spring,
pp. 40-47.
Snodgrass, W. D.
1959. "Spring Verse Chronicle," Hudson Review Spring, pp.114-
17.
1965. " 'That Anguish of Concreteness': Theodore Roethke's
Career," in Theodore Roethke: Essays on the Poetry, ed.
Arnold Stein, pp. 78-93. Seattle: Univ. of Washington Pr.
Sullivan, Rosemary
1975. Theodore Roethke: The Garden Master. Seattle: Univ. of
Washington Pr.
Wain, John
1958. "Half-way to Greatness," Encounter Apr., pp. 82-84.
1965. "The Monocle of My Sea-Faced Uncle," in Theodore
Roethke: Essays on the Poetry, ed. Arnold Stein, pp. 54-77. Seattle: Univ. of Washington Pr. Appeared as "Theodore Roethke,"
in Critical Quarterly, pp. 322-38. Winter, 1964.
Wilbur, Richard
1973. "Poetry's Debt to Poetry," Hudson Review Summer, pp.
273-94.
Williams, Harry
1977. "The Edge Is What I Have." Lewisburg: Bucknell Univ. Pr.
Wolff, George
1981. Theodore Roethke. Boston: Twayne.

Additional Reading

Arnett, Carroll
1957. "Minimal to Maximal: Theodore Roethke's Dialectic,"
College English May, pp. 414-16.
Blessing, Richard A.
1971. "The Shaking That Steadies: Theodore Roethke's 'The
Waking,' " Ball State University Forum 12, 4, pp. 17-19.
Bly, Robert
1958. "Five Decades of Modern American Poetry," Fifties
pp. 36-39.
Bogan, Louise
1959. New Yorker Oct. 24, pp. 195-96.

Breit, Harvey
1954. "Pulitzer Poet," <u>New York Times Book Review</u> May 16, p. 8.
Cole, Thomas
1954. "The Poetry of Theodore Roethke," <u>Voices</u> Sept.-Dec., pp. 37-40.
Davis, William V.
1975. "The Escape into Time: Theodore Roethke's 'The Waking,' " <u>Notes On Contemporary Literature</u> 5, 11, pp. 2-10.
Deutsch, ᴅabette
1958. "Roethke's Clear Signature," <u>New York Herald Tribune Book Review</u> Dec. 7, p. 3.
Ely, Robert
1976. "Roethke's 'The Waking,' " <u>Explicator</u> 34, item 54.
Flint, F. Cudworth
1959. "Seeing, Thinking, Saying, Singing," <u>Virginia Quarterly Review</u> Spring, pp. 312-13.
Husband, John Dillon
1954. "Some Readings in Recent Poetry," <u>New Mexico Quarterly</u> Winter, pp. 446-47.
Janik, Del I.
1973. "Roethke's 'The Boy and the Bush,' " <u>Explicator</u> 32, item 20.
Keil, H. Charles
1958. "Among the Happy Poets," <u>Cadence</u> Winter, pp. 7-9.
Lee, Charlotte I.
N.D. "Roethke Writes about Women," <u>Literature in Performance: A Journal of Literary and Performing Arts</u> 1, 1, pp. 23-32.
Maxwell, Emily
1961. "The Smallest Giant in the World, and the Tallest Midget," <u>New Yorker</u> Nov. 18, p. 237.
Mills, Ralph J., Jr.
1959. "Keeping the Spirit Spare," <u>Chicago Review</u> Winter, pp. 114-22.
1962. "Roethke's Garden," <u>Poetry</u> Apr., pp. 54-59.
Muir, Edwin
1958. "New Verse," <u>New Statesman</u> Jan. 18, pp. 76-77.
Murphy, Richard
1955. "Three Modern Poets," <u>Listener</u> Sept. 8, pp. 373-75.
Napier, John
1961. "Poetry in the Vernacular and Otherwise," <u>Voices</u> Sept.-Dec., p. 54.
Nemerov, Howard
1954. "Three in One," <u>Kenyon Review</u> Winter, pp. 148-54.
Roethke, Theodore
1954. The Waking: Poems 1933-1953. Garden City, N.Y.: Doubleday.
1962. <u>Words for the Wind.</u> New York: Folkways, FL9736.

Rosenthal, M. L.
1959. "Closing In on the Self," Nation Mar. 21, pp. 258-60.
Schap, Keith
1978. "A Syntactic Figure in Two Poems by Theodore Roethke," Language and Style: An International Journal 11, pp. 238-46.
Schott, Penelope Scambly
1975. " 'I Am!' Says Theodore Roethke: A Reading of the Nonsense Poems," Research Studies 43, 103-12.
Scott, Winfield Townley
1959. "Has Anyone Seen a Trend?" Saturday Review Jan. 3, p. 13.
Skelton, Robin
1958. "Poets' Ways of Speech," Manchester Guardian Feb. 4, p. 4.
Spender, Stephen
1959. "Words for the Wind," New Republic Aug. 10, pp. 21-22.
Vanderwerken, David L.
1973. "Roethke's 'Four for Sir John Davies' and 'The Dying Man,' " Research Studies 41, pp. 125-35.

CHAPTER 5

The Poems of The Far Field

Theodore Roethke's last book of poems, The Far Field, was published in 1964, the year after he died. The Far Field contains
four parts: the six long poems of the "North American Sequence,"
thirteen "Love Poems," seventeen poems in a variety of modes collected into a "Mixed Sequence," and twelve formally conventional
poems that make up the "Sequence, Sometimes Metaphysical." Though
the most important poems in Roethke's last book, the "North American Sequence" and the "Sequence, Sometimes Metaphysical," can
be fit into the context of his ongoing attempt to come to terms
with himself, there are important differences between the two sequences. Roethke wrote the six poems of the "North American Sequence" in the long, unmetered line of Walt Whitman and T. S.
Eliot. The "sometimes metaphysical" poems are stanzaically organized, metered, and rhymed. More significantly, in the "North
American Sequence" Roethke carries out an especially penetrating
and vigorous examination of the meaning of life and death amid the
concrete particulars of his native land. In style and content,
then, the "North American Sequence" is somewhat analogous to the
Lost Son narratives, though in the "North American Sequence" the
protagonist is older, more philosophical, and more psychologically
secure than his counterpart in the Lost Son narratives. In contrast, the twelve poems of the "Sequence, Sometimes Metaphysical"
correspond in style and tone to the Love Poems of Words for the
Wind. Instead of examining his feelings for a woman in this sequence, though, Roethke explores, often in religious terms, the
nature of a relationship with God. In the "Sequence, Sometimes
Metaphysical," Roethke's journey takes him into the more abstract
landscape of the individual soul. As we will see in the first
part of this chapter, some of the first reviewers of The Far
Field found Roethke's explicit statements of affirmation in the
"North American Sequence" and the "Sequence, Sometimes Metaphysical" to be compelling and logical outgrowths of his previous poetry,
while others remained unconvinced by what they saw as Roethke's
forced and derivative metaphysical appeals.
Ever since the publication of The Lost Son and Other Poems in
1948, some of Roethke's critics have expressed reservations about

157

the breadth and range of his poetic vision. The matter surfaced with a special insistence over Roethke's ability to "personalize" the Love Poems of Words for the Wind, and it emerged yet again in The Far Field because the "North American Sequence" can be seen as Roethke's definitive response to his times, to his historical circumstances. Some critics think the "North American Sequence" is an inadequate refutation of the persistent charge, however; they continue to find in the poetry too little reference to external circumstances and thus conclude that Roethke's poetic vision remains, to the end, essentially self-involved. An explicit stance on a political issue or even an explicit reference to an event does not make a political or socially responsive poetry, however, and as we shall see in the second part of this chapter, others think Roethke's poetry is a worthy response to his times, though a response primarily by the method of indirection.

While the "North American Sequence" has been the focus of much discussion of Roethke's involvement with his times, the "Sequence, Sometimes Metaphysical" is a different kind of step beyond the self for Theodore Roethke. In the "Sequence, Sometimes Metaphysical," Roethke explores the journey of the soul toward God. The mystical vision he presents in the "Sequence, Sometimes Metaphysical," and to lesser degree in the other two sequences of The Far Field, is different from the less conventional and less explicit mysticism suggested in the Greenhouse poems and in the Lost Son narratives, however. In the "Sequence, Sometimes Metaphysical," Roethke resorts to a traditional religious imagery and theological framework not apparent elsewhere in his poetry. While critics do not doubt that Roethke believed in the mystical experiences he describes in his poetry and prose, they are for the most part reluctant to agree that the "Sequence, Sometimes Metaphysical" effectively conveys that experience, as the third part of this chapter indicates. In fact, better evidence of what might be termed Roethke's spirituality lies in poems unencumbered by theological concepts and religious terminology.

Roethke's use of the style and voice of William Butler Yeats in Words for the Wind created considerable controversy over the strength of Roethke's poetic identity, and it should be no surprise that that issue carries over into discussions of The Far Field. Where critics hear the voice of Yeats in the poems of the 1950s, those of Walt Whitman and T. S. Eliot speak from the poems of the 1960s. Indeed, there are definite echoes of T. S. Eliot in the "North American Sequence" especially, cited in the fourth section of this chapter, but Roethke competes with Eliot in a way he did not with Yeats, and he echoes Eliot's verse in order to establish important contrasts between their poetic visions. In the "North American Sequence," Roethke does not deny the things of this world, as Eliot eventually does. In fact, though Eliot's voice does not loom largely in the "Sequence, Sometimes Metaphysical," the mystical vision Roethke presents in those poems more closely approximates that of the Nobel Laureate.

The enduring and unique quality of Roethke's poetic vision is perhaps best illustrated by his influence on poets of a later generation, however, not by his relationship to the poets of the past. As a classroom teacher, Roethke inspired and affected the work of a number of important contemporary poets, but his more lasting and widespread influence, of course, has come through the medium of his published poetry. Roethke's effect on younger poets has been considerable and various. Beyond his influential innovations in technique, voice, and form cataloged in the fifth part of this chapter, one of Roethke's most distinctive contributions has been his success at evoking the life and experience of nature's plants and animals. At the same time, though, Roethke's ability to identify with other beings is not total. Roethke's ambivalence before dissolution of the self, an ambivalence that stands as a boundary, an obstacle, to further poetic vision, recurs throughout his poetry. Interestingly, that unwillingness to lose the self has itself been influential, for poets inspired by Roethke's work typically make complete "immersion" a central part of their poetry.

Reviews and Overviews

After Words for the Wind in 1958, Theodore Roethke published two collections of children's poetry, I Am! Says the Lamb (1961) and Party at the Zoo (1963), and a limited edition of the Sequence, Sometimes Metaphysical (1963). With the posthumous publication of The Far Field in 1964, however, readers had yet another serious and widely distributed collection of poetry before them, but this time with the knowledge that it would be Theodore Roethke's last. In responding to The Far Field, and in responding to the Collected Poems published in 1966, many critics cast retrospective glances over Roethke's poetry and his career and evaluated his stature in twentieth-century American poetry. In commenting on Roethke's last poems, reviewers of The Far Field and The Collected Poems had endings very much in mind, therefore, and they devoted special attention to the resolutions, the endings themselves, of Roethke's poems. Some reviewers thought these conclusions were contrived and unconvincing, and thus an ending unworthy of any great poet's career, while others were fascinated by the intriguing coincidence between Roethke's theme of immersion in his last work and the fact of his death by water in 1963. Still others of Roethke's supporters saw important thematic connections between The Far Field and the earlier work, and they argued that Roethke's last poetry was a fitting conclusion to a coherent poetic career.

In their focus on the matter of resolution to poems and career,

160   THEODORE ROETHKE

the reviewers were also responding to Theodore Roethke's own
emphasis in his last work. In "Requiem for God's Gardener,"
for example, his review of The Far Field in the Nation, Hayden
Carruth notes Roethke's preoccupation with death in the "North
American Sequence" and the "Sequence, Sometimes Metaphysical,"
especially, an obsession Carruth goes on to discern in Roethke's
poetry as a whole. Roethke's career is a "repeated failing defense
against the fear of dying" (p. 169), Carruth argues, but he thinks
Roethke avoided that truth in his last work in order to construct
an affirmation. Carruth sees a particular falsity in lines like
"I lose and find myself in the long water" (CP, p. 198) and "What
does what it should do needs nothing more" (CP, p. 235). Carruth
recognizes that Roethke wanted such phrases to "transcend poetry"
but they do not do so, he says; they are "statements only" (p.
169).

M. L. Rosenthal was similarly unpersuaded by the conclusions
of the last poems, but he found resolutions a problem in Roethke's
poetry as a whole. In his review of Roethke's career, "The Couch
and Poetic Insight," published in The Reporter in 1965 and later
in that year expanded for The New Poets: American and British
Poetry since World War II, Rosenthal argues that even in the
Lost Son narratives, Roethke repeatedly moves from "raw terror" to
a "final, calmly affirmative, but really unearned resolution" (p.
113). Rosenthal finds the "Rabelaisian gusto" of the Greenhouse
poems far preferable to the studied calm of The Far Field because
in the later work Roethke asserts an affirmation without satisfactorily establishing its grounds (p. 117). Rosenthal dismisses the
"very uneven last poems" in which Roethke resorts "to the stock
cosmic pieties of sagedom from Chuang-Tzu on down" (p. 113), but
he seems to have expected that the last work would be less effective than the Greenhouse poems. According to Rosenthal, Roethke's
poetic career alternates between formality and freedom, and he regrets that Roethke died while in the particular "phase" that pro-
duced The Far Field (p. 113).

In his discussion of the Collected Poems, "A Very Separate
Peace," Robert Boyers comments in more detail on the alternations
in Roethke's poetry that M. L. Rosenthal observes. Unlike those
who appreciated such alternations in the Lost Son narratives, however, Boyers thinks these later swings of mood are a barrier to
Roethke's poetic vision. Regress and progress and regression
again may have contributed to the unfolding story of the Lost
Son, but the reemergence of such alternations in Roethke's later
work is detrimental. According to Boyers. such motion eventually
wears one out. To that problem in Roethke's verse, Boyers adds
others: Roethke's range of subject matter is too narrow, his vision is too rural, too unresponsive to the modern world, and his
conclusions in the "North American Sequence" are unmotivated.
Boyers thinks Roethke is a more courageous poet than Hayden Car-

ruth does, however. He says Roethke's poetry expresses powerfully
the "tension between Roethke's desire to explore the depths of his
sensibility and his natural reticence before the specter of hideous
possibilities which may be revealed" (p. 684).

In his overview of the poetry, "Roethke: 'The Lost Son,' " published in The New Republic in 1966, Stephen Spender discerns three
stages in Roethke's career. Of the three, Spender prefers the
first two, Roethke's "poetry of isolation" and his poetry "bridg-
ing the gulf of self and not-self" through love. Roethke's best
work comes from his "early self-identification with an almost sub-
human world" and from his "later inability to relate inner and
outer worlds satisfactorily through exuberant moments of lovemak-
ing" (p. 25). The third phase of Roethke's poetry, an expression
of fulfillment, is in Spender's view the least successful because
Roethke's "genius lay in losing his way and being able incompar-
ably to express the sense of loss, rather than finding it along
the lines of great contemporaries" like T. S. Eliot and W. H.
Auden (p. 25). David Ferry reiterated Spender's point the following year in the Virginia Quarterly Review. According to Ferry,
Roethke's "seriousness is frequently too solemnly serious, his
lyrical qualities too lyrically lyrical. His mystical vein often
seems willed, forced, even made up for the occasion" (p. 169).
Precedents exist for those views, as we have seen, but Ferry's
judgment that the poem, "I Knew a Woman," is "embarrassing" as
love poetry (p. 169) is both unique and inexplicable.

It might be expected that other readers would see in Roethke's
last poems the culmination, the triumph, of his career, and that
is of course the case. In Roethke's last they see his finest af-
firmations. Some critics, in fact, directly connect the poems of
The Far Field to the facts of Roethke's untimely death. John G.
Fuller, for example, thinks Roethke "wrote as a prophet" (p. 10).
In describing the circumstances of Roethke's death, Fuller explains that "the water he loved so much closed quietly around him.
He never came to the surface alive. He did not drown; his heart
simply stopped beating" (p. 10). The event is prefigured in Roethke's poetry, Fuller suggests, in the lines from the "North American Sequence," "I lose and find myself in the long water" (CP,
p. 198) and "I sway outside myself/ Into the darkening currents"
(CP, p. 202). Thus, in Fuller's view, resolution of the life
and resolution of the poetry approach identity, a notion echoed
in Jay Parini's book, Theodore Roethke: An American Romantic.
Parini suggests that "one of the fascinating aspects of Roethke's
last years is his awareness of approaching death. . . . The effort
to atone with God (and Otto) takes on a new insistence in his work;
it is as if the poet knew of his death several years in advance.
These poems [of The Far Field] . . . are, in effect, preparations
for the final moment" (pp. 160-61). In what seems an effort to
make both poet and poetry somehow additionally important, Fuller

and Parini surround Theodore Roethke with mystery. While, in
fact, there is tantalizing coincidence between the content of some
of Roethke's last poetry and the circumstances of his death, pressing that coincidence too vigorously results in a mistaken image of
the poetry and the artist who made it.

The religious elements in Roethke's last poetry become an important part in a defense of his controversial resolutions, however,
as indicated by James G. Southworth's enthusiastic, though over-
simplified, discussion, "Theodore Roethke's The Far Field." Like
Stephen Spender, James Southworth thinks Roethke's poetry is
divisible by three, but that is the only common denominator between the two interpretations. Southworth observes that Roethke's
poetry expresses "three states of mind": "a strong desire for purity and the ideal, a demonic drive for the sensual, and the struggle for becoming" (p. 417). The last of the three is most evident
in Roethke's last poems, in the "Sequence, Sometimes Metaphysical," especially, where Southworth finds that "the struggle between the conflicting desires underlies each poem" (p. 417). Because the "Sequence, Sometimes Metaphysical" appears last in
The Far Field, and thus appears to be the last poetry Roethke
wrote, Southworth's argument based on those poems may satisfy a
prevalent desire for things to come out well, for affirmation to
win. However, Southworth narrows and oversimplifies Roethke's
vision in saying that the "Sequence, Sometimes Metaphysical" "describes the final stages in the fight between angels and the devils
for the poet's soul with temporary victories on both sides until
the angels are triumphant in the end" (p. 418). Indeed, Roethke
occasionally uses terms like "soul" in the "Sequence, Sometimes
Metaphysical," and in that respect he gestures toward the traditional Christian vision, but that is by no means the dominant perspective of his poetry. Where and when it appears, therefore, it
seems not central but suspect. In his review, "The Completed Pattern," poet Michael Benedikt identifies more accurately the religious tendency of Roethke's verse. Benedikt applauds Roethke's
nature mysticism, and notes that "in his ability to meditate convincingly upon the mystical realities of natural existence, in
seizing the unseen, Roethke has few parallels among poets in English" (p. 266).

In his several discussions of Roethke's poems, Ralph J. Mills,
Jr., handles the issue of religious affirmation compellingly
because he shows that Roethke's last poems are an outgrowth of tendencies expressed in earlier work. In his essay of 1962, "Theodore Roethke: The Lyric of the Self," Mills puts Roethke's work
into the historical perspective of the twentieth century, and he
discusses and praises Open House, the Lost Son sequence (and its
method), and the poems of The Waking and Words for the Wind.
In prefacing his generous evaluation of Roethke's poetry, Mills
observes the "closely woven pattern" of Roethke's poems, and he

argues that "there is built up a scheme of meanings and values, what we might call a universe of discourse, in which the poems themselves fit and are comprehended" (p. 4). Thus, even before Roethke's death, even before publication of his last work, Mills established in his first statement on Roethke that all of the different pieces of Roethke's poetry work together to compose a coherent whole.

The following year, Mills epitomized his position in Theodore Roethke, yet another survey of Roethke's verse exclusive of The Far Field. In that little book Mills declares that Roethke's poetic "growth was organic and true" and that his "sense of direction was bold and challenging yet unfailingly accurate" (p. 45). To support that assertion, Mills argues that Roethke's "poetry grew in distinct stages, each one with its peculiar qualities and aims, each one expanding and developing from its predecessor, each providing its own special means of furthering the poet's central themes and subjecting them to different modes of apprehension" (p. 7). Roethke might have approved the style as well as content of Mills's comment: it ventures only to return, returns in order to move forward. To solidify still further his view that Roethke's poetry evolved and developed, Mills concludes his little book with a triumphant reading of "Meditations of an Old Woman," at the time among the latest of Roethke's poems widely available, as if to show that inklings of the completion of the "pattern" inhered already even in the next-to-last of Roethke's poems.

The poems of Theodore Roethke's last book fit neatly into Mills's interpretation; they confirm his earlier observations about the direction in which Roethke was going. In his essay of 1965, "In the Way of Becoming: Roethke's Last Poems," Mills discusses the "North American Sequence" and the "Sequence, Sometimes Metaphysical," especially, poems he had not treated in Theodore Roethke. Roethke's last poems are not merely repetitions of previous work, Mills says. In the two sequences, "the poet exceeds the limits of previous development and sets forth on an arduous but successful quest for mystical illumination" (p. 115). By detecting the point behind the several stages of Roethke's poetic development, and the way that point comes into fruition in the last poems, Mills thus counters two important objections to Roethke's verse. Mills directs his increasingly vigorous defense of Roethke at those who deny that Roethke grew as a poet after the Lost Son narratives, and at those who find his last poems inadequately resolved.

The "North American Sequence"

Because the "North American Sequence" indicates in most detail Theodore Roethke's response to the world around him, the six poems it includes have earned a special place in Roethke criticism

164 THEODORE ROETHKE

in the past twenty years. They have been used to gauge how effectively and how extensively Roethke responds to the here and now,
to the world and historical circumstances. Indeed, the "North
American Sequence" contains some of Roethke's most memorable
descriptions of landscape, nowhere more triumphantly than in the
image that concludes "The Rose," the final poem:

> Near this rose, in this grove of sun-parched, wind-
>   warped madronas,
> Among the half-dead trees, I came upon the true ease
>   of myself,
> As if another man appeared out of the depths of my
>   being. . . .
> . . . . And I rejoiced in being what I was:
> In the lilac change, the white reptilian calm,
> In the bird beyond the bough, the single one
> With all the air to greet him as he flies,
> The dolphin rising from the darkening waves;
>
> And in this rose, this rose in the sea-wind,
> Rooted in stone, keeping the whole of light,
> Gathering to itself sound and silence--
> Mine and the sea-wind's.
>
> [CP, p. 205]

A sense of place, of landscape, is central to the "North American
Sequence," but things, usually animals, living in what Roethke considers significant spaces also figure prominently, as in this passage from the title poem, "The Far Field":

> For to come upon warblers in early May
> Was to forget time and death:
> How they filled the oriole's elm, a twittering
>   restless cloud, all one morning,
> And I watched and watched till my eyes blurred from
>   the bird shapes,--
> Cape May, Blackburnian, Cerulean,--
> Moving, elusive as fish, fearless,
> Hanging, bunched like young fruit, bending the end
>   branches,
> Still for a moment,
> Then pitching away in half-flight,
> Lighter than finches, . . .
>
> [CP, pp. 199-200]

Despite the strength and beauty of such individual evocations of
life and landscape, some critics think the "North American Sequence"
amounts to yet another example of Roethke's self-involvement, yet
another indication of the limitation of his poetry. According to

that perception, Roethke fails in his attempt to come to grips
with his native land and his historical moment in the "North
American Sequence." With their argument reinforced by the paucity
of examples of social or political concern exhibited elsewhere in
the poetry, opponents think Roethke's last work does not refute
the persistent charge that his poetic vision is essentially narrow.
Interestingly, few of Roethke's defenders have tried to counter
this view by suggesting that Roethke's poetry is full of direct
references to his times. In fact, examples do exist in the poetry
and the prose, but most of Roethke's defenders agree that Roethke
was not a topical poet or a poet of occasions. Though he did not
write poems about war or politics or poverty, Roethke was himself
aware of those things, and the poems he did write were affected
by them. Roethke responded to his times by indirection, in the
"North American Sequence" in particular, his defenders argue, so
the relative absence of explicit reference to political or social
matters is no diminishment of his poetry.

Kenneth Burke was one of the first to address the general issue
of Roethke's subject matter, his "range," in his essay, "The Vegetal Radicalism of Theodore Roethke." Though Burke's essay was
published in 1950, and thus written well before both Words for the
Wind and The Far Field, his comments about the subjects available
for any poet remain relevant. In his essay, Burke identifies what
he calls three "motives" that shape what a poet chooses to address
in his poetry. These include "a realm of motives local to the body,"
motives "derived from the Ground of All Existence, whatever that
may be," and things "in between . . . the motives of man-made institutions, motives located generally in the terminologies of tech-
nology, business, politics, social institutions, and the like" (p.
276). Since the three "motives" taken together include virtually
everything, Burke asks "how much of human motivation is the poet
to encompass in his work . . . directly, explicitly, and how
much by implication, by resonance derived from sympathetic vibra-
tions in the offing?" (p. 277; Burke's italics). Burke does not
answer his question by establishing proportions of directness and
indirectness, but he does think this "problem" can be handled by
a variety of "methods," and Burke finds that Roethke's approach
in The Lost Son and Other Poems, at least, "has thoroughly and
imaginatively exemplified one of them" (p. 277). Roethke's solution to the matter of "human motivation" is the more impressive,
Burke says, because it compares so favorably with T. S. Eliot's:
"Eliot added winds of doctrine," Burke says. "Roethke 'regressed'
as thoroughly as he could, even at considerable risk, toward a
language of sheer 'intuition' " (p. 277).

Burke does point out areas of narrowness in Roethke's poetry. He
recommends, for example, that Roethke more completely "personalize" his verse, as we have seen, but on the specific matter of
Roethke's response to the events of his day, Burke is not critical.
"There comes a time, in life itself, when one flatly confronts the

realm of social hierarchy (in the scramble to get or to retain or to rewardingly use money, position, prestige)," Burke says (p. 277). The poet can choose to present his response to events of the day explicitly, Burke says, or he can choose to suggest or imply such response by "antithesis," by indirection. Neither is better nor worse, Burke concludes, for "it is not for critics, in their task of characterization, to legislate for the poet here" (p. 277). History penetrates any poetry, in other words, and part of the critic's task in reading a poet is detecting how that happens.

Both direct and indirect responses to historical circumstances exist in Roethke's poetry and prose, but his explicit references are easier to cite because, it must be acknowledged, they are few in number. Some of the most obvious include the vaguely antiwar poem, "Lull (November 1939)," probably patterned on W. H. Auden's more vigorous response to the Spanish Civil War, "September 1939" (CP, p. 31); Roethke's poem "Dolor," which dramatizes the numbing effect upon students and teachers alike of educational institutions (CP, p. 46); and the fourth of the "Meditations of an Old Woman," which contains grim characterizations of women led to lead useless lives (CP, p. 169). To these instances should be added, of course, the variety of references Roethke makes in the "North American Sequence."

Roethke also directs attention to historical circumstances in his prose. In his address, "On 'Identity,' " Roethke cites "four principal themes" the poet can and probably should address: "(1) The multiplicity, the chaos of modern life; (2) . . . the means of establishing . . . a self in the face of that chaos; (3) The nature of creation, that faculty for producing order out of disorder . . . and (4) The nature of God Himself" (SP, p. 19). Roethke treated the second theme most exhaustively in his Lost Son narratives, the third he discussed explicitly in his essays, and the fourth he considered in the "Sequence, Sometimes Metaphysical." The first of the four themes Roethke ignored, however, some critics think, and his subsequent comments about modern life in "On 'Identity' " may have been intended to correct that perception.

In "On 'Identity,' " Roethke notes two major problems in American life, materialism and the threat to individuality. "We continue to make a fetish of 'thing-hood,' we surround ourselves with junk, ugly objects endlessly repeated in an economy dedicated to waste," Roethke says, but this is contrary to our spirit because Americans long for "a purity, a final innocence" (SP, pp. 19-20). To elaborate upon his second point, Roethke quotes lines from the poem, "Dolor," which expresses, he says, the deleterious effects of "the institution that overwhelms the individual man." Roethke rejects any "bigness, the firm, the university . . . the organized team effort" because it can be "disastrous to the human psyche" (SP, p. 20). Roethke's several statements are worth mentioning and important to consider, but the quantity of his explicit references to the "chaos of modern life" is simply not overwhelming. Ralph J. Mills, Jr., has included Roethke's little review, "And Spain Sings: Fifty Loyalist Ballads" (1938) in On the Poet and His Craft primarily, one suspects, to add yet more evidence that Roethke was touched by the world's events.

Hilton Kramer was among the first to attempt to explain why Roethke's poetry contains so few direct references to historical circumstances. In "The Poetry of Theodore Roethke," Kramer acknowledges that Roethke's poetic range is narrow, but he thinks that is a necessary consequence of Roethke's innovative purpose and method. Roethke's preoccupation with prehistory limited his possibilities, Kramer says, and that can best be illuminated by contrast with the greater opportunity a preoccupation with history offered Robert Lowell. According to Kramer, "Lowell's poetry is bound to have a greater range, for that is what history is: the whole range of life as we recognize it objectively." On the other hand, prehistory is inherently limited to "those stages by which the psyche seeks to free itself from the bondage (and the security) of its first dwelling-place (the slime, the womb)." By taking history as his subject, Lowell has in front of him "a spectacle of great variety," Kramer argues, but by taking as his subject prehistory Roethke has only a "single episode in the human drama" (p. 132).

Other critics have been less forgiving than Hilton Kramer in his early essay, however. Like Kramer, John Wain sees also the significant redeeming qualities of Roethke's work, but he concludes in his essay, "The Monocle of My Sea-Faced Uncle," that Roethke "is not, and we must say it plainly, one of those poets in whose work we encounter the whole range of life" (p. 76). In his book, The New Poets: American and British Poetry since World War II, M. L. Rosenthal writes still more plainly that "we have no other modern American poet of comparable reputation who has absorbed so little of the concerns of his age into his nerve-ends, in whom there is so little reference direct or remote to the incredible experiences of the age" (p. 118). These omissions ruin Roethke for Rosenthal, but they do not ruin him for Randall Jarrell. In The Third Book of Criticism, he says that one "looks in vain" in Roethke's poetry "for hydrogen bombs, world wars, Christianity, money, ordinary social observations, his everyday moral doubts," (p. 326), but Roethke remains for Jarrell a "forceful, delicate, and original poet" (p. 327). Robert Phillips sides with Rosenthal, however, in his book The Confessional Poets. He expresses incredulity in noting that Roethke "flourished during the years of the Great Depression, World War II, the atom bomb, the Korean War, and more--and yet made no mention of them" (p. 107).

In his essay of 1968, "The Poetry of Theodore Roethke," John Lucas agrees that "the world of men engages him [Roethke] very little," but Lucas suggests that Roethke "made a wise decision in deciding to abandon the effort to look outward" (p. 46). Lucas finds Roethke's poems about the "social world" to be "at best pallid and derivative, at worst disastrous" (p. 46), an evaluation with which Karl Malkoff agrees in Theodore Roethke: An Introduction to the Poetry. Malkoff thinks the poems of part 5 of Open House, which he says place the self into its social context, are the "least successful part of the book," and he notes that "for some reason, Roethke was never able to write very good poetry about society, or even about the individual's relation to society" (p. 30). Malkoff does not concur with Jay Parini, however, who says in Theodore Roethke: An American Romantic that Roethke "was, say his friends, comically uninformed on political matters" or "only vaguely aware of the international catastrophe that had been gathering wind over Europe for a decade" (p. 24). Malkoff maintains that Roethke's "position was quite clear, both in domestic issues, and in the international affairs that drew the commitment of other poets such as [W. H.] Auden, [Stephen] Spender, and [Archibald] MacLeish" (pp. 30-31).

In his 1968 biography of Roethke, The Glass House, Allan Seager adds yet more evidence that Roethke was "not unaware" of international events, but more importantly, perhaps, he provides a clue to Roethke's silence on world events in a one-sentence paragraph following quotation of a politically motivated poem. Seager writes, "By 1942 Ted had been classified 4-F in the draft as a result of his stay in Mercywood [Sanitarium] so there was no question of any direct participation in the war" (p. 122). Roethke was committed to writing poetry out of his own experience, and thus he may have felt it dishonest and perhaps presumptuous to comment on the war imaginatively. Such comment might also have called attention to Roethke's nonparticipation, to his deferment, to its reason, and that may have been personally and perhaps professionally embarrassing to him.

The relative absence in Roethke's poetry of a clearly articulated concern for the world turning around him troubles some for yet another reason. For example, in his essay "Roethke's Broken Music," Denis Donoghue says that Roethke's poetry is so barren of explicit references to his native land that it is possible to read Roethke without recognizing that he is an American poet. Donoghue does not have the same problem in reading Wallace Stevens, Robert Frost, William Carlos Williams, or Robert Lowell. In these poets, he finds the "insistent element" he can call American, but it should be added that Donoghue can place the other poets mentioned in one of the two "dominant traditions in American poetry--New England and the South" (p. 163). Since Roethke does not fit either of these traditions that help to define his concept of "American," Donoghue admits the two traditions themselves may no longer be conceptually viable.

C. W. Truesdale disagrees with Donoghue in his 1968 essay,

"Theodore Roethke and the Landscape of American Poetry." Truesdale finds in Roethke the same "passion for exact knowledge" that he sees in Thoreau, Natty Bumppo, and Mark Twain (p. 352), and he finds in Roethke "above all the sense of the land--the vast, the particular, the wasted, the utterly beautiful and the utterly exploited landscape of America, the motherland of Thoreau, Whitman, Twain, even Cooper" (p. 351). In contrast to Donoghue, Truesdale thinks Roethke is a "distinctly 'American' poet" and Truesdale fits him easily into the American Romantic tradition because of his journey motif, his self-absorption, and paradoxically, his universality (p. 357). Truesdale admits that, like Whitman's, Roethke's poetry is "limited" (p. 357), but at the same time his limitation is a distinctively American one. In Roethke's poetry, Truesdale observes a "natural or pastoral freudianism in which the land is always maternal, abundant, abused by the pragmatic, indifferent, work-a-day paternal spirit, and desiccated by artificial boundaries called property. In this paradigm, the poet is always the 'lost son' who seeks a fresh birth in a new America" (pp. 351-52). The central themes of Roethke's poems support Truesdale's argument, and so do Roethke's comments in "On 'Identity' " about materialism and individuality.

Brendan Galvin does not address the specifically American aspects of Roethke's poetry, but he does think Roethke was much concerned about the exploitation and abuse of the American landscape. In his essay, "Theodore Roethke's Proverbs," Galvin suggests that evidence of Roethke's ecological consciousness helps to refute the charge that he was uninterested in the things going on around him. Citing lines that appear early in the narrative poem, "The Long Alley," Galvin argues that Roethke was "aware of the social ramifications involved in environmental pollution" (p. 39). The opening lines of the first poem in the "North American Sequence" reinforce Galvin's assertion, but such details of imagery do not, it must be said, constitute a subject matter or a central part of Roethke's vision of the American landscape. In the Lost Son narratives and in the "North American Sequence," imagery depicting environmental despoilment usually reveals the observer's damaged condition rather than the other way around.

Instead of entering what is probably a losing battle over the quantity of his references to the issues of the day, however, most of Roethke's supporters have insisted, to greater or lesser degree, that Roethke's larger concerns come through his poems by, as Kenneth Burke would put it, "antithesis" or indirection. Some critics have addressed that matter specifically, while others have themselves been indirect and have focused on the strength and implication of Roethke's controversial resolutions. In his essay of 1964, "The Rose in the Sea-Wind: A Reading of Theodore Roethke's 'North American Sequence,' " Hugh Staples argues that the sequence is primarily a "quest for salvation, a kind of contemporary Pil-

grim's Progress" (p. 198), and he notes that the "journey moves
from hell to heaven, from negation to affirmation" (p. 193). Despite the conventional religious terminology Staples uses, he
thinks Roethke's is an unorthodox spiritual quest because his poems proceed "in a manner that suggests counterpoint in music,"
what Staples calls the "principle of alternation" (p. 192). By
the very nature of that principle, Staples implies, a certain
amount of failure is built into the poems. However, Staples believes such "blind alleys and circuitous detours" are essential
to Roethke's unconventional means of reconciling body and soul,
for "only through such a principle of alternation can the process
of spiritual education commence" (p. 194). By being "much concerned with water, the symbol of process and formlessness," by
confronting the opposite of his goal, Staples says, Roethke finally discovers "the meaning of form" in the concluding image of
the rose in the sea-wind. Thus, Roethke succeeds in his "search
for form, and for its implications at all levels of human experience, individual and collective" (p. 191), and by indirection
he does address and resolve a pervasive American concern in the
"North American Sequence."

Richard Blessing also thinks that Roethke's poetry contains an
implicit response to the issues of his day. In his 1972 essay,
"Theodore Roethke: A Celebration," Blessing observes that "the
essential experience of modern life is speed, movement, energy,
whirl, a sense of unceasing and often violent motion." The distinctively "dynamic" qualities of Roethke's poetry both respond to
and illuminate modern experience, Blessing says, because Roethke
was "wise enough to sense that the historical events that swirled
around him were but varied forms of the same energy which drove
him in his personal evolution as a man and an artist" (p. 170).
In his 1974 book devoted to that issue, Theodore Roethke's Dynamic Vision, Blessing sees in the "North American Sequence"
one of the finest examples of Roethke's "dynamic vision" at work,
but he disagrees with Hugh Staples that Roethke's "search for
form" in the "North American Sequence" culminates in the final
image of its last poem, "The Rose." According to Blessing, there
are no angels or devils in the sequence, no heaven and hell. In
the end of the last poem, Blessing argues, there is no "ultimate salvation or 'final epiphany' " as Staples suggests (p. 148).
"For Roethke," Blessing says, "such experiences are never 'final'; they are merely events that repeat themselves again and
again. . . . There is no need to invalidate the moment of spiritual awakening in 'Journey' ["Journey to the Interior," the first
poem in the sequence] simply because other such moments occur later in the sequence" (p. 148). Blessing agrees with Staples that
the concluding imagery in "The Rose" constitutes one such epiphany. He agrees that "the energy of life is nowhere more felt
in Roethke's poetry than in these strange images of moving stillness, of terrific repose" (p. 121), but he insists that Roethke's

ultimate allegiance is to an enduring dynamism in life erupting
repeatedly in epiphanies that "must give way to make room for the
next" (p. 148).

Harry Williams offers a narrower reading of the "North American Sequence" in his book, "The Edge Is What I Have," but his
view provides an interesting contrast to Blessing's focus on the
"dynamic vision." Like Blessing, Williams argues that the rose
image should not be read as the culminating "emblem of mystical
ecstasy" in the "North American Sequence" (p. 118), but Williams
stresses the static rather than the dynamic quality of the rose
and of similar imagery. Williams says that at the end of "The
Lost Son," for example, Roethke "perfects a sense of stasis,
that is, a mystical sense of stillness for its own sake" (p. 66).
(Similarly "still" images appear in the Greenhouse poem, "Carnations," and at the end of "The Rose" in the "North American Sequence.") Such stillness is a threat to life, however. According
to Williams, Roethke's "regenerative animism is conditioned by
the reality of death and stasis" (p. 67), and in his subsequent
discussion of poet Robert Bly, Williams observes that "animism,
as seen with Roethke sometimes, can be easily transformed into a
death-wish, and not necessarily death as nourishment" (p. 172).
In Roethke's poetry, however, "fidelity to natural processes
approaches an inclusiveness that does not tolerate abstractions
about beauty" (p. 120), but Williams thinks Roethke willfully constructs such static images and abstractions nonetheless: he "continually creates these forms of stasis as a threat to his identity"
(p. 112). That keeps him going, keeps him on the journey toward
self-definition. Roethke creates static imagery, Williams says,
"as if to bait himself and the reader to see how far into a sense
of stasis and being he could go 'without courting silence'" (p.
112). When Roethke "does court the realm of abstraction," Williams says, "it is more a matter of escape, a respite, which
readers have come to look upon as points of stasis in the poetry"
(p. 120).

In her essay, "The Explorer's Rose: Theodore Roethke's Mystical Symbol," Susan R. Bowers focuses on the concluding imagery
of the "North American Sequence." She argues that the key to
understanding the mystical experience represented in the sequence
lies in the nature of Roethke's symbolism of the rose. In the
course of her essay, Bowers points out that the rose of Roethke's
"North American Sequence" is wild, and thus different from the rose
of the Greenhouse poems and of the Lost Son narratives, and she
charts the evolution of rose imagery in Roethke's poetry. With
his North American rose, however, Roethke is not symbolizing one
specifiable, reducible thing, Bowers says; its situation "near
the convergence of fresh and salt water . . . on the edge between
water and earth, between wild and domesticated nature . . . implies the resolution of contraries" (p. 45). In concluding that
"Roethke's mystical experience . . . is his encounter with the life

force" and the rose is "the symbol of that life force" (p. 47),
Bowers evokes Blessing's notion of the "dynamic vision," but like
Staples she thinks the imagery of "The Rose" is the fitting culmination of the "North American Sequence." In Bowers's view
the rose implies "neither transcendence over nor re-integration
with things, but re-integration with relations between and among
things" (p. 47; Bowers's emphasis).

Cary Nelson's reading of the "North American Sequence" appears
as the second chapter in Our Last First Poets: Vision and History
in Contemporary American Poetry, a book devoted to the contemporary poet's response to American cultural history. In comparison
to the more overtly political poetry he discusses in his introductory chapter, "Whitman in Vietnam: Poetry and History in Contemporary America," Roethke's must seem a strange selection, a point
Nelson recognizes. Nelson observes that "until late in his career
he [Roethke] gives little overt evidence of an attempt to come to
terms with his national origin" (p. 31), but instead of continuing to evade or neglect history in the "North American Sequence,"
Roethke locks it into a specific historical moment that is distinctive and unique. Thus the long poem is "threatened by its exposure
to American culture" (p. 32). Were it to have appeared only a
few years after it did, Nelson says, it "would have been undone
by too many bitter ironies." For example, "Roethke could barely
describe the rippling tide as 'burnished, almost oily' without being literal and therefore unintentionally comic" (p. 47). (Nelson
does not think, therefore, that such imagery indicates what Brendan Galvin sees as "ecological consciousness.") Part of Nelson's
aim, then, is to show that Roethke's "North American Sequence"
is a distinctively American response to its American moment. According to Nelson, Roethke's is a "poetry, grounded in loss and
courting failure, that in many ways anticipates the poetry of the
1960s" (p. 32).

In that it comprehends what Nelson calls "Roethke's polarized
poetics of nature" (p. 33), the "North American Sequence" is
the culmination of Roethke's poetry, Nelson says. At one extreme of this polarity are "spaces of enclosed germination" that
Nelson connects with the Greenhouse poems (p. 33) and the "intro-
spective values" characteristic of them: "meditation, repose,
retreat to the womb, death and germination in darkness" (p. 35).
The emblem of this "space" in the "North American Sequence" is
the image of the stone, according to Nelson. Opposing the stone
is the image of light, emblem of the other extremity of Roethke's "polarized poetics." In contrast to the greenhouse enclosure,
Roethke posits the "field, meadow, and plain"; these have what
Nelson calls a "ravishing openness" (p. 33). Though the greenhouse
enclosure offers a "retreat," and the field offers "growth," Nelson says, Roethke values neither space above the other. Each
space also contains its menace: the greenhouse enclosure presents
the possibility of a "smothering, claustrophobic death" while the

field presents the "risk of death through overextension" (p. 34). Between the two, Nelson says, "stands a poet whose vertical flowering would link them both" (p. 35) or, as he puts it elsewhere, Roethke tries to "occupy the verbal shoreline, the textuality, between self and other" (p. 50). The ground upon which the poet stands is the poem itself, the "textuality the poem maps out for itself" (p. 57).

In a place itself, then, and not on a map of a place, "Roethke works out verbally a synthesis not available elsewhere in human experience," but Nelson believes that Roethke saw the limitations of such a synthesis and did not expect it to "change his life" (p. 60). The "North American Sequence" is a "highly self-conscious verbal artifice," Nelson says (p. xii), and he stresses the "quality of sheer performance" which is "central to the experience of the poem" (p. 53). Seen in that light, the authenticity of Roethke's mystical perspective, for example, is not at issue because "we no longer have to believe that the vision exists outside the poetry," he says. "We only have to recognize that Roethke wants the vision to succeed and that his desire is characteristically American" (p. 54). Nelson is aware that his reading makes Roethke's "North American Sequence" a less grand response to modern life than some critics would prefer, but he refers his interpretation to Roethke's personal history ("For a man at times unhinged by guilt and self-doubt, the poignancy and necessity of a vision that is wholly a willed artifice should be apparent" [p. 60]), and in the course of his book, Our Last First Poets, to the diminishing expectations of twentieth-century American culture as a whole. Cary Nelson's is the most extended and persuasive discussion of Roethke's response to his times by "antithesis," and it will probably be welcomed by many of Roethke's adherents. However, Nelson's essentially agnostic approach to Roethke's mystical emphasis is at odds with the prevailing tendency in the criticism first to characterize that vision and then to establish (or deny) its believability. The "North American Sequence" figures in these efforts to be sure, but Roethke's explicit treatment of mysticism in the "Sequence, Sometimes Metaphysical" figures still more prominently.

The "Sequence, Sometimes Metaphysical"

As we saw in discussion of the Greenhouse poems and the Lost Son narratives, Theodore Roethke does not explicitly align his poetic vision with any traditional religious or philosophical perspective, nor have Roethke's critics come to agreement on whether his vision in those poems is essentially animistic, pantheistic, or mystical. All of the terms appear in the critical literature. Roethke's spiritual position is hard to define because he is so reluctant to release the world, to become spirit alone. However,

in the twelve poems of the "Sequence, Sometimes Metaphysical,"
the fourth and final part of The Far Field, and in essays relevant
to that sequence, Roethke articulates most explicitly his commitment to a mystical vision. For that reason, much of the discussion of the issue of Roethke's mysticism, its character, origins,
and authenticity, has turned around the "Sequence, Sometimes Metaphysical."

   Though the poems of the metaphysical sequence again record a
personal spiritual journey, they are uncharacteristically conventional in form, theme, and imagery. In the third stanza of "The
Marrow," for example, Roethke writes:

> Godhead above my God, are you there still?
> To sleep is all my life. In sleep's half-death,
> My body alters, altering the soul
> That once could melt the dark with its small breath.
> Lord, hear me out, and hear me out this day:
> From me to Thee's a long and terrible way.
>   [CP, p. 246]

In addition to borrowing its distinctive terminology, Roethke
looks to Christian theology for the basic shape of his spiritual
journey. In the concluding stanza of "Infirmity," Roethke fore-
goes the stirring image of resolution he offered at the end of
the "North American Sequence" to reiterate the categories of
Open House and a philosophical bias toward the spirit:

> Things without hands take hands: there is no choice,--
> Eternity's not easily come by.
> When opposites come suddenly in place,
> I teach my eyes to hear, my ears to see
> How body from spirit slowly does unwind
> Until we are pure spirit at the end.
>   [CP, p. 244]

   It is possible to see Roethke's recourse to a traditional religious outlook and imagery in the "Sequence, Sometimes Metaphysical" as analogous to his exploration of his native land in the
"North American Sequence." In both sequences, Roethke steps
outside the self, in the one case toward the landscape, in the
other toward God, or at least toward religious language. In that
respect, the two sequences clarify and make more public Roethke's
otherwise private universe. In the "North American Sequence,"
however, Roethke remains enamored of the concrete particulars of
the landscape, and as we have seen, one of Roethke's strengths
as a poet is to evoke the individual entity, the specific locale.
Roethke's journey in the "Sequence, Sometimes Metaphysical" occurs in the especially rarefied atmosphere of the soul, a place

that remains abstract and ethereal despite Roethke's efforts to make it real. When carried over into the "Sequence, Sometimes Metaphysical," then, and presented in a language that borrows heavily from religious and philosophical discourse, the individual's quest for the Father, so compellingly presented in the Lost Son narratives, gets overwhelmed by the Christian imagery of the soul's journey toward God. There is reason to question the success of Roethke's metaphysical poems, therefore, but that is not the same thing as questioning Roethke's commitment to mystical experience.

Of the twelve poems of the "Sequence, Sometimes Metaphysical," the first of them, "In a Dark Time," has received the most attention. Probably none other of Roethke's poems has inspired so many of the titles of critical essays and critical books:

> In a dark time, the eye begins to see,
> I meet my shadow in the deepening shade;
> I hear my echo in the echoing wood--
> A lord of nature weeping to a tree.
> I live between the heron and the wren,
> Beasts of the hill and serpents of the den.
>
> What's madness but nobility of soul
> At odds with circumstance? The day's on fire!
> I know the purity of pure despair,
> My shadow pinned against a sweating wall.
> That place among the rocks--is it a cave,
> Or winding path? The edge is what I have.
>
> A steady storm of correspondences!
> A night flowing with birds, a ragged moon,
> And in broad day the midnight come again!
> A man goes far to find out what he is--
> Death of the self in a long, tearless night,
> All natural shapes blazing unnatural light.
>
> Dark, dark my light, and darker my desire.
> My soul, like some heat-maddened summer fly,
> Keeps buzzing at the sill. Which I is I?
> A fallen man, I climb out of my fear.
> The mind enters itself, and God the mind,
> And one is One, free in the tearing wind.
>   [CP, p. 239]

Theodore Roethke delivered two statements that are helpful in understanding "In a Dark Time" and the "Sequence, Sometimes Metaphysical." In "On 'Identity' " (1963), comments made at a panel discussion at Northwestern University, Roethke speaks openly and easily of mysticism, and he draws subtle distinctions between aspects of the experience. For example, Roethke notes a difference between the "heightening and awareness of one's own self" which can give rise to love, as we saw in chapter 4, and a "feeling of the oneness of the universe" (SP, p. 25). Roethke says the first feeling can be "induced . . . simply by intensity in the seeing" (SP, p. 25), by careful focusing on the object, an attentiveness whose results are everywhere evident in Roethke's verse. The second feeling can also be "induced," Roethke says, and

> the "oneness," is, of course, the first stage in mystical illumination, an experience many men have had, and still have: the sense that all is one and one is all. This is inevitably accompanied by a loss of the "I," the purely human ego, to another center, a sense of the absurdity of death, a return to a state of innocency.
>
> This experience has come to me so many times, in so many varying circumstances, that I cannot suspect its validity: it is not one of the devil's traps, an hallucination, a voice, a snare. I can't claim that the soul, my soul, was absorbed in God. No, God for me still remains someone to be confronted, to be dueled with: that is perhaps my error, my sin of pride. But the oneness, Yes! [SP, p. 26]

Roethke gives an example of such mystical experience in his discussion of "In a Dark Time" in Anthony Ostroff's symposium on the poem in The Contemporary Poet as Artist and Critic. Roethke's essay is a line-by-line commentary on the poem that rivals in its detail the "Open Letter," his discussion of the Lost Son narratives. In "On 'In a Dark Time,' " Roethke provides a historical context for the composition of the poem reminiscent of his startling description of the origins of "The Dance." He says "In a Dark Time" was "a dictated poem, something given, scarcely mine at all. For about three days before its writing I felt disembodied, out of time; then the poem virtually wrote itself, on a day in summer, 1958" (p. 49). In recounting its mysterious origins, Roethke takes no credit for the poem, but in his concept of the poem, its place in the "Sequence, Sometimes Metaphysical," and the sequence as a whole, he forcefully asserts his will: "In a Dark Time" "is the first of a sequence, part of a hunt, a drive toward God: an effort to break through the barrier of rational experience; an intention not unmixed with pride . . . accompanied by a sense of exhilaration, and only occasional seizures of humility" (p. 49).

Reconciling Roethke's motive for the poem with the gift of the poem is complicated by Roethke's special commitment to the experience behind "In a Dark Time." Elsewhere, Roethke has insisted upon a poet's "fidelity to his subject" (SP, p. 83), but in the case of "In a Dark Time," "fidelity" becomes ferocious, even blinding, loyalty: "I was granted an insight beyond the usual," he writes. "To speak of it further is a betrayal of the experience. . . . One defiles whatever purity has been achieved" (p. 49). By definition, mystical experience is inexpressible, and most mystics have little confidence in language. Paradoxically, silence rather than speech authenticates the mystical experience. In his essay, Roethke comes close to the mystic's contempt for language. The problem for him, of course, was that he was a poet, a maker and user of language. Other poets like William Blake and Walt Whitman circumvented that difficulty by claiming their own visions or realizations prompted them to speak, to prophesy. It is revelation, not mysticism, that affords the poet the authority to practice his craft, but Roethke's metaphysical subject did not present itself that way. Thus, according to the reading of "In a Dark Time" that Roethke offers in his essay, the poems of the "Sequence, Sometimes Metaphysical" betray their very origins by being poems.

Alongside Roethke's reading of "In a Dark Time" in Anthony Ostroff's symposium appear analyses by John Crowe Ransom, Babette Deutsch, and Stanley Kunitz, critics historically sympathetic to Roethke's poetry. As might be expected, the three critics disagree on a variety of points of interpretation, but more remarkably Ransom, Deutsch, and Kunitz agree there are significant problems in the poem. In his essay, "On Theodore Roethke's 'In a Dark Time,' " John Crowe Ransom notes a "theological strain" in Roethke's poetry, an "intellectualism" that has become especially strong in "In a Dark Time" (p. 30). Ransom thinks the poem is a "tremendous poem, but a religious or philosophical poem" (p. 35); he respects Roethke's "reckoning with God" but he regrets that "In a Dark Time" is "not slowed by the sweet clang and clog of some profuse conventional rhetoric, which we may have come to expect for our greater ease when we are being persuaded to religious themes" (p. 26). Roethke is a "poet dedicated to pure images," Ransom observes, and a poem such as "In a Dark Time," a poem "classical in the history of religion rather than the history of poetry," needs more directly to "draw upon a multitude of familiar images" (pp. 30-31).

Ransom notes how the "theme of death" figures prominently in "In a Dark Time" (p. 29), and in her reading, which bears the same title as Ransom's, Babette Deutsch suggests that this specter overwhelms the poet and reduces the strength of his concluding affirmation. According to Deutsch, "the release is less fully realized than the conflict and the dread that haunts it. . . . The change from appalled uncertainty to what one might call 'the comfort of the resurrection' . . . is too sudden to be quite convincing" (p. 40). Where Ransom objects to the abruptness of the imagery in the poem as a whole, Deutsch objects to "abruptness of [the] reversal" which constitutes the pivotal moment, the leap of faith, in the poem (p. 40).

In his essay, "The Taste of Self: On Theodore Roethke's 'In

a Dark Time,' " Stanley Kunitz agrees with Deutsch that there is nothing in the poem to prepare "for so pat a resolution" (p. 48), but Kunitz's major objection to "In a Dark Time" concerns its "style of oracular abstraction" (p. 41). Like the other readers, Kunitz can find precedents for Roethke's poem in religious and literary history, but in comparison to a poem of John Clare's that Kunitz cites, he thinks Roethke's poem "curiously less affecting." "One longs for the artless human touch," Kunitz writes. His primary quarrel with the poem is its "clinically analytical tone, which jars on the ear that has been listening to a stranger music" (p. 47).

As we have seen, Roethke's response to the readings of Ransom, Deutsch, and Kunitz does not sufficiently answer their objections to "In a Dark Time," a matter John Hobbs takes up in his essay, "The Poet as His Own Interpreter: Roethke on 'In a Dark Time.' " Hobbs thinks most readers would organize the poem in their minds very differently from the way Roethke does, and he notes in particular that "In a Dark Time" offers no access to the crucial autobiographical information Roethke provides in his essay. Hobbs stresses also that Roethke interprets the experience behind "In a Dark Time" in Ostroff's Symposium; he does not interpret the poem he offers as representation of that experience. For example, instead of explaining how and why the last stanza of the poem is successful, Roethke refers to the experience it depicts and the concepts that experience implies. Roethke admits that the "conclusion puts a heavy burden on language, most certainly" (p. 52), but in discussing the phrase, "And one is One," Roethke writes:

> This seems a genuine double, at the least. In the Platonic sense, the one becomes the many, in this moment. But also-- and this is what terrified me--the one not merely makes his peace with God . . . he--if we read One as the Godhead theologically placed above God--transcends God: he becomes the Godhead itself, not only the veritable creator of the universe but the creator of the revealed God. This is no jump for the timid, no flick from the occult, no moment in the rose garden. Instead it is a cry from the mire, and may be the devil's own. [p. 53]

Roethke may well have intended to squeeze all these theological subtleties into his concluding stanza, but those subtleties are not readily available in the poem. In a narrow respect, however, Roethke's "In a Dark Time" may do odd justice to its mystical experience, for as the analyses of Ransom, Deutsch, Kunitz, and Hobbs illustrate, Roethke's language could not adequately compass it.

Despite the problems of "In a Dark Time," many critics take the matter of mysticism in Roethke's life and in the poems of The Far Field seriously, though cautiously. As noted earlier, for example, Ralph J. Mills, Jr., thinks that Roethke's poetic vision as a whole tends toward "mystical illumination" (p. 115), though he emphasizes in his 1963 book Theodore Roethke that Roethke is reluctant to deny "the validity of the natural in favor of the transcendental" (p. 24), a point Grosvenor E. Powell reiterates in his review, "Robert Lowell and Theodore Roethke: Two Kinds of Knowing." Powell concludes that there are two kinds of mystic, the Christian and the Romantic. The former (like Lowell) is a "poet of distinctions and definitions, not [like Roethke] a poet trying to merge with nature" (p. 181). Karl Malkoff also notes "expressions of sympathy with the mystic's point of view throughout Roethke's poetry" (p. 139) in his book, Theodore Roethke: An Introduction to the Poetry, but because of Roethke's refusal to give himself over to the transcendental, a final affirmation is never easy. As Malkoff explains, Roethke must "again and again turn to confront the threat of nonbeing, of death" (p. 164).

While most critics think Roethke's is thus an unconventional mystical perspective, his replication of the stages of mystical experience does parallel those of classical mysticism, according to William Heyen's extended discussion of the issue in "The Divine Abyss: Theodore Roethke's Mysticism," published in 1969. Heyen focuses on Roethke's long poem, "The Abyss," a work Roethke might have included in the "Sequence, Sometimes Metaphysical" were it not for its formal differences from those poems. As it is, "The Abyss" opens the "Mixed Sequence." Heyen believes it constitutes a "striking summary of Roethke's mysticism," and that the five parts of "The Abyss" parallel stages of mystical experience documented by William James and Evelyn Underhill (pp. 1052-53). In The Varieties of Religious Experience, William James uses four criteria by which to evaluate the authenticity of mystical experience, ineffability, a noetic quality, transiency, and passivity, and Heyen thinks "The Abyss" satisfies those standards. Roethke's poem more closely follows the five stages that lead to mystical awakening which Evelyn Underhill describes in her 1910 book, Mysticism: A Study of Man's Spiritual Consciousness, Heyen argues, however. Underhill's five stages include the awakening of the self, the purification of the self, an experience of illumination, a period of despair known as the "dark night of the soul," and a final experience of mystical union (p. 1053). Heyen shows convincingly that Roethke relied on Underhill's book: the source of the last line of "The Abyss," "Being, not doing, is my first joy" (CP, p. 222), Heyen finds in Underhill's sentence, "Being, not doing, is the first aim of the mystic" (p. 1067). In addition, Heyen offers valuable insights about mysticism in general in his essay, but in fact "The Abyss" does not follow Underhill's five stages so neatly as Heyen suggests or would prefer. To be true to Underhill, the fourth section of the poem should present the nadir of the experience, the famous "dark night of the soul," but Heyen notes truthfully (and with some surprise) that "Roethke does not seem to emphasize intense suffering here" (p. 1064). Heyen wants him to,

however, so he helps the section conform to Underhill's mystical
path by inferring that "the mental anguish, despair, and finally
the heroic resignation in the face of this anguish and despair of
the speaker . . . point to a quiet desperation" (p. 1064). That
is quite different, of course, from the abject terror of the "dark
night of the soul."

Though "The Abyss" must be distorted to conform to Evelyn Underhill's five stages, Heyen thinks her book is helpful in reading
other of Roethke's poems, those in the "Sequence, Sometimes Metaphysical," of course, but also "Meditations of an Old Woman" and
the "North American Sequence." "If 'The Abyss' is the prototyp-
ical mystical poem in the Roethke canon," Heyen says, "all these
others presuppose much of the information in Underhill's book that
the poet absorbed" (p. 1068). And yet Roethke's mystical poems do
not derive solely from Underhill's book, Heyen argues. Roethke
went to Underhill to "bulwark his intimations of mysticism with
a formal understanding of its tradition" (pp. 1067-68), though at
times Heyen implies a heavier borrowing, a fact he seems to recognize. After his enthusiastic observation that "it is seldom that
a single book [Underhill's] sheds so much light on a major portion
of a poet's work," Heyen qualifies his remark with "though, certainly, 'The Abyss' is not a literary exercise in which Roethke
sets out to parallel Underhill" (p. 1068). Though Heyen thinks
Underhill's treatise on mysticism illuminates "The Abyss" and some
of Roethke's other poems, he does puts the mystical emphasis in
Roethke's poetry into perspective. Near the outset of his essay,
he notes that Roethke was primarily a poet, and not "a man who
dedicates his life to educating himself to achieve union with God"
(p. 1052).

Richard Blessing would probably agree with William Heyen's introductory statement, but Blessing thinks Roethke's "drive toward
God" in the "Sequence, Sometimes Metaphysical" involves greater
conflict than Heyen acknowledges. Blessing believes that Theodore Roethke was himself interested in mysticism, and in his 1974
book, Theodore Roethke's Dynamic Vision, Blessing cites David
Wagoner's report "that perhaps the strongest impression that one
brings away from the notebooks is that of how desperately Roethke
sought to find God" (p. 58). However, Blessing says that "if on
the one hand he [Roethke] felt drawn by the love of God and by a
desire to come at last face to face with transcendent reality, on
the other hand he feared the encounter might utterly destroy him"
(p. 198). In the "Sequence, Sometimes Metaphysical," Blessing
sees a "protagonist torn between the desire which reaches out and
the fear which clings to what one has and is" (p. 199). Because of
Roethke's reluctance to immerse himself finally, Blessing concludes
that "Roethke was not much of a mystic if, indeed, he was one at
all" (p. 60). Despite that, Roethke's interest in mysticism had
an impact on his poetry, and in Blessing's opinion it is important

that Roethke "believed that the search for God and the search for poems reflecting a greater intensity of life were closely related" (p. 60).

In her book, Theodore Roethke: The Garden Master, Rosemary Sullivan is also careful to note the difference between Roethke's vision and classical mysticism. Again and again, she notes, like Orpheus his Eurydice, Roethke strained to return himself to the senses, to the world. At the same time, however, Sullivan complicates her discussion by referring to Roethke's "mystical experience" (p. 197), and by drawing close connections between his "private psychic experiences" and his "interest in mysticism" (p. 125). "If, through the experience of psychological disorder, Roethke came to fear madness," she says, "he nevertheless discovered what he felt to be a natural propensity for mystical insight" (p. 124). However, Sullivan thinks Roethke's own "mystical moments were states of feeling rather than of intellect"; compelling though they were, those experiences do not meet all of the criteria the mystical tradition has established: they had "no specific intellectual content," answered no questions, and thus "the fall from assurance, the oscillation between moments of ecstasy and despair, is . . . almost inherent in the experience itself" (pp. 108-9). Sullivan concludes that Roethke's poetic vision is a compromise position, a "secular mysticism," and she notes that Evelyn Underhill cites precedents for that compromise in the mystical tradition (pp. 126-28).

Though it is generally agreed that Theodore Roethke's personal commitment to and interest in mystical experience was considerable, especially later in his life, it is clear also that Roethke's expression of that commitment in his poetry is incomplete. In his last poems, Roethke uses explicitly religious images and terms, and some of his works parallel in structure the stages of classic mystical experiences, but despite his effort to articulate a sense of mystical resolution with his world, in fact he rejected the total dissolution of the self, the union with the All, that is the goal and defining characteristic of mysticism. In his book, The Quest for Being: Theodore Roethke, W. S. Merwin, and Ted Hughes, Daniel Liberthson attempts to explain Roethke's reluctance before immersion by suggesting that Roethke is an "Orphic" poet, "a poet who through the living power of his language connects--via poetic song--mind and spirit with the presences of nature and so overthrows loss and rescues life from death, being from nothingness" (p. 8). Since he will not reject the world, the problem of death, and of fear of death, repeatedly assails the Orphic poet's faith. As a result, according to Liberthson, the Orphic poet must find "possibilities of life in death, of gain in loss--he must bring death to life" (p. 37). A characteristic of the poets influenced by Theodore Roethke is a greater willingness to lose the self, but "The edge is what I have," Roethke says in "In a Dark Time" (CP, p. 39), and that juncture between life and death,

between self and other, between the one and the All, remained his
fundamental vantage-point.

Literary Backgrounds and Sources

In much the way that Jessie L. Weston's book, From Ritual to
Romance, helps illuminate the themes and structure of T. S.
Eliot's The Waste Land, Evelyn Underhill's Mysticism: A Study
of Man's Spiritual Consciousness helps reveal similar features
of Theodore Roethke's most metaphysical poetry, but to find the
origins of the style and voice of Roethke's last poems, particularly the "North American Sequence," critics have looked to more
specifically literary precedents.   Roethke wrote the six poems
of the sequence in a long-lined free verse reminiscent of the
meditative sections of the Lost Son narratives and of "Meditations of an Old Woman," and as C. W. Truesdale points out in
"Theodore Roethke and the Landscape of American Poetry," this
line can be traced to Walt Whitman.   Truesdale notes that Roethke is "least explicit" and "most circumspect" about his indebtedness to Whitman, but he rectifies that in his last poems where
"the acknowledgement of Whitman as primary source, as the well-
spring of American poetry, is affirmed in many ways, not the least
of which is Roethke's use in the longer poems (and mastery) of the
long, sinuous, Whitmanesque line" (p. 349).   The "North American
Sequence" thus represents a return to stylistic innovation for
Roethke and a departure from the rhymed and metered verse of Words
for the Wind and the "Sequence, Sometimes Metaphysical."   In
that respect, the poems of the "North American Sequence" are
nearer to prose, Roethke's attempt, as he says in his 1960 essay,
"Some Remarks on Rhythm," to "recapture" for poetry "what it
has lost to some extent to prose" (SP, p. 83).

And yet the lines of the sequence are anything but "unmeasured
and inexact," as Donald Wesling observes in his essay of 1970,
"The Inevitable Ear: Freedom and Necessity in Lyric Form, Wordsworth and After" (p. 125).   Wesling notes, for example, that the
lines from "Meditation at Oyster River," "the doe with its sloped
shoulders loping across the highway" and "the ice piling high
against the iron-bound spiles" (CP, p. 190-91) are "limber and
inevitable" (p. 125).   Just as Roethke measures the individual
line, so he measures the poem as a whole, Harry Williams points
out in his discussion of "The Rose" in "The Edge Is What I Have."
While Williams does not stress Roethke's allegiances to Whitman,
he does note that the last poem of the "North American Sequence"
"is composed of sections approximately equal in length," and each
section contains three verse paragraphs.   These interacting sym-
metries work to highlight the importance of the word "Stays,"
Williams observes, the "only monosyllabic line in the sequence" (p.

THE POEMS OF THE FAR FIELD

116). For Williams, Roethke shapes "The Rose" so that it becomes a " 'final perspective' comprehending both past and present in the thinking mind of the poet" (p. 116).

Charles Molesworth increases the number of literary sources for the "North American Sequence" in his chapter on Roethke in The Fierce Embrace. Molesworth thinks "the language of the 'North American Sequence' gathers up the exfoliating parts of Roethke's sensibility," and he detects in its poems "biblical rhythms, the long line and catalogue of Whitman, the ecstatic litany of Smart, the meditative energy of Stevens, and the commonplace grandeur of Eliot's Four Quartets" (p. 30). Several voices from the tradition are thus detectable in the poems, according to Molesworth, but in fact the majority of the critical discussion of literary influence in the "North American Sequence" concerns Roethke's indebtedness to T. S. Eliot.

In his review of the Collected Poems, "Recent Poetry: Roethke, Warren, and Others," Louis Martz notes specific echoes of T. S. Eliot in the "North American Sequence." He cites Roethke's lines, "Old men should be explorers?" (CP, p. 189), "I have come to a still, but not a deep center" (CP, p. 201), "There are those to whom place is unimportant" (CP, p. 202), and Roethke's concluding vision in "The Rose." All suggest particular sites in Eliot's Four Quartets, Martz says, but in his opinion, Roethke echoes Eliot as a way of indicating how his vision differs from Eliot's. Martz answers the issue of literary influence in Roethke's poetry by concluding that Roethke practiced "creative imitation, in which the heart of the older poet is absorbed and then transformed into an expression of the poet's own self" (p. 295). According to Bernard Heringman, however, Roethke's relationship to T. S. Eliot was qualitatively different from his relationship to William Blake or W. B. Yeats. It was "less comfortable," Heringman writes in his essay, " 'How to Write like Somebody Else.' " "There is no open, confident acknowledgement or friendly wrestling" between the two, Heringman says, and "Roethke even seems a little grudging in his attitude" to Eliot (p. 36). Two years after Heringman's discussion, Richard Blessing contradicted that view in his book, Theodore Roethke's Dynamic Vision. Blessing suggests that Roethke's trying "to outdo T. S. Eliot in writing about the same paradox [of 'terrific repose'] is . . . part of the fun" (p. 121). Heringman is right, though, that there is little "fun" to some of Roethke's published comments about T. S. Eliot; in his letters, he is occasionally obscene. Indications of antipathy alone, however, do not mean Eliot's voice overpowers Roethke's, though Harold Bloom does arrive at that conclusion by way of a different method.

Bloom does not devote much space to discussion of Roethke's poetry in his book, The Anxiety of Influence: A Theory of Poetry, but he does state forcefully that the voices of Whitman, Yeats, Eliot, and Wallace Stevens are too pronounced in Roethke's later

poetry. "There is late Roethke that is the Stevens of Trans-
port to Summer," Bloom says, "and late Roethke that is the Whitman of Lilacs but sorrowfully there is very little late Roethke
that is late Roethke" (p. 142). According to Bloom, the apophrades, what Roethke would call the "great dead," "came as dev-
astation, and took away his strength, which nevertheless had been
realized. . . . Of apophrades in its positive, revisionary sense,
he gives us no instance; there are no passages in Yeats or Eliot,
in Stevens or Whitman, that can strike us as having been written
by Roethke" (p. 142).

No one has yet refuted Harold Bloom's conclusion by locating
"passages" of Theodore Roethke in the works of the poets he mentions, but his view of Roethke's uneasy relationship to T. S.
Eliot has been challenged on other grounds, most comprehensively
by Jenijoy La Belle in her book, The Echoing Wood of Theodore
Roethke. According to La Belle, Roethke summarizes and epitomizes his attitude toward literary tradition in the "North American Sequence." As he had in his earlier poems, La Belle says,
Roethke "strengthens" in the "North American Sequence" "the
sense of his own past by re-echoing some of the writers to whom
he was particularly attracted" (p. 141). Thus fortified, Roethke
can transform his personal quest for identity into the more sweeping, even mythic, journey he undertakes in the "North American
Sequence." The echoes of other poets one hears in reading the sequence, La Belle says, result from the fact that in his travels,
Roethke "finds not only places but companions," and Roethke specifically populates his sequence with "those other poets who have
also journeyed from interior to periphery and back again" (p. 150).
The "companions" most prominent in the "North American Sequence"
are, of course, Walt Whitman and T. S. Eliot; the distant "an-
cestor" Whitman is mediated to the son Roethke through the "parent" Eliot, La Belle explains (p. 135), through the medium of technical and "rhythmic" similarities, the details of which La Belle
borrows from S. Musgrove's book, T. S. Eliot and Walt Whitman
(pp. 128-30). While La Belle establishes that Whitman, Eliot,
and Roethke use similar poetic devices that cause them to sound
at times similar, her major intention is to show Roethke's uniqueness, how his echoing of T. S. Eliot in particular illustrates that
uniqueness.

La Belle acknowledges that Eliot's verse and some of his ideas
appealed to Roethke. She shows, for example, that both Roethke
and Eliot consider the concept of "place" particularly important.
Both poets use actual place names in their poems, and those places
usually have both historical and personal import. History and
autobiography thus intersect in each poet's work, but the notion
of place assumes even larger significance, La Belle says, because
"within the journey and within the rose [the significant figure
for both Eliot and Roethke] is a point that has as its temporal
dimension eternity and as its spatial dimension infinity" (p. 158).

Whereas Eliot describes this point of intersection "in terms of time" in "Burnt Norton" ("Only through time time is conquered" [p. 120]), Roethke describes the point "in terms of space" ("All finite things reveal infinitude" [CP, p. 201]) (p. 158). Both poets "find solace, if not ultimate fulfillment, within a perception of the moment that reveals the eternal and in a union with things beyond the self that expand that self to give a glimpse of eternity" (p. 159), La Belle concludes, but each comes to that resolution and each phrases that resolution in his own way.

On a more fundamental issue, however, La Belle thinks Roethke's vision differs importantly from Eliot's. His echoes of Eliot in the "North American Sequence" are meant to emphasize such difference. Though the two share a sense of the significance of place (and of time intersecting with it), La Belle says that "Eliot is pervasively religious, even theological, in his interests, and thus he finally must move from the physical world and the imagery of that world to a spiritual world in which abstract concepts replace images from nature" (pp. 156-57). Roethke refuses to take that step, La Belle observes. Unlike Eliot and Yeats, Roethke was "never so willing to desert the natural world" (p. 157), and despite his gesture toward the transcendental in the "Sequence, Sometimes Metaphysical," he came to terms with himself "not by leaving the woods and the waters but by penetrating more deeply into their interiors" (p. 157). Though Roethke does indeed pay homage to T. S. Eliot by echoing his verse in the "North American Sequence," and elevates his own poem to the level of Eliot's meditative seriousness by so doing, Roethke also questions Eliot and differs with him, La Belle says. In the end, Roethke answers Eliot's own more abstract, rarefied, and theologically conventional poetic vision by rededicating himself to the world Eliot's poetry renounces.

Theodore Roethke's Literary Influence

When literary critics spoke of the issue of literary influence in Roethke's poetry before his death in 1963, they invariably meant the extent to which his work was affected, for better or worse, by poets he borrowed from and echoed, Wordsworth, Whitman, Yeats, Eliot. Recently, however, critics cite the influence of Theodore Roethke, not the influence on his work of other poets. More and more readers are beginning to see that Roethke's influence on younger poets has been considerable. It occurred directly in his own lifetime through his teaching, and it continues to occur through the presence of his poetry. Teaching students to write poems was a second career for Roethke, a career he took very seriously. Since his death, his reputation as an inspiring, demanding, and effective teacher of creative writing has assumed legendary proportions. A sense of Roethke's pedagogical approach can be found in his essays, "The Teaching Poet" (SP, pp. 44-51) and "A Word to the Instructor" (SP, pp. 52-56), and an idea of the energy and enthusiasm with which Roethke approached teaching emerges from his wild statement, "Last Class" (SP, pp. 96-104). In addition to Roethke's own essays and his comments on teaching in his letters, Carolyn Kizer describes in her 1956 article, "Poetry: School of the Northwest," the Poetry Workshop at the University of Washington that Roethke conducted; she attributes to the efforts of Theodore Roethke the wealth of talent attracted there and the enthusiasm generated. In "Theodore Roethke: Personal Notes," Roethke's department chairman at the University of Washington, Robert B. Heilman, gives an interesting reminiscence of Roethke as teacher, including an appreciative defense of Roethke's equally legendary noncomformities. Allan Seager provides a comprehensive account of Roethke's experiences and techniques in the classroom in his biography, The Glass House, and in his review of Seager's biography, "Theodore Roethke, Teacher," Peter F. Neumeyer offers a sympathetic appraisal of Roethke's teaching, and he offers up Roethke's methods in the classroom as examples for other teachers of writing to follow.

The power of Roethke's teaching performance was enormous: his students included the now well-known poets Carolyn Kizer, James Wright, David Wagoner, and Richard Hugo, but his more widespread and enduring influence on succeeding generations comes through his published poetry. In the last decade, several studies have emerged that outline important connections between the works of Roethke and prominent contemporary poets. For example, in "The Edge Is What I Have," Harry Williams argues that Roethke has been given "little or no credit . . . for initiating in this country, largely on his own, a poetry of the deep image, especially its innovative beginnings in 'The Lost Son' sequence" (p. 153). Williams seeks to rectify that by showing how Roethke's poetry influences the work of James Dickey, Sylvia Plath, Ted Hughes, James Wright, and Robert Bly. Of this group, according to Williams, James Dickey shows the least successful assimilation of Roethke's influence. Though Dickey is the "most self-expressed admirer" of Roethke in his prose reviews of the poet, Dickey's poetry itself is "merely derivative for the most part," Williams says (p. 174). He notes that "Dickey's poetry expresses an explosion of personality," what Williams calls "multiple I's . . . in an attempt to facet the given personality of the poet," but Dickey does not refract those I's off another, as Roethke does. Williams suggests that where Roethke seeks to and then succeeds in exploding the shell of the self, Dickey simply offers "an ego in need of expression" (pp. 174-75), the kind of charge at times leveled at Roethke. Both Sylvia Plath and Ted Hughes more successfully assimilate the influence of Roethke, Williams says. From Roethke's descriptions of nature, from his depiction of the

THE POEMS OF THE FAR FIELD   187

"heaven and hell" that is the greenhouse, Plath and Hughes derive
their own imagery, Plath invoking "the floral in nature to image
a poetry that is essentially nihilistic," and Hughes invoking "the
animal in nature to image the nihilistic" (p. 192). For Williams,
however, Roethke's student and friend James Wright is the most
able and significant of poets influenced by Roethke. "Wright has
absorbed his influences," Williams says, and he points particularly
in Wright's poetry to the "close attention paid to verbal precision
and sound forms employing much assonance and consonance" (p. 163).
Williams suggests that Wright's best-known poem, "A Blessing,"
which he characterizes as "intensely animistic," could not "have
been written without the Roethkean model preceding it" (p. 161).
    In The Fierce Embrace, Charles Molesworth lengthens the list
of those influenced by Roethke to include A. R. Ammons, John
Ashbery, Galway Kinnell, Denise Levertov, W. S. Merwin, Gary
Snyder, Mark Strand, and Diane Wakoski. Molesworth thinks it
plausible to view Roethke "as the father of the next generation
of poets," and he argues that "deep imagery, confessionalism, neo-
surrealism, and the return to a kind of pastoral ecstasy, as well
as the use of mythical parable," all can be found in and traced
to parts of Roethke's poetry (p. 35). Molesworth concludes that
"it is difficult to be either traditional or as modern as possible,
to write either spiritual autobiography in a heroic vein or natur-
alistic lyrics with anonymous ease, without borrowing something
from Roethke's poetry" (pp. 35-36). In his book, Our Last First
Poets, Cary Nelson indicates the continuities of some of Roethke's
concerns in the works of poets Galway Kinnell, Robert Duncan,
Adrienne Rich, and W. S. Merwin. Since his major aim is to discuss each poet's distinctive response to the cultural context,
however, Nelson does not elaborate direct or extensive influences,
as such. Nelson does show, though, that for each of the younger
poets he discusses, Roethke's poetry has itself become part of the
cultural context.
    It would be misleading to suggest that all critics see Roethke's
influence as beneficial, however. Some of those poets cited by
Williams, Molesworth, and Nelson have been lumped into and derided
as what William H. Pritchard calls the "somnambulistic school" in
his essay, "Wildness of Logic in Modern Lyric." (The term "somnambulistic" may come from James Dickey's review of Words for the
Wind [1961] where Dickey uses the word approvingly to indicate
Roethke's commerce with the "deep well of unconscious cerebration"
[p. 148].) Members of this "school," Pritchard says, "eschew an
ironic social tone and choose a purer toneless voice which would
somehow encompass life itself" (pp. 143-44). In his book, The
Situation of Poetry, Robert Pinsky offers a similar criticism
in observing that "one of the most contemporary strains in contemporary poetry is often interior, submerged, free-playing, elusive,
more fresh than earnest, more eager to surprise than to tell."
This "strain" Pinsky connects with a distinctively " 'surrealist'

diction" that "sometimes suggests, not a realm beyond surface reality, but a particular reality, hermetically primitive, based on
a new poetic diction: 'breath,' 'snow,' 'future,' 'blood,' 'silence,'
'eats,' 'water' and most of all 'light' doing the wildly unexpected"
(pp. 162-63). Eric Torgerson repeats Pritchard's and Pinsky's
charge and brings it up to date in his 1983 essay, "Inflation and
Poetry." He argues that the diction of the "somnambulists,"
which they owe to Roethke, is now predictable and wearying. Torgerson writes, "I think we have allowed grand, vatic conceptions of
poetry to go to our heads, and settled too often for poetry that
flatters our egos rather than addressing the circumstances of our
lives." One of the central criticisms of Roethke's verse surfaces
again, leveled this time not at Roethke but at his inheritors. Torgerson thinks the future of American poetry lies "in more modest
description," in "stressing craft" (p. 13). Ironically, if Torgerson is right, future poets may look with redoubled interest at
Roethke's carefully crafted and much criticized formal lyrics,
precisely those which some in his own more experimental generation
decided to scorn.

A more compelling discussion of Roethke's influence on the next
generation of poets is Anthony Libby's penetrating 1974 essay,
"Roethke, Water Father." Libby is not an uncritical enthusiast
of Roethke's poetry, however. He thinks Roethke "one of the
most uneven poets ever called 'great' in serious critical writing.
He consistently explored new territory only to retreat into the
security of old and often secondhand styles" (p. 267). Libby
also criticizes Roethke for omitting political content from his poems, a lack one finds especially noticeable when contrasting Roethke's work with that of Robert Bly. Despite those objections, and
we have seen that these are common objections to Roethke's work,
Libby notes that his poetry "reverberates into the future." Libby
wants to show that Roethke is a "dominant influence on most of
our recent mystical or oracular poets, poets of transcendent landscapes and magical transformations" (p. 267).

Unlike other critics who have observed connections between
Roethke and the generation of postmodern poets, Libby is not content to catalog the "shallow convergences, similarities in phrase,
word, image" that are readily noticeable in their works (p. 268).
Libby does note that the figure of the female frequently assumes
an important role in the mystical illuminations of this group of
poets; he notes that these poets (Dickey "almost obsessively") use
the figure of the animal to "represent a way of knowing uncorrupt-
ed by rational consciousness" (p. 280); and he notes that to indicate achievement of an "illuminating darkness" these poets frequently invoke the image of the "impenetrable stone" (p. 280). But
Libby is less interested in these tantalizing similarities than he
is in articulating the larger poetic vision such imagery implies.
Libby can refer that vision to psychoanalytic thinking, for "one
logical extension of Jung's theory of archetypes is the idea that

a particular cluster of images, and even a particular attitude toward those images, may dominate the psyches of the inhabitants of a given period of history" (p. 287), but he more convincingly connects the poetic vision to the "water father," Theodore Roethke.

Roethke's impact on the next generation of poets is more complicated and more fundamental than most critics have thus far allowed, according to Libby. Roethke did not simply perfect a style and delineate a subject from which other poets learn and borrow. Rather, in his best poems he expressed intimations of a vision, "a new mysticism, one opposed to the mysticism of transcendence," but Roethke was himself unsure of the implications of that vision, and in a sense he feared what he was moving toward (p. 279). As a result, some of his last poems "fail . . . because they seek--through abstract statement and the clichés of orthodoxy--too easy a resolution of his ambivalence toward the mystical experience" (p. 276). "The imagery of his most effectively mystical poetry," Libby argues, "poetry not of transcendence but of physical immersion, combined darkness and light in a union ambiguously beautiful" (p. 276). Libby cites "In a Dark Time" as one of the most successful of such combinations. The controversial conclusion of the poem is not forced but exemplary of Roethke's innovative vision, Libby says, for "unlike the traditional mystic, the contemporary visionary often locates himself not in an imagined area of cosmic peace but at the center of a storm" (p. 276).

The way to that center is a dark way, though, a move "into watery darkness . . . into the depths of the self" (p. 279). In Roethke's "earthbound mysticism" (p. 273), one penetrates the earth and its waters, not the sky and its light, and Libby notes that a characteristic figure for such a pilgrim's progress is "death by drowning, burial in a watery earth" (p. 278). Though "drowning forms a constant metaphor in Bly, Plath, and Dickey," Libby points out, "Roethke seldom used the image so literally as the younger poets; he tended to stop with suggestions of immersion" (p. 278). Roethke's "dark revelation" is more fully explored by the later poets, Libby says, because Roethke himself "fell away from its mystical truths" (p. 276).

To a degree, Libby is correct on the point: we have seen in some detail in the Love Poems of Words for the Wind that Roethke resists the loss of self, the "immersion" necessitated by love. In his last poetry, Roethke uses a "drowning" imagery more frequently and explicitly than Libby suggests, however. In the "North American Sequence," for example, Roethke writes, "I lose and find myself in the long water" (CP, p. 198), and "I sway outside myself/ Into the darkening currents,/ Into the small spillage of driftwood,/ The waters swirling past the tiny headlands" (CP, p. 202). Were such citations insufficient to challenge Libby's conclusion, some critics might want to go further to observe the dramatic coincidence between the imagery of Roethke's last poetry and the circumstances of his own death in water.

Roethke's ambivalence toward immersion is eventually undeniable, however, because it itself, for Theodore Roethke, is an essential "mystical truth." His ambivalence signals most importantly his allegiance to the body and the physical world. Libby seems to fault Roethke for this allegiance, oddly enough, but in fact such resistance prevents Roethke's vision from becoming a worship of death or yet another version of the traditionally transcendental. As the poem "In a Dark Time" can illustrate, Roethke availed himself of the transcendental option, it must be said, but he did so to his own poetic peril. In his more innovative though less obtrusively mystical work, in his Greenhouse poems and in the Lost Son narratives, for example, Roethke did not so easily forego the world. He embraced it instead. He entered it and he spoke from it. By so doing, he intimated the influential result that Anthony Libby aptly terms Roethke's "earthbound mysticism" (p. 273).

There is a side to Theodore Roethke that values the end of the "journey out of the self," and that side emerges in his last poetry. In The Far Field, in the "North American Sequence" especially, Roethke offers poems that balance the contradictions of self and other, and mount to a final poise in that relationship, but Roethke was at root a poet of beginnings, not ends, of journeys, not arrivals, of beginning again after each end. His poetry as a whole shows that he would not commit himself for long to any resolution of the "journey out of the self." All ends necessitate new beginnings for Roethke, a characteristic at once the strength and limitation of his poetic vision. With that in mind, and with a notion of the kind of poet Theodore Roethke was, the poems of The Far Field seem fitting conclusion to a career directed more toward discovering origins than ends.

The poems of The Far Field reiterate the central themes of Roethke's poetry; they also generate, yet again, the major issues important in previous critical discussions of his verse. Though he gathered to his poetry a world of elemental things, plants and animals, and people he loved, to the end Roethke's central theme remained the self; his ability to reach beyond that self was not limitless and, some argue, not considerable. Nonetheless, Roethke's last poems show, primarily by indirection, that he could respond to the variety of things that formed his world. Not the least of such responses was his reaction to the various objections leveled at the scope and nature of his work. Against the charge that he could write convincingly only of the self, for example, Roethke aimed to "personalize" the Love Poems of Words for the Wind and The Far Field, and against the charge that he was unaffected by his historical circumstances (in fact, an absurd charge) he ventured to come to terms, in what way those circumstances allowed, with his moment and his geographic place in the poems of the "North American Sequence."

And yet Roethke's last poems are no capitulation to earlier

criticism of his work. They show courage and the constancy of
his method and intent. After his controversial appropriation of
the poetic voice of William Butler Yeats in his poems of the
1950s, Roethke dared to compete with another influential poet,
T. S. Eliot, in his last volume of poems. To do so was quite in
accord with his theoretical commitment to the value of writing
by imitation. It might also be said that had Roethke not acknowledged his indebtedness to Yeats so directly, his echoes of T. S.
Eliot in the "North American Sequence" might register more faint-
ly on the critical ear. In addition, Roethke's last volume shows
that the formal poems of the 1950s were not anomalous, no dead
end. Formal poetry appears again in the "Sequence, Sometimes
Metaphysical," and those poems thus extend and vindicate to a
degree the controversial lyrics of Words for the Wind. Though
the self-consciously mystical vision and the theological language
of the "Sequence, Sometimes Metaphysical" raise questions, the
presence of the sequence itself in Roethke's last volume does
help throw into relief the various formalist tendencies in his
poetry.

In addition to the traditionally styled poems of the "Sequence,
Sometimes Metaphysical," of course, Roethke included in The Far
Field the looser, less conventional poems of the "North American
Sequence." There is thus something of formal verse and something
of free in Roethke's last volume, something for anyone he may,
in the course of his career, have alienated by his bewildering
diversity. However, Roethke's summary of technique in his last
poems has not and probably will not undo the particular problem
caused by his reversion to traditional forms in the 1950s, a reversion made the more striking because Roethke himself had advanced to the forefront of experimental poetry by originating the
form for his voice and vision in The Lost Son and Other Poems.

Though Roethke's most innovative poetry and his distinctive
vision have demonstrably affected poets of the succeeding generation, it is nonetheless true that Roethke did not capture for an
age a vision of the world as Dante did, as Milton did, as T. S.
Eliot did. In assessing that fact, we must remember, of course,
that Eliot demonstrated, at least at one point in his career, that
the comprehensive vision is no longer possible. Negative reaction to Theodore Roethke's own vision may articulate some lingering
frustration over the truth of what Eliot showed. Roethke's vision
remains influential, however, and without doubt his poems will
continue to be read. Very few other American poets of the twentieth century have contributed so many and such a variety of poems
worthy of standing alone in the standard anthology. It is less
easy to say whether Roethke will in the future become a central
figure in American poetry. The constant revisions to Roethke's
own position in literature offer yet another example of how such
ranking is affected by the turn of historical circumstance. However, the fact that important poets of the current generation

look to Roethke's voice and vision, and the fact that literary critics are starting to recognize the nature and extent of his influence, suggest that Roethke's reputation as a poet will grow rather than diminish in coming years. Roethke's prose, too, will remain of interest. The essays illuminate his poems, his intentions in writing his poems, and they provide insights about the psychology and experience of a poet worth the attention of anyone who wants to write poems or see how poems get written. In these respects, Theodore Roethke might be remembered as a poet's poet, but unlike others who have earned that sometimes daunting title, Roethke is also a poet for the general audience. In addition to containing his thematically original and technically innovative explorations of the self, Roethke's volumes include many remarkably accessible, expertly crafted, and somehow inevitable poems. If for nothing else, he should be remembered for his evocations of the large lives of the small things we often ignore.

Bibliography

Benedikt, Michael
  1967. "The Completed Pattern," Poetry Jan., pp. 262-66.
Blessing, Richard A.
  1972. "Theodore Roethke: A Celebration," Tulane Studies in English, pp. 169-80.
  1974. Theodore Roethke's Dynamic Vision. Bloomington: Indiana Univ. Pr.
Bloom, Harold
  1973. The Anxiety of Influence: A Theory of Poetry. New York: Oxford Univ. Pr.
Bowers, Susan R.
  1980. "The Explorer's Rose: Theodore Roethke's Mystical Symbol," Concerning Poetry 13, 2, pp. 41-49.
Boyers, Robert
  1967. "A Very Separate Peace," in The Young American Writers, ed. Richard Kostelanetz, pp. 27-34. New York: Funk and Wagnalls.
Burke, Kenneth
  1966. "The Vegetal Radicalism of Theodore Roethke," in Language as Symbolic Action, pp. 254-81. Berkeley: Univ. of California Pr. Appeared in Sewanee Review, pp. 68-108. Winter, 1950. Reprinted in Profile of Theodore Roethke, ed. William Heyen. Columbus: Merrill, 1971.
Carruth, Hayden
  1964. "Requiem for God's Gardener," The Nation Sept. 28, pp. 168-69.

Deutsch, Babette
1964. "On Theodore Roethke's 'In a Dark Time,' " in The Contemporary Poet as Artist and Critic: Eight Symposia, ed. Anthony Ostroff, pp. 36-40. Boston: Little, Brown.
Dickey, James
1961. "Correspondences and Essences," Virginia Quarterly Review Autumn, p. 640.
Donoghue, Denis
1965. "Roethke's Broken Music," in Theodore Roethke: Essays on the Poetry, ed. Arnold Stein, pp. 136-66. Seattle: Univ. of Washington Pr. Reprinted in Connoisseurs of Chaos: Ideas of Order in Modern American Poetry. London: Faber and Faber, 1965.
Eliot, T. S.
1971. The Complete Poems and Plays 1909-1950. New York: Harcourt, Brace & World.
Ferry, David
1967. "Roethke's Poetry," Virginia Quarterly Review 43, pp. 169-73.
Fuller, John G.
1965. "Trade Winds," Saturday Review Mar. 27, pp. 10-11.
Galvin, Brendan
1972. "Theodore Roethke's Proverbs," Concerning Poetry 5, pp. 35-47.
Heilman, Robert B.
1964. "Theodore Roethke: Personal Notes," Shenandoah Autumn, pp. 55-64.
Heringman, Bernard
1972. " 'How to Write like Somebody Else,' " Modern Poetry Studies 3, pp. 31-39.
Heyen, William
1969. "The Divine Abyss: Theodore Roethke's Mysticism," Texas Studies in Literature and Language Summer, pp. 1051-68. Reprinted in Profile of Theodore Roethke, ed. William Heyen. Columbus: Merrill, 1971.
Hobbs, John
1971. "The Poet as His Own Interpreter: Roethke on 'In a Dark Time,' " College English 33, 1, pp. 55-66.
Jarrell, Randall
1969. The Third Book of Criticism. New York: Farrar, Straus & Giroux.
Kizer, Carolyn
1956. "Poetry: School of the Pacific Northwest," New Republic July 16, pp. 18-19.
Kramer, Hilton
1954. "The Poetry of Theodore Roethke," Western Review Winter, pp. 131-46.
Kunitz, Stanley
1964. "The Taste of Self: On Theodore Roethke's 'In a Dark Time,' " in The Contemporary Poet as Artist and Critic: Eight

Symposia, ed. Anthony Ostroff, pp. 41-48. Boston: Little,
Brown.
La Belle, Jenijoy
1976. The Echoing Wood of Theodore Roethke. Princeton:
Princeton Univ. Pr.
Libby, Anthony
1974. "Roethke, Water Father," American Literature Nov., pp.
267-88. Revised version reprinted in Mythologies of Nothing:
Mystical Death in American Poetry, 1940-1970, pp. 101-25.
Urbana: Univ. of Illinois Pr., 1984.
Liberthson, Daniel
1977. The Quest for Being: Theodore Roethke, W. S. Merwin,
and Ted Hughes. New York: Gordon.
Lucas, John
1968. "The Poetry of Theodore Roethke," Oxford Review, 8, pp.
39-64.
Malkoff, Karl
1966. Theodore Roethke: An Introduction to the Poetry. New
York: Columbia Univ. Pr.
Martz, Louis
1966. "Recent Poetry: Roethke, Warren, and Others," Yale
Review Winter, pp. 275-77.
Mills, Ralph J., Jr.
1962. "Theodore Roethke: The Lyric of the Self," in Poets
in Progress: Critical Prefaces to Ten Contemporary Poets, ed.
Edward Hungerford, pp. 3-23. Evanston: Northwestern Univ. Pr.
Reprinted as "Theodore Roethke" in Mills's Contemporary American Poetry, pp. 48-71. New York: Random House, 1966.
1963. Theodore Roethke. Minnesota Pamphlets on American
Writers, no. 30. Minneapolis: Univ. of Minnesota Pr.
1965. "In the Way of Becoming: Roethke's Last Poems," in Theodore Roethke: Essays on the Poetry, ed. Arnold Stein, pp. 115-
35. Seattle: Univ. of Washington Pr. Reprinted in Creation's
Very Self: On the Personal Element in Recent American Poetry,
pp. 48-66. Fort Worth: Texas Christian Univ. Pr., 1969.
Molesworth, Charles
1979. "Songs of the Happy Man: The Poetry of Theodore Roethke," in The Fierce Embrace, pp. 22-36. Columbia: Univ. of Missouri Pr.
Musgrove, S.
1952. T. S. Eliot and Walt Whitman. Wellington, New Zealand:
University Pr.
Nelson, Cary
1981. Our Last First Poets: Vision and History in Contemporary American Poetry. Urbana: Univ. of Illinois Pr.
Neumeyer, Peter F.
1976. "Theodore Roethke, Teacher," Journal of Aesthetic
Education 10, 1, pp. 109-12.

Ostroff, Anthony, ed.
1964. The Contemporary Poet as Artist and Critic: Eight Symposia. Boston: Little, Brown. Originally appeared as "The Poet & His Critics," New World Writing 19, pp. 189-219, 1961.
Parini, Jay
1979. Theodore Roethke: An American Romantic. Amherst: Univ. of Massachusetts Pr.
Phillips, Robert
1973. "The Inward Journeys of Theodore Roethke," in The Confessional Poets, pp. 107-27. Carbondale: Southern Illinois Univ. Pr.
Pinsky, Robert
1976. The Situation of Poetry. Princeton: Princeton Univ. Pr.
Powell, Grosvenor E.
1967. "Robert Lowell and Theodore Roethke: Two Kinds of Knowing," Southern Review Jan., pp. 180-85.
Pritchard, William H.
1970. "Wildness of Logic in Modern Lyric," in Forms of Lyric: Selected Papers from the English Institute, ed. Reuben A. Brower, pp. 127-50. New York: Columbia Univ. Pr.
Ransom, John Crowe
1964. "On Theodore Roethke's 'In a Dark Time,' " in The Contemporary Poet as Artist and Critic: Eight Symposia, ed. Anthony Ostroff, pp. 26-35. Boston: Little, Brown.
Roethke, Theodore
1964. "On 'In a Dark Time,' " in The Contemporary Poet as Artist and Critic: Eight Symposia, ed. Anthony Ostroff, pp. 49-53. Boston: Little, Brown. Originally appeared as "The Poet & His Critics," ed. Anthony Ostroff, in New World Writing 19, pp. 189-219, 1961.
1965. On the Poet and His Craft: Selected Prose of Theodore Roethke, ed. Ralph J. Mills, Jr. Seattle: Univ. of Washington Pr.
1966. The Collected Poems of Theodore Roethke. Garden City, N.Y.: Doubleday.
1968. Selected Letters of Theodore Roethke, ed. Ralph J. Mills, Jr. Seattle: Univ. of Washington Pr.
Rosenthal, M. L.
1965. The New Poets: American and British Poetry since World War II, pp. 112-18. New York: Oxford Univ. Pr. A portion of Rosenthal's discussion appeared as "The Couch and Poetic Insight" in The Reporter Mar. 25, 1965, pp. 52-53.
Seager, Allan
1968. The Glass House: The Life of Theodore Roethke. New York: McGraw-Hill.
Southworth, James G.
1966. "Theodore Roethke's The Far Field," College English Feb., pp. 413-18.

Spender, Stephen
1966. "Roethke: 'The Lost Son,' " New Republic Aug. 27, pp. 23-25.
Staples, Hugh
1964. "The Rose in the Sea-Wind: A Reading of Theodore Roethke's 'North American Sequence,' " American Literature May, pp. 189-203.
Sullivan, Rosemary
1975. Theodore Roethke: The Garden Master. Seattle: Univ. of Washington Pr.
Torgerson, Eric
1983. "Inflation and Poetry," American Poetry Review July-Aug., pp. 7-13.
Truesdale, C. W.
1968. "Theodore Roethke and the Landscape of American Poetry," Minnesota Review, pp. 345-58.
Wain, John
1965. "The Monocle of My Sea-Faced Uncle," in Theodore Roethke: Essays on the Poetry, ed. Arnold Stein, pp. 54-77. Seattle: Univ. of Washington Pr. Appeared as "Theodore Roethke," in Critical Quarterly, pp. 322-38. Winter, 1964.
Wesling, Donald
1970. "The Inevitable Ear: Freedom and Necessity in Lyric Form, Wordsworth and After," in Forms of Lyric: Selected Papers from the English Institute, ed. Reuben A. Brower, pp. 103-26. New York: Columbia Univ. Pr.
Williams, Harry
1977. "The Edge Is What I Have." Lewisburg: Bucknell Univ. Pr.

Additional Reading

Atlas, James
1969. "Roethke's Boswell," Poetry Aug., pp. 327-30.
Blessing, Richard A.
1972. "Theodore Roethke's Sometimes Metaphysical Motion," Texas Studies in Literature and Language 14, pp. 731-49.
Bogan, Louise
1964. New Yorker Nov. 7, p. 243.
Bullis, Jerald
1970. "Theodore Roethke," Massachusetts Review 11, pp. 209-12.
Burke, Kenneth
1968. "Cult of the Breakthrough," New Republic Sept. 21, pp. 25-26.
Ciardi, John
1963. "Theodore Roethke: A Passion and a Maker," Saturday Review Aug. 31, p. 13.

1969. "Comments on Theodore Roethke," Cimarron Review 7, pp. 6-8.
Ciardi, John, Stanley Kunitz, and Allan Seager
1967. "An Evening with Ted Roethke," Michigan Quarterly Review 6, pp. 227-45.
Cohen, J. M.
1960. Poetry of This Age 1908-1958. London: Hutchinson, pp. 249-53.
Corrigan, Matthew
1971. "A Phenomenological Glance at a Few Lines of Roethke," Modern Poetry Studies 2, pp. 165-74.
Creeley, Robert
1971. "Interview," Unmuzzled Ox Dec., p. 34.
Davie, Donald
1964. "Two Ways Out of Whitman," The Review Dec., pp. 14-17.
Davison, Peter
1965. "Madness in the New Poetry," Atlantic Jan., p. 93.
Dickey, William
1964-5. "Poetic Language," Hudson Review Winter, p. 596.
Donoghue, Denis
1966. "Aboriginal Poet," New York Review of Books Sept. 22, pp. 14-16.
Driver, C. J.
1968. "Theodore Roethke: The Soul's Immortal Joy," Tracks Aug., pp. 43-48.
Everette, Oliver
1969. "Theodore Roethke: The Poet as Teacher," West Coast Review Spring, pp. 5-11.
Fiedler, Leslie
1964. "A Kind of Solution: The Situation of Poetry Now," Kenyon Review 26, pp. 63-64.
Garrigue, Jean
1964. "A Mountain on the Landscape," New Leader Dec. 7, pp. 33-34.
Goodheart, Eugene
1968. "The Frailty of the I," Sewanee Review 76, pp. 516-19.
Gustafson, Richard
1966. "In Roethkeland," Midwest Quarterly Jan., pp. 167-74.
Heaney, Seamus
1968. "Canticles to the Earth," Listener Aug. 22, pp. 245-46.
Heringman, Bernard
1970. "Theodore Roethke," Earlham Review Spring, pp. 20-30.
1973. "Images of Meaning in the Poetry of Theodore Roethke," Aegis 2, pp. 45-57.
Heyen, William, ed.
1971. Profile of Theodore Roethke. Columbus, Ohio: Merrill.

Hirsch, David H.
1978. "Theodore Roethke," Contemporary Literature 19, pp. 243-48.
Hoffman, Steven K.
1979. "Lowell, Berryman, Roethke, and Ginsberg: The Communal Function of Confessional Poetry," Literary Review 22, pp. 329-41.
Hugo, Richard
1979. "Stray Thoughts on Roethke and Teaching," in The Triggering Town: Lectures and Essays on Poetry and Writing, pp. 27-36. New York: Norton.
Jaffe, Dan
1970. "Theodore Roethke: 'In a Slow Up-Sway,' " in The Fifties: Fiction, Poetry, Drama, ed. Warren French, pp. 199-207. Deland, Fla.: Everett Edwards.
James, Clive
1970. "Tough Assignments," The Review Sept.-Nov., pp. 47-53.
Kinzie, Mary
1981. "Two Lives," American Poetry Review Mar.-Apr., pp. 20-21.
Kennedy, X. J.
1964. "Joys, Griefs, and 'All Things Innocent, Hapless, Forsaken,' " New York Times Book Review Aug. 5, p. 5.
La Belle, Jenijoy
1976. "Out of the Cradle Endlessly Robbing: Whitman, Eliot, and Theodore Roethke," Walt Whitman Review 22, pp. 75-84.
Levi, Peter, S.J.
1964. "Theodore Roethke," Agenda Apr., pp. 11-14.
Lit, A.
1967. "Notes on Roethke's Poetry," Topic Fall, pp. 21-29.
Malkoff, Karl
1965. "Cleansing the Doors of Perception," Minnesota Review Oct.-Dec., pp. 342-48.
Martz, Louis
1964. "Recent Poetry: The Elegiac Mode," Yale Review Dec., pp. 285-98.
McMichael, James
1971. "Roethke's North America," Northwest Review: Theodore Roethke Special Issue Summer, pp. 149-59.
Meredith, William
1965. "Cogitating with His Finger Tips," Book Week July 18, pp. 4, 15.
Mills, Ralph J., Jr.
1964. "Roethke's Last Poems," Poetry Nov., pp. 122-24.
Paschall, Douglas
1973. "Roethke Remains," Sewanee Review 81, pp. 859-64.
Pinsker, Sanford
1979. "An Urge to Wrestle/ A Need to Dance: The Poetry of Theodore Roethke," CEA Critic 41, 4, pp. 12-17.

Ramsey, Paul
1964. "A Weather of Heaven," Shenandoah Autumn, pp. 72-73.
Roethke, Theodore
1939. "Random Political Reflections," New Republic Mar. 1, p. 98.
1961. I Am! Says the Lamb. Garden City, N.Y.: Doubleday.
1963. Nine Pulitzer Prize Poets Read Their Own Poems. Phonodisc. Washington, D.C.: Library of Congress.
1963. Party at the Zoo. New York: Crowell-Collier.
1963. Sequence, Sometimes Metaphysical. Iowa City: Stone Wall Pr.
1964. The Far Field. Garden City, N.Y.: Doubleday.
1964. In a Dark Time. Poetry Society of San Francisco Film.
1972. Theodore Roethke Reads His Poetry. New York: Caedmon Records, Caedmon TC 1351.
1973. Dirty Dinkey and Other Creatures: Poems for Children, ed. Beatrice Roethke and Stephen Lushington. Garden City, N.Y.: Doubleday.
Romig, Evelyn M.
1978. "An Achievement of H. D. and Theodore Roethke: Psychoanalysis and the Poetics of Teaching," Literature and Psychoanalysis 28, pp. 105-11.
Rosenthal, M. L.
1965. "Throes of Creation," New York Times Book Review July 18, p. 4.
Schumacher, Paul J.
1970. "The Unity of Being: A Study of Theodore Roethke's Poetry," Ohio University Review 12, pp. 20-40.
Skelton, Robin
1967. "The Poetry of Theodore Roethke," Malahat Review 1, pp. 141-44.
Slaughter, William R.
1968. "Roethke's 'Song,' " Minnesota Review 8 pp. 32-44.
Smith, William J.
1964. "Two Posthumous Volumes," Harper's Oct., pp. 133-34.
Snodgrass, W. D.
1964. "The Last Poems of Theodore Roethke," New York Review of Books Oct. 8, pp. 5-6.
Stein, Arnold
1971. "Roethke's Memory: Actions, Visions, and Revisions," Northwest Review: Theodore Roethke Special Issue Summer, pp. 19-31.
Stoneburner, Tony
1964. "Ardent Quest," Christian Century Sept. 30, pp. 1217-18.
Sullivan, Rosemary
1975. "A Still Center: A Reading of Theodore Roethke's 'North American Sequence,' " Texas Studies in Literature and Language 16, pp. 765-83.

Swann, B.
1973. "Theodore Roethke and the Shift of Things," Literary Review Winter, pp. 269-88.
Tate, Allen
1963. "In Memoriam: Theodore Roethke 1908-1963," Encounter Oct., p. 68.
Tillinghast, Richard
1969. "Worlds of Their Own," Southern Review Spring, pp. 594-96.
Vanderbilt, Kermit
1979. "Theodore Roethke as a Northwest Poet," in Northwest Perspectives: Essays on the Culture of the Pacific Northwest, ed. Edwin R. Bingham and Glen A. Love, pp. 186-216. Seattle: Univ. of Washington Pr.
Waggoner, Hyatt Howe
1968. American Poets: From the Puritans to the Present. Boston: Houghton Mifflin.
Walsh, Chad
1965. Saturday Review Jan. 2, p. 28.
Warfel, Harry R.
1966. "Language Patterns and Literature: A Note on Roethke's Poetry," Topic Fall, pp. 21-29.
Willingham, John R.
1964. Library Journal Sept. 15, p. 3320.

Index

Adams, Léonie: poetic influence on Roethke, 22, 24, 148
Agee, James: compared to Roethke, xi
Ammons, A. R.: Roethke influence on, 187
Arrowsmith, William, 74
Ashbery, John: Roethke influence on, 187
Auden, W. H., xi, 29, 95; comment on Roethke, 4, 5, 21; compared to Roethke, 161, 168; poetic influence on Roethke, 21, 22, 84, 166
Augustine, see St. Augustine
Ayo, Nicholas, 132, 133

Baldanza, Stephen, 5
Beaudelaire, Charles: compared to Roethke, 51, 54, 60
Belitt, Ben: Roethke letter to, 11
Benedikt, Michael, 162
Bennett, Joseph, 120
Bergson, Henri, 128
Berryman, John, 145
Bible: as source, 78, 97, 138, 183
Blake, William, 139, 147; as source, 99-100, 101; compared to Roethke, 60, 93, 177; poetic influence on Roethke, 109, 183
Blessing, Richard, 6, 10-11, 22, 29-31, 54, 65-66, 80, 84, 107-9, 127, 148, 170-71, 180-81, 183
Bloom, Harold, 25, 183-84
Blunden, Edmund: poetic influence on Roethke, 21
Bly, Robert: compared to Roethke, 171, 188, 189; Roethke influence on, 186
Bodkin, Maud: intellectual influence on Roethke, 78
Boehme, Jakob, 54
Bogan, Louise, 95; comment on Roethke, 74, 80, 106-7; poetic influence on Roethke, 22, 122, 148
Bogen, Don, 11
Bowers, Neal, 9-10, 92, 94-95
Bowers, Susan R., 171-72
Boyd, John D., 43-44, 53, 64
Boyers, Robert, 160-61
Bradley, F. H., 128
Brantley, Frederick, 74
Brown, Dennis E., 128-29
Buber, Martin, 55, 129, 130
Burns, Robert: as source, 100
Buttel, Helen, 132, 133
Burke, Kenneth, 28, 51-52, 61-62, 65, 88, 91, 104, 125, 165-66; influence on Roethke criticism, xvi, 53, 56, 64, 76, 109, 121, 123; influence on Roethke, 78, 84;

Roethke, 96, 189; Roethke
influence on, 186-87
Poe, Edgar Allan, 60
Pope, Alexander: as source,
146
Porter, Katherine Anne: Roeth-
ke letter to, 11
Pound, Ezra, xi, xiii; com-
pared to Roethke, xiv, xvi,
23, 147
Powell, Grosvenor E., 179
Pritchard, William H., 187

Ralegh, Sir Walter: as source,
140, 141
Ramsey, Jarold, 40, 44, 45, 46
Ransom, John Crowe, 126, 145,
177
Rexroth, Kenneth, 120
Rich, Adrienne: Roethke influence on, 187
Rimbaud, Arthur: compared to
Roethke, 60, 74, 93
Rodman, Selden: Roethke letter
to, 95
Roethke, Beatrice Lushington
(wife), xi, 93
Roethke, Charles (uncle), 38
Roethke, Otto (father), xiii,
12, 18, 38, 88-91, 96
Roethke, Theodore Huebner:
alienation, in poems of, 1-2,
14-15, 71, 75; allusive method
of, 23, 147; ambivalence, in
poems of, 1-4, 9, 12-13, 15,
19, 20, 49-50, 56, 89, 118,
126-27, 131, 134-39, 150, 159,
180-82, 190; anima, in poems
of, 125-26 (see also woman);
animism, in poems of, 52, 54,
55, 171; archetype, in poems
of, 76, 78, 80, 99-100, 101;
as American poet, 168-69,
173; as apprentice poet, 5,
29-31; as literary critic,
xvi-xvii, 62, 175-77, 178;
as teacher, ix-x, 13, 31,
39, 92, 159, 185-86; associative method of, 30-31;

awards and fellowships of,
ix-x, 121; career of, x-xiv;
children's poetry of, ix, 2-
3, 119; Christianity, in poems of, 4, 78, 162, 174-5,
179; competitiveness of, 62,
148-9, 183; correspondence,
in poems of, 51-52, 54-55,
81; death, in poems of, 8,
9, 14, 43-44, 50, 118, 131,
136, 145-46, 160, 161-62,
171, 173, 177, 179, 181, 189;
death of, xi-xii, 160, 161;
diction, in poems of, 28, 30-
31, 45, 59, 61-63, 65-66,
104-5, 108-9, 149, 187-88;
ecology, in poems of, 169,
172; education of, ix; ego-
centricity of, 118, 164-65;
family, in poems of, 12-13,
18; father, in poems of, 12-
13, 18, 26, 27, 31-32, 88-
91, 96, 126, 175 (see also
Roethke, Otto); flesh, in
poems of, see neoplatonism;
form, in poems of, x, 6, 27-
29, 31-32, 59, 60-62, 64-65,
148-49; God, in poems of, 4,
14, 17, 75-76, 89, 91, 128,
139, 150, 157, 158, 162,
166, 174-78, 180-81; growth
(theme), in poems of, 40-43,
75-77, 80-82; guilt of, 2,
90, 173; identity (theme),
in poems of, 41-42, 71, 166,
179; see also self; imagery,
in poems of, 3, 17-19, 39-
40, 50, 53, 71, 80-81, 81-
82, 98, 99-100, 104-6, 108-9,
123-27, 129-30, 170-173,
188-89; imitative method
of, 24, 29-31, 32, 142; immersion (theme), in poems of,
125, 159, 189-90; inaccuracy
of, xvi-xvii; individuation,
in poems of, 76; infancy narratives of, 1, 40, 72, 105-7,
144; influence on others, 4,
39, 159, 185-89; intuition,

129-30, 131-35, 146 (see also
personalization)

POETRY

"The Abyss," 179-80
"Academic": quoted, 15
"The Adamant," 6, 23, 29;
  quoted, 5
"The Bat," 137; quoted, 15
"Big Wind," 42, 54, 65;
  quoted, 49, 63-4
"Bring the Day!" 98, 100;
  quoted, 1, 110
"Carnations," 43, 46, 49, 50,
  62, 171; quoted, 44-45
"Child on Top of a Green-
  house," 44, 120; quoted, 42
"Country Summer": Roethke com-
  ment on, 24
The Collected Poems of Theo-
  dore Roethke, 159-60; tex-
  tual problem in, 46-48, 82-
  84, 86, 87, 106
"Cuttings," 11, 38, 43, 53,
  64; quoted, 41
"Cuttings (later)," 43, 56;
  quoted, 41
"The Dance," see "Four for Sir
  John Davies"
"Death Piece," 8
"Dolor," 166; quoted, 13
"Double Feature," 13, 14
"The Dream," 125
"The Dying Man," 91, 118,
  140, 145, 146, 149
"Elegy for Jane," xvii, 97,
  123, 133; Roethke comment
  on, 110
"Epidermal Macabre," 4, 8, 10;
  quoted, 9
"The Far Field": quoted, 164
The Far Field: 84, 89, 117,
  121, 126, 128, 137, 150;
  primary discussion of, 157-
  200; literary backgrounds
  and sources for, 182-85;
  "North American Sequence"

in, 163-73; reviews of,
  159-63; "Sequence, Sometimes Metaphysical" in,
  173-82; Roethke's literary influence in, 185-90
"Feud," 8, 18, 27; quoted,
  24-25
"A Field of Light," 85, 100
"The Flight," see "The Lost
  Son"
"Flower Dump," 44, 64, 65;
  quoted, 43
"Forcing House," 43; quoted,
  65
"Four for Sir John Davies,"
  118, 119, 125, 145, 149,
  176; quoted, 140; Roethke
  comment on, 140-41
"Frau Bauman, Frau Schmidt,
  and Frau Schwartze," 39,
  42, 45, 117, 119; quoted,
  46-47
"Genesis," 11
"The Gentle," 8
"The Gibber," see "The Lost
  Son"
"Give Way, Ye Gates," 77,
  100
Greenhouse poems: 2, 8, 11,
  15, 17, 19-20, 27, 30, 32,
  71-72, 91, 117, 119, 128,
  129, 134, 143, 158, 160,
  171, 172-73, 190; primary
  discussion of, 38-70; literary backgrounds and
  sources for, 57-60; overviews and organizations of,
  40-48; poetic method and
  technique in, 60-66; Roethke's minimal mysticism in,
  48-57
"Heard in a Violent Ward,"
  147
"The Heron," 137
"Highway: Michigan," 10
I Am! Says the Lamb, ix, 159
"I Cry, Love! Love!" 83, 100,
  124
"I Knew a Woman," 119, 125,

128, 129, 137, 148, 149,
162, 168, 174; primary
discussion of, 1-33; literary backgrounds and sources
for, 21-27; minimals in,
17-19; misanthropy in,
15-16; poetic breakthrough
in, 11-12; poetic methods
and techniques in, 27-32;
reviews of, 4-5, 21; struc-
ture of, 10-11; themes of,
6-10
"Orchids," 41, 43
"Orders for the Day," 18
"Otto": quoted, 89
Party at the Zoo, ix
"Pickle Belt," 13
"The Pit," see "The Lost Son"
"Plaint," 139
"Poetaster," 15
"Praise to the End!" 58,
75, 83, 86; Roethke com-
ment on, 124
Praise to the End! xii, xiii,
40, 51, 122, 123; see also
Lost Son narratives
"Prayer," 8; quoted, 17-18
"Prayer before Study," 9
"The Premonition," 6, 8, 18,
23; quoted, 31-32
"Prognosis," 18
"The Pure Fury": quoted, 135-
36
"The Reminder," 10, 18
"The Renewal": quoted, 31-32
"Reply to Censure," 16
"The Return," 13; quoted, 14
"The Return," see "The Lost
Son"
"River Incident": quoted, 19
"Root Cellar," 43, 53-54,
64; quoted, 61
"Sale," 10, 18, 27; quoted,
25-26
"Sensibility! O La!" 77, 100
"The Sensualists," xvii, 136;
quoted, 135
"Sequence, Sometimes Meta-

physical," 2, 48, 127, 150,
157-59, 162, 163, 166, 173-
82, 185
"The Shape of the Fire," 50,
83, 85, 100, 105; quoted,
99, 107; Roethke comment
on, 95-96
"The Signals," 8, 18; quoted,
19
"Silence," 16
"The Siskins," 121
"Slug," xvii, 121; quoted,
137-39
"Snake," xvii, 121
"The Swan," 135
"To My Sister," 16, 21;
quoted, 15
"Transplanting," 43, 46, 47,
48
"Unfold! Unfold!" 100
"The Visitant," xvii, 119
"The Voice," 125
"The Waking," xvii, 119,
120
The Waking, x, xii, 4, 31,
38, 46, 71, 79, 83, 87,
112, 162; see also Words
for the Wind
"Weed Puller," 51; quoted,
50
"Where Knock Is Open Wide,"
1, 77, 81-82, 83, 85-
86, 87, 88, 90, 100,
119; quoted, 72, 105-6
"Words for the Wind," 29,
118, 125; Roethke comment
on, 124
Words for the Wind: x, xii,
xvi-xvii, 4, 13, 14,
19, 27, 29, 31, 38, 46,
82, 83, 86, 87, 106, 157,
162, 182, 189; primary
discussion of, 117-150;
influence of Yeats in,
139-49; love's progress in,
131-39; problem of personalization in, 123-31; re-
views of, 119-23

Randall Stiffler holds a Ph.D. in English from the University of Illinois and is currently an assistant professor in the Division of Rhetoric, College of Basic Studies at Boston University. His poems and articles have appeared in Shenandoah, Literary Review, and Modern Poetry Studies.

Designed by Vladimir Reichl

Title lettered by Jack Sugioka

Composed by Jaymes Anne Rohrer
in Madeleine on a Tandy 2000
Personal Computer. Display type,
Janson, composed by Pearson
Typographers.

Printed on 60-pound Glatfelter,
a pH-neutral stock, and bound
in 10-point Carolina cover stock
by Cushing-Malloy, Inc.